W9-BMS-822

Ex Líbrís
© APCo

Henri Stierlin
Photographs: Anne and Henri Stierlin

GREECE

From Mycenae to the Parthenon

TASCHEN
KÖLN LISBOA LONDON NEW YORK PARIS TOKYO

Page 3
A gargoyle in the form of a lion's head at the Temple of Hera, Metapontum (southern Italy), dating from the sixth century B.C. This drawing, taken from the book by the Duc de Luynes and F. Debacq, was published in Paris in 1833, during the so-called "polychromy controversy".

Page 5
At the top of a tall votive column with an Archaic Ionic capital stands the Sphinx of the Naxians, from the Sanctuary of the Earth at Delphi. It was created in about 575–550 B.C. (Delphi, Museum)

Hohenzollernring 53, D-50672 Köln

Editor-in-chief: Angelika Taschen, Cologne
Edited by Susanne Klinkhamels, Caroline Keller, Cologne
Design and layout: Marion Hauff, Milan
English translation: Simon Pleasance & Fronza Woods, Lagrasse

Printed in Germany
ISBN 3-8228-8578-9

Contents

Introduction

Greek Architecture – a Source of Aesthetics

Women at the fountain
This 24 cm high Athenian *hydria,* or water-jar, in the style of Nicoxenus, dated 530–520 B.C., is decorated with black figures with white highlights. The girls are coming to fetch water in a small building with slender Ionic columns housing an outlet in the form of a lion's head from which the spring gushes forth.
(Rome, Villa Giulia Museum)

The monuments of ancient Greece have a vital place in the history of architecture. The Greek orders – as systems which codify forms – have played a paramount role in the stylistic expression of western architecture. For most authors, from the sixteenth century on, the distinctive features that best identify buildings – based on the Doric, Ionic and Corinthian orders – form the very vocabulary of the art of building.

There can be no doubt that Greece and her temples had a far-reaching influence on Rome, where the system of orders was borrowed, but endowed with an accent that was more decorative than structural in effect. Subsequently, as a result of the considerable boost given to it by the building activities of the Roman Empire, ancient architecture continued to have a discreet influence on the medieval world, before really coming back into its own with the achievements of the Renaissance and the Baroque and Neo-classical periods.

This almost mythical Greece which re-emerged as a source of architectural language was nevertheless profoundly altered by the historical perspective of the times and by the contagious spread of Roman forms. Naturally enough, it was the orders which survived, and not the very stuff of which buildings are made. In the mean time, however, the function of buildings had changed, as had the nature of man's requirements and needs.

For Greece had asserted a language based on columns and porticoes. Although the Greeks may have devised an architectural décor based on sculpted friezes, metopes and tympana, they had done little to develop inner areas, which were of no use in relation to the role played by temples, where the room forming the naos was designed solely to house the statue of the deity.

Nor did Greek classicism give full rein to civic buildings, no matter how emblematic, and the great palaces did not make their appearance until the Hellenistic period. Where theatres were concerned, with their open *cavea,* they did little to foster the development of spatial concepts. Only the formula of the hypostyle *telesterion* (a room which was used for initiation ceremonies) would produce huge covered halls.

In addition to temples in their many and varied forms – ranging from buildings with a surrounding colonnade (peripteral porticoes) to small treasuries, to underground or round sanctuaries *(tholos)* – we should mention such conspicuous features as theatres, porticoes *(stoai)* encircling the *agora,* monumental gateways *(propylaea)* and *exedrai,* not forgetting the creation of places of a political nature *(ecclesiasterion, bouleuterion),* designed for meetings, technical buildings (tool repositories) where warships and other vessels were built, and military constructions (walls, towers, posterns, and bastions).

The principal phenomenon is nevertheless the flourishing of temples, illustrating all the creative genius of Greek architects. In these buildings full rein was given to the aesthetic options of the Greeks, based on philosophical concepts of which architecture was merely a reflection.

Themes and Classification

Broaching a theme as "Classical" as Greek architecture, whose outward manifestations are not easy to encapsulate in any summary way, we must arrange our study both geographically and chronologically, so as to situate the contributions of both place and time, and gain a clearer grasp of the various structural and formal developments.

It is only in the last fifty years that we have learned that the people who, in the middle of the second millennium B.C., gave birth to the Mycenaean civilization, spoke Greek. So the impressive buildings of Mycenae and Tiryns, with their walls, domed tombs and palaces, had to be included, even if they had had virtually no influence on Archaic and Classical works.

When we deal with the features of the Greek temple, it would seem that the essential contribution of the Greeks to architecture lies in the portico surrounding the cella of the temple. This ring of columns needs interpreting in any semiological approach to building. Archaeology helps us to trace the genesis of this form, and at the same time simplifies the role and significance of peripteral structures.

We shall take a look at the continuous series of temples of Magna Graecia in order to emphasize the transition from Archaic expression to Classical formulations, bound by the dictates of proportion and number, based on Pythagorean concepts. These buildings offer a most rewarding area of study. For they make up nothing less than a museum of Doric architecture, with remarkably well preserved examples at Paestum, Agrigentum and Segesta, covering the period stretching from the mid-sixth century to the end of the fifth century B.C.

Over and above the upheavals and destruction caused by the Persian Wars, which pitted the Ionian Greeks and the Athenians, on the one hand, against the armies of the kings of the Achaemenid Empire of Persia, on the other, it is interesting to follow the often fundamental advances made by Ionian thinkers and architects. Whether on Samos or the shores of Asia Minor – at Ephesus, Miletus, Priene and Halicarnassus – they designed temples and grandiose mausolea, while at the same time working out an altogether original style.

The "Basilica" at Paestum: maturity of the Archaic style
South of Naples, in the city of Posidonia (Paestum) – founded by the Sybarites in 650 B.C., the large Doric temple, which is known as the "Basilica", is dedicated to the goddess Hera. It dates from *circa* 540 B.C. Its powerfully curved columns support broad capitals. The façade, distinctive for the uneven number of shafts (nine), has lost its pediment. All that now remains on the architraves is a layer of blocks once decorated with triglyphs and metopes.

Temple E at Selinunte: a classical façade
Temple E at Selinus (now Selinunte), in Sicily, which dates from the first half of the fifth century B.C., lay in ruins on the ground. It has been completely rebuilt by archaeologists. This reconstruction from fallen parts, called anastylosis, shows us the perfection of a Doric sanctuary in Magna Graecia.

The Frieze of the Tributaries at Persepolis
These scenes depicting the procession of the peoples bringing their tribute to Darius were carved during the last quarter of the sixth century B.C. to the glory of the empire of the Achaemenids by Ionian and Lydian artists in the service of the Great King. They combine the Severe style of Greek art with the influence of Assyrian sculpture.

An ancient fortress at Aegosthena
The fortifications of Attica are clear evidence of the endless wars waged by the Greek cities to gain supremacy. They form a powerful defensive chain, dating from the fourth century B.C. Here, the "keep" within the walls of Aegosthena, on the Gulf of Corinth, stands more or less unscathed.

The Greek world
Map showing the principal sites either referred to or illustrated in this book

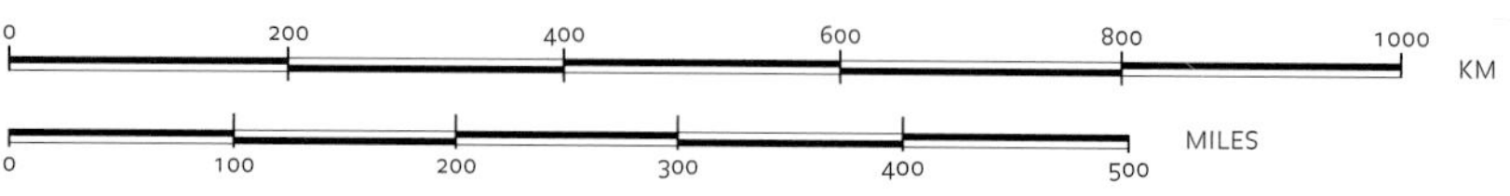

Euboea
Lefkandi
Eretria
Thermum
Delphi
Thebes
Eleutherae
Aegosthena
Eleusis
Athens
Peloponnese
Corinth
Mycenae
Olympia
Epidaurus
Tiryns
Dendra
Aegina
Sunium
Bassae
Messene
Sparta
Pylos
Vaphio
Aegean Sea
Smyrna
(Izmir)
Sardis
Klaros
Ephesus
Ionia
Priene
Samos
Miletus
Didyma
Labranda
Cyclades
Delos
Paros
Halicarnassus
Cnidus
Thera
Santorini
Rhodes
Lindus
Rhodes
Crete
Cnossus
Mallia
Gournia
Hagia Triada
Minor
Al-Mina
Ras Shamra (Ugarit)
Syria
Euphrates
Tigris
Susa
Babylon
Pasargadae
Persepolis
Persian Gulf
Red Sea

The Parthenon crowning the Acropolis
The eight columns of the east façade of the Temple of Athena Parthenos thrust their elegant Doric shafts skyward at the top of the small rocky plateau where the original city of Athens was built, in the Mycenaean period.

It is no less thrilling, however, to look into the contributions made by the Ionians and the Lydians in the flowering of this great symbolic and prestigious architecture represented by the palaces of Pasargadae, Susa and Persepolis. For on closer inspection, they turn out to have played a crucial part in the design of hypostyle halls. Furthermore, the bas-reliefs forming the Procession of the Tributaries reflect a Greek influence. So it is out of the question to overlook and not comment on the amazing works of the Achaemenids – in which the Greeks had a decisive hand – on the pretext that the two "nations" were at loggerheads.

It is clear to see that continental Greece offers a whole series of buildings, including some very well preserved ones, which help us to understand the breakthrough of architecture beyond Athens in the Greek metropolises at Aegina, Sunium, Delphi, Bassae, Lindus, and Epidaurus. Unity and diversity attest to the outpouring of art in the most elaborate forms conceivable. What is more, the permanent war footing that raged throughout the whole Classical era between the various Greek cities (Athens, Sparta, Thebes, Eretria, Megara, and Corinth) led the warring parties to erect powerful fortifications. These form a whole raft of spectacular structures – walls, towers, posterns, and so on – which still stand at sites like Messene, Aegosthena and Eleutherae, and, to the north of Syracuse, at Euryalos, and at Velia, near Paestum.

The incredible town-planning and architectural operation embarked upon by Pericles to obliterate all trace of Darius' sacking of the Acropolis of Athens will round off this study of the Greek art of building. For this complex – which includes the Parthenon, the Propylaea, the Temple of Athena Nike and the Erechtheum buildings – forms a coherent whole, conceived with an eye to mass gatherings and dazzling rituals. In the wake of the victories scored against the Persians, these monuments mark the zenith of Greek design, from both an aesthetic and a numerical standpoint. And this is without mentioning the wide iconographic range offered by the friezes and metopes which encircle sanctuaries with a whole vocabulary of mythological symbols and legends, all imbued with deep meaning.

Such is our approach, which is devised to lend the architecture of ancient Greece an overall image, while contributing one or two essential keys to its interpretation.

A shell-shaped theatre dedicated to the tragedians
The most perfect of all the Greek theatres, built into a hillside at Epidaurus, in about 330 B.C., could accommodate an audience of 15 000 spectators at festivals held in honor of Asclepius, the god of healing.

The Caryatid Porch on the Acropolis
Combining sculpture directly with architecture, and giving the columns which support the canopy of the Erechtheum the appearance of young women, these caryatids illustrate the refinement and elegance of Classical art. Dating back to 421 B.C., this Ionic structure stands facing the northern portico of the Parthenon.

Mycenaean Architecture

Fortifications, Tombs and Palaces of the "Homeric" World

Page 15
Heirs of the Minotaur
The Mycenaeans – the first properly so-called Hellenic people to settle in Greece – derived considerable advantage from the Cretan civilization which they inherited. Their art reflects this influence – and in particular this silver rhyton in the form of a bull's head with gold horns, discovered in a tomb at Mycenae. It is not always easy to tell such objects from those made by Minoan goldsmiths. This work, dating from the sixteenth century B.C., is 15.5 cm high. (Athens, National Museum)

The "Mask of Agamemnon" from Mycenae
"Agamemnon's mask" was the name given to this gold funerary mask by the archaeologist and excavator Heinrich Schliemann when it was unearthed in one of the graves forming the circle of royal tombs at Mycenae. This 32 cm high effigy of a sixteenth century B.C. Achaean king nevertheless predated the Trojan War, described by Homer, by several centuries. (Athens, National Museum)

Might it not be improper to describe as "Homeric" the monuments built in Greece between the sixteenth and twelfth centuries B.C., when the *Iliad* and the *Odyssey* – the great epic poems of Homer – date no further back than the eighth century? The fact is that the fortifications, tombs and palaces of Mycenae and Tiryns match perfectly the poet's descriptions when he evokes the war scenes, funeral rites and palace life at the time of the Trojan War.

It was, moreover, a painstaking reading of the writings of Homer which led the self-taught German scholar, Heinrich Schliemann, to embark on his literally ground-breaking excavations in the Peloponnese, in 1876, once he had explored the ancient city of Hissarlik, at the mouth of the Dardanelles. At Mycenae he discovered what he believed to be the Palace of Agamemnon, the Tomb of Clytemnestra and the Treasury of Atreus. What was actually happening was the exhumation of the origins of the Greek world.

The accuracy of his verdicts was not confirmed until 1952. The archaeological world had in fact to wait until the script known as Linear B was deciphered by the English architect Michael G. Ventris, with the assistance of John Chadwick, to be quite certain that the inhabitants of Mycenae – who had hitherto been classified among the pre-Hellenic societies – were really Greeks. Based on tablets unearthed at Pylos, researchers have managed to show that the language spoken by the Mycenaeans was a form of early Greek. From that moment on, it became quite acceptable to set the birth of the history of the Greeks at Mycenae.

It had long seemed that the Mycenaeans were so closely related to the Cretan civilization and to the art of Cnossus – ruled over by the legendary King Minos – that they must have been part of the same ethnic stock. But the decipherment of the Linear B script showed that the Mycenaeans were newcomers – the new arrivals were confused with the Achaean invaders.

The Achaeans, who form the oldest population of Greek origin, reached Greece in around 2200 B.C. They found their way to the Peloponnese, where they settled before 1600. The pantheon which they worship is the same as that of Classical Greece: their principal gods are Zeus, Hera, Poseidon, Hermes, Athena, and Dionysus. The Mycenaeans are in fact the Achaeans, as Homer depicted them in his work.

The Mycenaeans were warriors. They occupied fortresses perched on acropolises surrounded by mighty walls. They formed a military aristocracy in a Greece that was divided up into small territories. Their petty kings reigned over districts whose main resources were farming and livestock. They set up a "feudal" system based on trade and plunder, and surrounded themselves with luxury which stood in stark contrast to their coarse, manly customs.

As contemporaries of the New Empire of Egypt, the Hittites of Anatolia and the Mitanni of northern Mesopotamia, the southern neighbour of the Mycenaeans was the maritime empire of the Cretans. The Mycenaeans were in no time at war with the kingdom of Cnossus, which they assailed with plundering forays.

Skilled goldsmiths' work from Vaphio and Mycenae
The beauty of the pieces recovered from Mycenaean tombs dating from around 1500 B.C. is clear evidence of an outstanding mastery of the goldsmith's craft. *Left*: The technical brilliance of this goblet found in a *tholos* tomb at Vaphio, in Laconia, celebrates the Cretan theme of the bull. *Right*: A *kantharos* – or deep cup with handles – from Mycenae is characterized by the sobriety of its lines. (Athens, National Museum)

The Myceneaean armies were also responsible for the sudden decline of the Minoans. Their troops landed on Crete between 1450 and 1400, and set fire to the palaces dotted about the large island.

Some decades earlier, on the Aegean island of Thera (Santorini), a fearsome volcanic eruption had levelled the city of Akrotiri – the site where, in 1967, the archaeologist Marinatos would discover the dazzling evidence of a Minoan-type culture, with its sumptuous frescoes buried beneath the ash – just as would happen 1500 years later to the Roman cities of Pompeii and Herculaneum.

This natural catastrophe which struck Santorini was probably followed by a huge tidal wave, the after-effects of which seem to have wiped out the fleet of Cnossus. From then on, Cretan hegemony dwindled and left the field open to the vessels of the Mycenaeans. The Achaeans made the most of this chance, and took control of Crete, adopting, as they went about the task, many of the characteristics peculiar to their predecessors.

An Artistic Merger

Before looking at Mycenaean architecture, it might be helpful to establish the artistic context in which this architecture flourished. In this respect, there is much to be learned from the arts and crafts unearthed by archaeological excavations in both Crete and continental Greece.

There are close symbiotic links between the art of the Minoans and the art of the Mycenaeans. The treasures discovered in pit and shaft graves and *tholoi* at Mycenae, Vaphio, Dendra and so on are often so akin to those unearthed at Cnossus that it is impossible to tell these structures apart. The similarities are especially striking in the working of gold, bronze, ivory and rock crystal. Chalices, cups, goblets, *rhytons,* and daggers may sometimes pass for artefacts imported from Minoan Crete, and sometimes for objects created in workshops located in Mycenaean Greece. Experts often decline to favour one hypothesis over the other.

It would certainly seem that part of the treasures with which the Mycenaeans surrounded their dead in the tomb came from raids carried out in Crete. But other scenarios are also conceivable. The lords of Mycenae might well have got Cretan craftsmen to manufacture the objects they coveted – as the wealthy chieftains of Thrace would do later, ordering their finery from Greek goldsmiths at Lampsacus.

So there are several possible answers. Either the workshops of Cnossus did work on request, and were paid when an actual deal was struck (archaeology shows us

A script deciphered in 1952
As a result of the decipherment of the Linear B script, we now know that the Mycenaeans were Greeks and that they were thus different from their neighbors, the Cretans of Cnossus. This terracotta tablet bears signs from a syllabic system which appeared in about the fifteenth century B.C. representing an early form of the Greek language.

He lived thirty-five centuries ago
This 30.5 cm high funerary "portrait" made of chased gold comes from a tomb at Mycenae excavated by Schliemann. Beyond death itself, the facial expression of the beardless person reveals an enigmatic smile. (Athens, National Museum)

that Minoan objects found their way all over the eastern Mediterranean, from Cyprus and Palestine to the Egypt of the Pharaohs), or the Mycenaeans, returning home from a campaign, brought with them – along with the objects which they seized – Minoan craftsmen who were entrusted with the manufacture of jewellery and decorative finery which was thenceforth produced in continental Greece.

We can also imagine how Greek apprentices rubbing shoulders with skilled Cretan gold- and silversmiths would have been quick to learn the Minoan skills. Workshops would thus have started to spring up in the Peloponnese, headed by accomplished "bosses" from the islands.

It is probably this latter hypothesis which was at work in the particular instance of gold funeral masks, for this type of symbolic attire was not known in Crete.

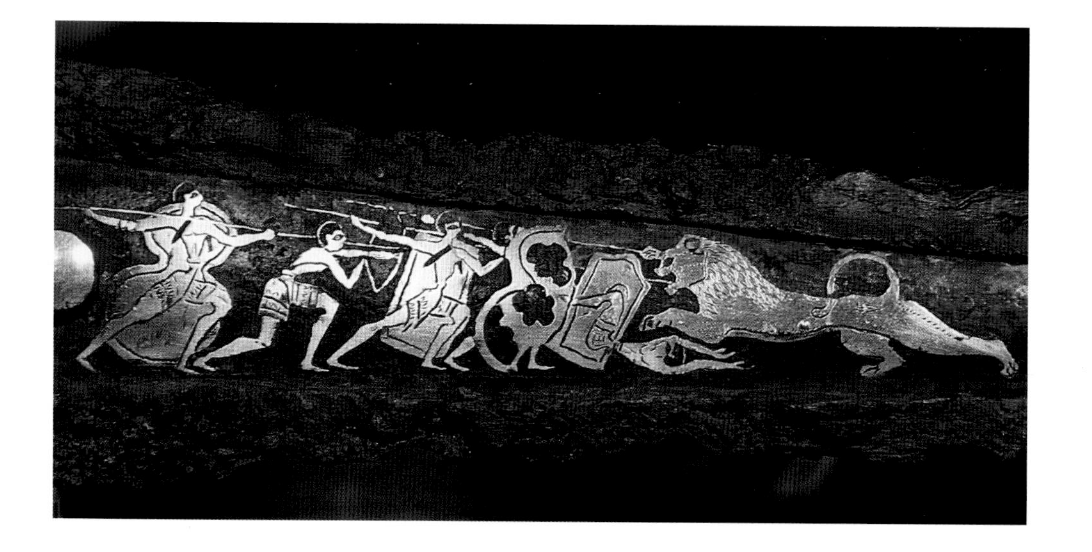

A lion-hunt in the Peloponnese
This scene depicting men armed with spears, bows and shields battling with lions decorates the blade of a 23.7 cm high bronze dagger set off by gold and niello inlay. The dagger is a ceremonial weapon from the sixteenth century B.C., coming from the Circle of Royal Tombs at Mycenae. (Athens, National Museum)

A bucolic scene decorating a ring
This carved 3 cm high bezel, found in a grave at Mycenae, embellishes a gold ring. It is possible to make out three women in a garden. Two of them, standing, seem to be paying homage to the third, who is seated and holding a bouquet of flowers. This is possibly a Cretan religious scene. (Athens, National Museum)

Thanks to this ritual Mycenaean practice, we now have intriguing effigies which have made the art of Mycenae so famous. For, down the ages, they re-create for us the expression of those early Greek warriors, the Achaeans, of whom Homer was so fond.

A Series of Masterpieces

Whether the fruit of looting, or produced in Crete and imported, or, last of all, made in Greece, the treasures unearthed in Mycenaean tombs and graves represent an impressive inventory of assets. They reveal the artistic concerns of their owners. The elegance of stemmed chalices, made from a single sheet of gold, and decorated with wild creatures; the amazing formal beauty of the Vaphio goblets, with their reliefs depicting bulls using the repoussé or embossed method; the vitality of the scenes of a lion hunt which appear on the blade of a dagger; the refinement of the mountings and settings of gold rings delicately chased with hunting and religious scenes; all this culminates in the effigy of the mythical bull of Minos, a sumptuous silver *rhyton* in the shape of a bull's head with gold horns and a rosette on the forehead, while the nose is covered with gold leaf. This magnificent object, whose origins seem to defy identification, raises once again the difficult enigma of the genesis of specifically Greek art.

The working of silver and gold, which demands not only the skilled virtuosity of deft-fingered experts, but also the sure eye of aesthetes and artists perpetuating a

The Acropolis of Mycenae
A general plan of the fortified city of Mycenae:
1 The Lion Gate
2 The Circle of Royal Tombs
3 The palace and *megaron*
4 An underground reservoir

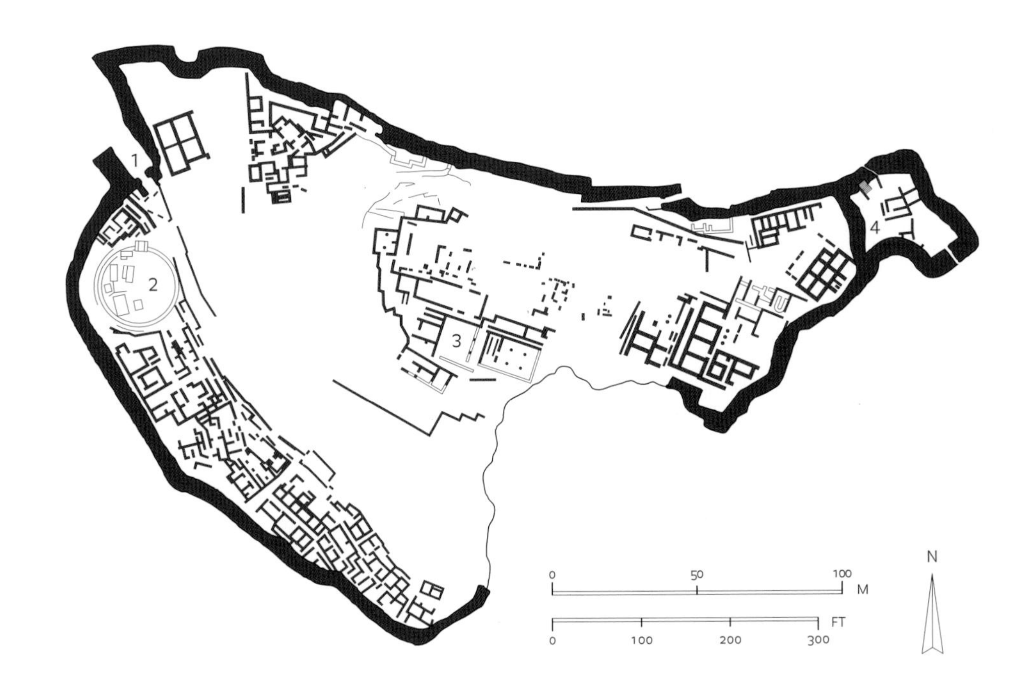

tradition, gives no hint of the nature of the Mycenaeans' architecture. For the art of building as practised by the Achaeans in no way carries on the constructions of Cnossus, Mallia, Gournia and Hagia Triada.

The Cretan palaces, with their countless rooms forming, in the legend of the Minotaur, the disconcerting labyrinth created by the mythical Daedalus, are quite the opposite of the megalithic and cyclopean monuments of the Mycenaeans.

Military Architecture

Unlike the huge ports and sprawling urban areas of Crete, the Mycenaean cities are fortified places. They are often strategically positioned and easy to defend. For their own safety, the Greek kings placed powerful entrenched walls on high ground, with soaring curtain-walls and monumental gateways. This military architecture reached its high point in the thirteenth century B.C., culminating in remarkable cyclopean walls, made of large polygonal stones – Mycenae offering the finest example of this style.

The defensive system of this stronghold city went through two stages: the first dates back to the fourteenth century and must have involved large boulders and blocks of stone with an outermost cladding formed by a stockade, according to Homer's description. Later, in the thirteenth century, the area was extended southwards to enclose a series of tombs. At the same time, the surrounding wall was considerably improved to cope with the threat of Dorian raids which marked the "return of the Heraclidae", to borrow the poet's turn of phrase.

During the second phase of these works, the Mycenaeans inaugurated an impressive building technique: they deployed huge polygonal blocks of stone, weighing several tons, and assembled without mortar. To explain the sheer size of each block, we have come to understand that the use of large stones is the most economical and offers the greatest solidity. In the Bronze Age, metal was still rare and the quarryman's work was done with hard stone sledgehammers. So it was easier to move heavy loads with rollers, sleds and quite large teams of manual labour than to erect quantities of parallelepipedal blocks with which to form regular courses.

The towering walls of Mycenae enclose a triangular area measuring 300 by 200 m. They cover a steep-sided hill, which is particularly sheer on the slope where

Arriving at Mycenae
This print, showing Mycenae in 1805, was made by the English painter Edward Dodwell and published in 1821. The site has hardly changed, despite the excavations.

there is a plunging ravine. This fine construction, attributed by Greek tradition to the Cyclopes, because of the volume of the stone blocks used to build it, already contained all the features of military architecture, as it would later be developed by Classical poliorcetics (the art of laying and resisting sieges).

When the assailant reached Mycenae, he had no choice but to take the least steep slope along the thoroughfare hewn from the rock which led to the main entrance to the city. He thus followed the steps leading to the main gate, which was accessible to horses and carts. In so doing, he followed a rocky outcrop with a bastion built on top. A continuous curtain wall, set firmly in the rock, surveyed the thoroughfare on his left.

Before him then rose the Lion Gate, preceded, to the right, by a projecting postern, enabling those within to keep attackers at bay in the crossfire. The Lion Gate is justly famous. It is an amazing construction, where polygonal blocks are replaced by colossal, even stones. The trapezoidal opening is formed by three enormous stones: the two upright stones are surmounted by a lintel weighing 20 tons. Above this monolith rises a relieving arch with, on either side, four large blocks in horizontal courses. These stones are corbelled, with one jutting out beyond the next to form a triangular bay. By reducing the staggered effect of each course, the Mycenaeans carefully outlined the contour of the arch, in which they then set a fantastic tympanum, made of a single block of finely carved limestone.

This tympanum, after which the gate is named, is decorated with two large wild animals which rear up, symmetrically, on either side of a column. These lions, with their well-delineated bodies and vigorous musculature, are – alas! – headless, the top of the sculpture having been hammered away by victorious foes keen to destroy the symbol of Mycenaean might.

As far as the central column is concerned, it rises up on a three-levelled base, which probably suggests the city itself. This column has similarities with the shafts of Cretan buildings; its smooth shaft is slightly flared towards the top – like those restored by Sir Arthur Evans in the palace of Cnossus. The shaft supports a moulded capital, with a projecting echinus, surmounted by a square abacus. Above, a row of cylindrical elements, set beneath an abacus, calls to mind the stepped roofing system using dressed beams. On the other side of the entrance, the uprights have holes for fitting reinforcement bars behind the wooden leaves – which were probably covered in bronze.

Mycenae, dominated by the Achaean fortress
The access road leading to the Lion Gate at Mycenae runs alongside the imposing cyclopean wall, from which those defending the city would bombard their foes. This wall dates from 1350 B.C.

Lastly, to withstand sieges, the Mycenaeans invested a great deal of effort to hew – by hand – in the rock a narrow underground passage leading to a deep spring. As a result of the techniques used by Bronze Age miners, the city enjoyed a constant supply of water.

Apart from Mycenae, other great constructions also attest to the technology achieved by these builders. A citadel such as Tiryns, with its steps rising between two walls up to the first courtyard in front of the palace, is a formidable creation, with walls soaring to a height of 6–7 m. The bastions are punctuated by loopholes. Its corbel-vaulted casemates and its hidden passages are impressive. To the south, the wall reaches a height of 16 m. This is an example of defensive architecture which heralds not only the fortifications of Classical Greece, but also the strongholds of medieval Europe.

Tholos-Tombs and Graves

Once inside the city of Mycenae, we find, to the right of the steps, the Royal Circle, formed by large upright slabs which ring the site, beneath which is a series of

The impressive bulk of the Lion Gate

Wedged between the city-wall (on the left) and the fortified spur of the outer postern (on the right), the gate with its pair of surmounting lions includes a lintel weighing 20 tons. It used to control access to the Acropolis of Mycenae in about 1250 B.C. The opening, measuring about 3 x 3 m, was defended by a huge wooden gate with two leaves covered with bronze "armor-plating".

Page 27
The Circle of Royal Tombs at Mycenae
This view shows the works undertaken by the Mycenaeans when the Lion Gate was built, in order to protect pit graves (shown here in the foreground) housing the treasures and remains of their sovereigns.

The defensive system of Tiryns
As at Mycenae, the Acropolis of Tiryns had an access road lined by imposing walls.
Below: Greek builders chose to erect the foundations of their cyclopean walls directly on the natural rock.

Dressed stone slabs
The Circle of Royal Tombs at Mycenae is formed by "shuttering" made of large upright stones (orthostats), between which a fill surmounted by horizontal slabs was designed to provide protection for the burial places, while at the same time forming a circular area intended for funerary rites.

A concentric arrangement
The complex architecture of the tomb circle shows the importance which the Mycenaeans attached to the burial places of their sovereigns. At a later stage, the *tholos*-tombs – vaulted underground structures – would replace these pits. But they were built outside the walls bordering the Acropolis.

Mycenae: the monumental entrance to a *tholos*
A road running between tall walls, called a *dromos,* leads to the domed tombs of Mycenae. Here, the entrance to what is known as the "Tomb of Clytemnestra" – as Schliemann called it – leads to the façade which is surmounted by a tall relieving triangle. This underground structure was erected in about 1220 B.C. The sunken roadway, 6 m wide, is 37 m in length.

several burial places. These are pit-and-shaft graves dating back to the sixteenth century B.C., carefully preserved during the rebuilding undertaken in the thirteenth century. They are located within an enclosure with a diameter of 26.5 m. It is here that Schliemann unearthed a series of intact burial places, whose treasures have duly revealed the art and gold- and silverwork of the Minoans and Mycenaeans, found together, somewhat pell-mell, in these royal tombs.

Another grave circle has been unearthed to the south of the city, below the walls. As far as the history of architecture is concerned, however, these are so-called *tholos*-tombs, with their corbelled dome, and they are the most phenomenal constructions of Mycenaean Greece. Their shape has sometimes been likened to primitive straw beehives. The Greek word *tholos* means, in essence, a round, columned religious edifice, described as monopteral (having just a single ring of columns), but it also applies to the large vaulted burial places of the Mycenaean period.

At Mycenae there are several domed tombs. Schliemann called the two best preserved examples the "Tomb of Clytemnestra" and the "Treasury of Atreus". These constructions beneath *tumuli* date back to *circa* 1250–1220 B.C. All buildings of this type have essentially the same layout: a straight, uncovered access way called the *dromos*, forms a deep trench in the ground. This horizontal cavity is bordered by tall walls in fine stonework. It leads to a large door giving access to the actual *tholos*. Behind this door lies the round area beneath the dome which houses the burial places.

The "Treasury of Atreus" is the largest of these Mycenaean funerary *tholoi*. Its *dromos* is 36 m long and 6 m wide, and the side walls rise to a height of 14 m. The monumental door, 5.4 m high, is surmounted by an impressive monolithic lintel. This great block, measuring 7 m by 6 and 1.4 m thick, has a total volume of almost 60 m^3, weighing more than 120 tons. It is topped by a triangular relieving arch, made of corbelled cyclopean stones, as in the Lion Gate. It is worth noting that

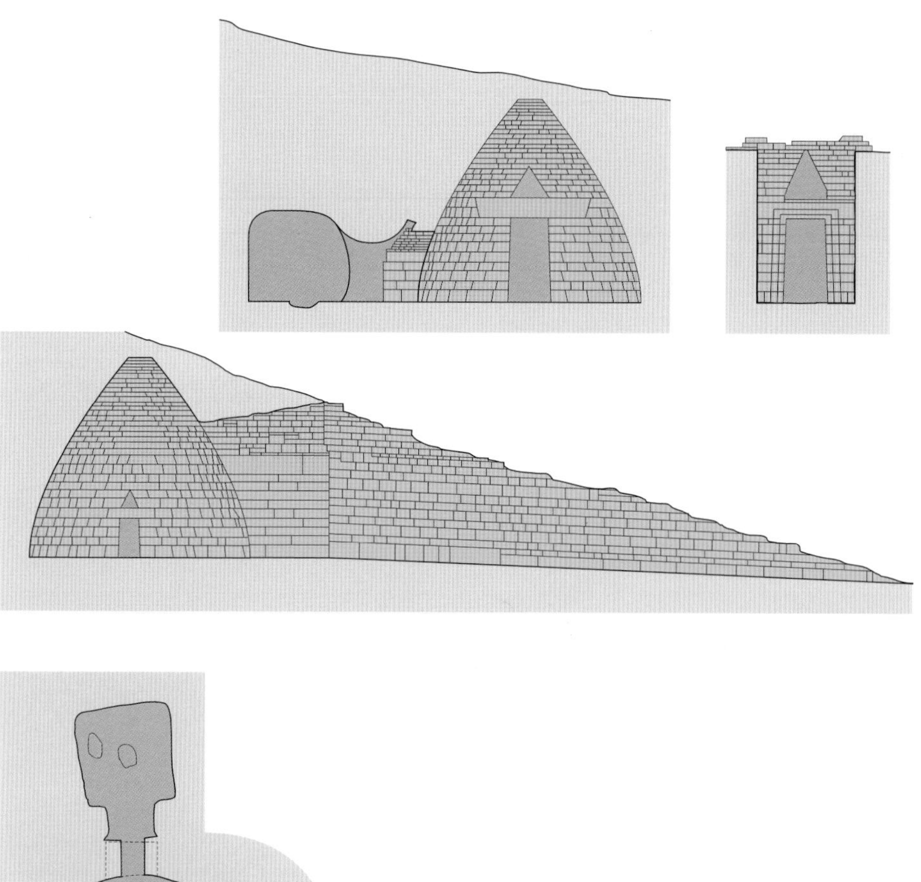

A gigantic portal
The façade of the "Treasury of Atreus", 10.5 m high, has a square, monolithic lintel measuring 7 m by 6, with a depth of 1.4 m, giving a total weight of some 120 tons. Once again, a triangular relieving arch, made using corbelled stones, absorbed the thrust above the door leading to the round chamber.

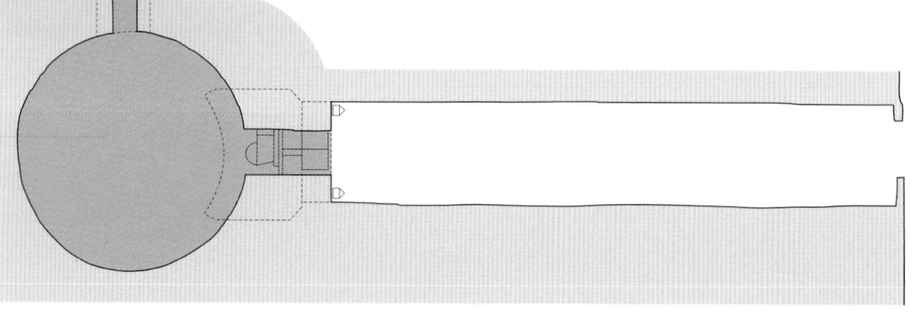

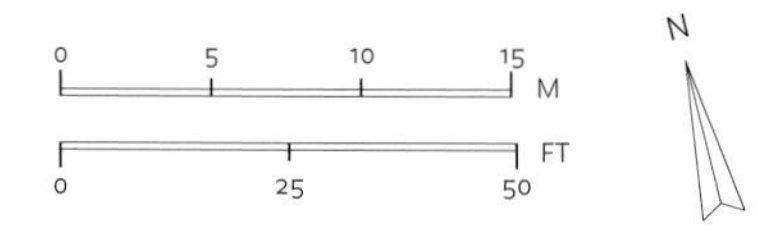

Page 31
The "Treasury of Atreus" at Mycenae
Schliemann thought he had discovered the Tomb of Agamemnon. This burial place, which marks the zenith of Mycenaean architecture, dates from 1250 B.C. These plans show the cross-section, the elevation of the doorway, the longitudinal section, and the plan of this superb *tholos* at Mycenae.

Mycenaean architects were not aware of, or familiar with, the true vault with radiating joints.

The same corbelling technique is used for the domed room. This measures 14.5 m in diameter and rises by way of a series of thirty-three concentric courses to the top of the building, at a height of 13.2 m.

The height of the courses is reduced with each successive level; their diameter becomes narrower and narrower. The outline of this "pointed" dome thus resembles a diagonal or cross-arch. The different levels between each block have been levelled in such a way that the *intrados* is strictly smooth and even. Traces of bronze tenons suggest the existence of metal decorative features (stars, perhaps), once embellishing this vault built to resemble the heavens.

The stability of this building stems from large quantities of material piled up outside the dome and which completely cover it. As the building gradually went up, fill was placed all around it. Buried beneath a *tumulus*, the dome thus receives an evenly distributed pressure over its entire outer surface, and this lends it both its cohesion

An accomplished interplay of buttressing
The lateral uprights – pilasters – at the entrance show the depth of the corbelled dome which crowns the "Treasury of Atreus". When the builders created this access to the vaulted area within, it was important that they did not weaken the circular structure.

Page 33
Like a huge hive
The conical shape of the chamber which forms the *tholos* of the "Treasury of Atreus" is produced by means of thirty-three concentric courses, corbelled one on top of the next. The dome, which has a diameter of 14.5 m at the base, rises to a height of 13.2 m. For 1300 years – until the Roman period – this building was the largest vaulted construction in the whole history of architecture.

and its strength. After being sunk into the ground, the *dromos* was filled in and the royal burial place vanished from mortal view.

Up until the Roman era – that is, 1300 years later – when the large brick, tufa and concrete cupolas of the imperial baths were erected, the Mycenaean *tholoi* would contain the largest inner areas with no intermediate supporting structure ever built in Antiquity. The perfection of their form, the technological mastery of their cyclopean stonework, and the quality of their corbelled vaulting all make these funerary structures the high point of the architecture of the second millennium B.C.

Palaces and the Question of the *megaron*

The palace which crowned the promontory of Mycenae has survived to this day in a state of preservation insufficient to provide any authoritative interpretation of its various areas. On the other hand, complexes such as Tiryns and Pylos (this latter

excavated by Blegen) reveal a palatial organization whose toothing stones on the ground are well preserved. They help us to grasp the particular distribution of the reception rooms forming what Homer called the *megaron*.

This is a standard plan to which every Mycenaean city brought its variations. It is well worth examining the plan of Pylos, which is among the most characteristic. The entire configuration is axial, and extends over some 40 m. A porch marks the main entrance, whose roof is supported by a lone column, set on the axis of penetration. Behind the door, an identical area with an axial column replicates the same configuration. The whole forms a kind of *propylaeum.* Next comes an oblong courtyard. This precedes a vestibule which opens behind the portico supported by two columns. It gives access to an antechamber which, in Pylos, has openings on each of the four sides.

Large axial doors lead to a large almost square room which forms the *megaron* proper. This area is 10 m wide by about 12 m long. Four columns surround the round hall. They hold up the roof which is fitted with a lantern designed both for letting smoke out and for ventilating the room. In the middle of the wall on the right of the entrance stands the king's throne. The ground is stuccoed and the walls are covered with frescoes.

Around this central complex, which forms the princely receptionroom, several chambers are accessible from corridors. These are private apartments, with bathrooms and bathtubs, as well as storage areas, some of which contain large storage jars or *pithoi*, used for wine, olives and other foodstuffs.

To the extent that the remains of the buildings permit any sure interpretation, it would seem that in the Mycenaean palaces only the basements were of masonry. The superstructures, on the other hand, like ordinary dwellings, were built with timber. The upper floor contained the women's quarters, called the *hyperoon*, which was entirely constructed with joists. The disappearance of these upper areas made from perishable materials deprives us of a great deal of information. It would therefore be interesting to know where the light that illuminated the rooms, and the throne room in particular, came from. If there were windows, they must have been above the solid basements, and no trace remains.

These wooden buildings – in particular the ceilings made of thick planks and logs, as well as the lantern surmounting the vestibule – linked palatial architecture to vernacular buildings. There are too few traces to enable us to imagine the details, because these buildings were all consumed by fire during the Dorian invasions.

The particular layout of the *megaron*, with its series of areas in a row – the vestibule preceded by a pair of columns, antechamber and main room – is an essential feature of Mycenaean architecture. This typical structure of the princely abode, as described by the epic tradition, thus applies above all to palaces. The Homeric Hymns also use the term *megaron* to denote certain underground sanctuaries dedicated to chthonian deities. This is why modern archaeologists have postulated an actual structural continuity between the *megaron* and the plan of the *naos* in the Greek temple. It so happens, however, that, between the decline of the Mycenaean civilization in the twelfth century B.C. and the flowering of Archaic art in the ninth and eighth centuries, there was a deep break. The invasion of the Dorian tribes was a catastrophe which once again plunged Greece into a period of upheaval and ruin.

Any tentative link between the palace room and the temple *cella* is called into question by a tangible silence lasting several centuries. Furthermore, as we shall see, the very nature of the area peculiar to these two types of construction is different. The plans of the new buildings appearing in the ninth century have an "apsidal" feature – rounded in shape – which was totally absent from Mycenaean buildings. Lastly, from the eighth century on, the major novelty resides in the creation of structures which excavators have christened "verandas". They are peripheral porticoes on wooden pillars which surrounded certain buildings. To all

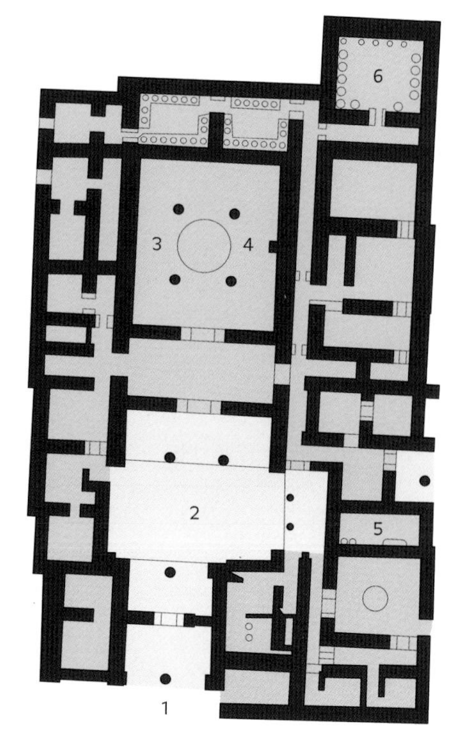

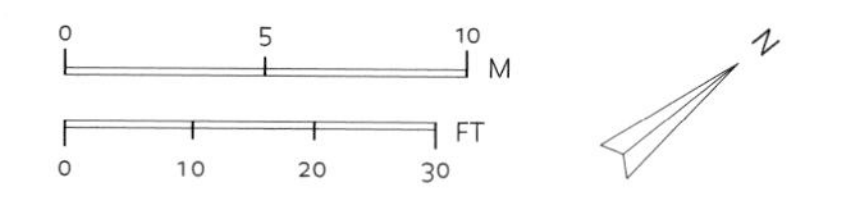

Pylos: a typical *megaron*
The plan of the Mycenaean palace of Pylos shows the features of the *megaron*, characteristic of the Achaeans. For many years, it was thought that the spatial organization of the Greek temple derived from the Mycenaean palace. It is worth noting, however, that the sovereign's throne produces an axis that is broken at 90° C, which has no counterpart in the Greek temple.

1 Entrance
2 Inner courtyard
3 Main hall, or *megaron*
4 Sovereign's throne
5 Bathroom for the apartments
6 Storerooms

A polychrome sculpture
This stuccoed woman's head, enhanced by polychrome features, was found at the foot of the Acropolis of Mycenae, and dates from the thirteenth century B.C. It points to the existence of a body of Achaean statuary, but, sadly, only rare examples of this have come down to us.
(Athens, National Museum)

appearances, these porticoes were harbingers of the peripteral colonnade which would be the major characteristic of Greek architecture. The original feature will be discussed in the chapter dealing with the "Origins of the Greek Temple".

It would in any event seem difficult to accept that the *naos* of the Greek sanctuaries is the direct heir of the Mycenaean *megaron*, mentioned by Homer. Any such proposition relies, as far as can be seen, on the desire to bring about a historical continuity, where the disruptions following the upsurge of the Dorian tribes rocked traditions. By plunging Greece into a long period of anarchy and chaos, these dramatic goings-on make any such link quite unlikely.

The Spread of Mycenaean Culture

After the Mycenaeans gained control of Crete in about 1450, they enjoyed a period of expansion between 1400 and 1200 B.C. Their influence – spurred on by busy maritime traffic in the eastern Mediterranean, reaching as far as Italy – was based on naval supremacy. In this respect, they first took the place of the Minoans themselves, then of the Phoenicians who, in about 1230, were overcome by the invasions

of the "Sea Peoples". But their hegemony was short-lived, for the Dorian raids (between 1150 and 1000 B.C.) wiped out the Mycenaean culture, and led to an impressive intermixing of peoples. After fierce battles and onslaughts mounted against the Mycenaean strongholds, the newcomers drove the Achaeans back towards the south and east. The Ionians, for their part, took possession of the shores of Asia Minor. There followed various highly complex movements which, towards the ninth century, would bring about a certain unity in Greece.

From then on, the period of the great migrations was over. "The Aegean is a Greek lake", and the names of the different peoples only continued to exist in the appellation of Greek dialects – Ionian spoken in Attica, Euboea and on Samos; Aeolian spoken on the northern coast of Anatolia and as far as Lesbos; Dorian used in the regions around Megara, Corinth and Argos, on Crete and in Cnidos; and Arcadian in Arcadia and on Cyprus.

The fact nevertheless remains that the Mycenaean expansion in the Mediterranean, followed by the intermingling of different tribes resulting from the last wave of invasions, are factors which prepared the Greeks for the great colonizing movement which got under way in the beginning of the eighth century B.C.

Discovered on the Acropolis of Mycenae
This fragment of a fresco, brought to light in 1970, is proof that the great pictorial art of the people of Cnossus or Akrotiri (Santorini) did not vanish under the rule of the Achaeans. Other examples of mural paintings have been discovered at Tiryns, thus confirming the existence, in the thirteenth century B.C., of an artistic link between Minoans and Mycenaeans. This woman's face, in profile, with its rich trimmings, helps us to imagine the decoration of the palaces of this period. (Athens, National Museum)

Page 37
Linear B
This Mycenaean syllabic script predates the appearance in the ninth century B.C. of the alphabet originating from the Phoenician coast. (Athens, National Museum)

From Linear B to the alphabet

It is thanks to an "amateur", the architect Michael Ventris, that we have known since 1952 that the texts transcribed using the so-called Linear B script belong to the Greek language group. They stand apart from Linear A documents, engraved on clay tablets found in Crete (Hagia Triada, Phaestus, Cnossus, Mallia) which probably encompass a Minoan language – which have not been deciphered. Linear A appeared from 1650 B.C. onward. Linear B writings, which have been found at Cnossus, Pylos and Mycenae, and which also come in the form of clay tablets, make up a syllabic system which appeared towards the end of the fifteenth century B.C. This script postdates the fire that gutted the palaces of Crete. We thus know that Greek has been spoken and written for at least 3 500 years.

Linear B consists of ninety signs, representing either vowels or syllables formed by a consonant and a vowel. In addition, certain symbols are ideographic. The texts found to date involve only administrative documents, repertories and accounts. They are essentially inventories, stock lists, fiscal records and statements of quantities of craft products and objects. Some signs also act as counting and measuring units. These numerals form a decimal system, with special signs for fractions. These texts thus shed little light on the culture and social preoccupations of Achaean society. On the other hand, they explain the commercial success of the "Mycenaean thalassocracy".

With the collapse caused by the Dorian invasions (1200–1000 B.C.), and with the disappearance of all writing, it was not until the ninth or eighth century that the Greeks finally adopted a new method of writing. This emerged from the contacts made in the Near East by Greek mariners with the Phoenicians. It was by way of the trading post (*emporion*) set up by the Greeks at Al-Mina, in Syria – on a site close to the port of Ras Shamra (Ugarit), where the first alphabet with thirty signs was invented – that Greece acquired an alphabetic script. The great leap forward here was in the notation of vowels, which no Semitic language recorded.

From that moment on, the Greek script, which would vary scarcely at all for millennia, was well suited to recording the subtleties of thought and language, whether of poetry or of philosophy. The Greeks thus managed – with greater ease than their Egyptian, Sumerian and Babylonian predecessors – to set down the great epic and mythical narratives of Hellenism.

Once they had their script, the Greeks lent a definitive form to the numerous versions that developed orally around the epics telling of the Trojan War and the seaborne adventures of Odysseus in the Mediterranean. This task of bringing together the two great epic cycles dating back to Mycenaean traditions was masterfully achieved by the poet Homer. It would seem that he was born in Smyrna, on the border of Aeolis and Ionia, where the two most important Greek dialects were spoken. It was the merger of these in Homer's work that created the *koine* – the basic language – that would guarantee its posterity.

The Origins of the Greek Temple

The Emergence of the Peripteral Colonnade

Page 39
An early affirmation of humanism, at Delphi
With the image of the *kouros* – a naked young man, standing – which glorifies the role of man in the presence of the gods, Greece expressed the power of its religiosity and the individualism of its attitude to fate. This small bronze *kouros*, which despite its height of 14 cm has a monumental hieratic quality, dates from the seventh century B.C. At Delphi, it is the earliest known example of this type. (Delphi, Museum)

The "Sulky Girl"
This *kore* – a statue of a standing girl in Archaic Greek art – discovered in 1882 on the Acropolis of Athens, dates from 490 B.C. She clearly illustrates the Severe style. Dedicated by Euthydicus, she is dressed in the Ionian style. Her heavy hairstyle frames a full face, on which there is no trace of the smile of earlier works. (Athens, Acropolis Museum)

When the final curtain went down on the Mycenaean world, during the twelfth century B.C., Greece was the scene of far-reaching upheavals. The country sank into a dark age of decline, and the art produced in it would only come to light 500 years later, around the middle of the eighth century B.C.

Everywhere there was destruction, fire and plunder, following the waves of invasions by peoples from the north. The rash of Dorian and Ionian migrations was followed by ruined palaces, looted tombs and abandoned cities.

The only glimmer – but it was a bright one! – still burning in the wake of these disasters, and illuminating the darkness of these turbulent "Middle Ages", was the work of Homer who, from Ionia in the late ninth century, bequeathed his all-encompassing epic poems to the Greek people. With the *Iliad* and the *Odyssey*, the poet fashioned the mind and thinking of the Greek world. He shaped and moulded – if we may use the term – Greekness. Together with the appearance of his works, there arose around the Aegean a cultural entity and a religious reality, complete with myths and gods, as well as a set of ideals shared by all Greeks. This was the sign of a complete renewal. Thanks to the Homeric Hymns, Greece would re-emerge from the old civilizations of Egypt and the Near East, regenerated, transformed, youthful and imaginative. She created an original conception and an approach all of her own to both man and the gods.

On these foundations, the Greeks would give birth to a new type of sanctuary which, over three centuries, would attain the fullness and harmony of outward form which we call beauty.

The Invention of an Architecture

The great structural innovation which is the original feature of Greek architecture is the outer colonnade which runs around the sanctuary. This ring of stone shafts forms a curtain – powerfully cadenced, but nevertheless "see-through" – around the hallowed *cella*, and is the major formal achievement of the Greeks. It is this colonnade which typifies the approach of builders constructing places of worship in the Archaic and Classical periods.

Paradoxically, the sources and significance of this feature peculiar to great Greek architecture have aroused very little curiosity among specialists. Art historians have not devoted their research to this architectural element. They have often contented themselves with recording this structure as an obvious fact, or a postulate. As a general rule, they have been happier to devote themselves to studying the "orders" and "styles", and the countless variations which were made to the peripteral colonnade down the centuries.

It can, indeed, be said that the Ionic style and the Doric style are only the vital element of Greek art because they represent the forms of expression of an architecture based on the peristyle. For the creation and flourishing development of this ring of outer columns surrounding the sanctuary marks the assertion of the altogether new formula of the Greek temple.

This dazzling peristyle, set hard against the light, like a screen between the outer world and the dark *cella* housing the sacred image of the deity, sets out the revolutionary formula of the Greek sanctuary. This encircling portico, with its theory of shafts supporting the temple roof, this series of stone cylinders standing side by side, and this effect of salience, all give the true stamp of the "Greek order". They imbue it with a specific seal and endow it with its powerful novelty.

What is there in the neighbouring civilizations, contemporary or earlier, which also shows a use of this particular support embodied by the column? Egypt – the pre-eminent source of so much artistic creation – made use of stone shafts in its funerary buildings from the Old Kingdom on (*circa* 2500 B.C.) – for example the palm-shaped stone columns of the lower temple at Abu Sir. Subsequently, porticoes stood at the entrance to sanctuaries and certain rock tombs in the Middle Kingdom. Colonnades were erected as façades to sweeping terraces set against the mountain of Deir el-Bahari, and other colonnades encircled the inner courtyard in the temples of the New Kingdom and the Late Period.

The most frequent use of the column culminated in the creation of hypostyle rooms. But there is no evident presence of peripteral colonnades in the vocabulary of Egyptian architecture, though there were pavilions and chapels surrounded by square pillars. But these porticoes on pillars which mark the boundaries of distinct buildings are generally part of the interior of a building surrounded by walls.

The civilizations of the Near East – with the exception of the Achaemenids, whom we shall be discussing in some detail in due course – also use hypostyles. By way of example, let us mention the so-called "Forest of Lebanon" room built by the Hebrews and mentioned in Solomon's Palace, and the symbolic columns, called Boaz and Yakin, which stand before the vestibule of the Temple of Jerusalem, constructed by Phoenician craftsmen. At Bogazkoy, on the Acropolis of Büyükkale, the Hittites built Palace D (fifteenth–fourteenth centuries B.C.) which included – or so it would seem from rediscovered foundations a square area with five by five wooden columns measuring 30 by 30 m. But once again this was a hypostyle room.

So the Greek peristyle colonnade has all the features of an outstandingly original creation in the context of cultures either preceding it or contemporary with its blossoming. How, then, was this encircling outer structure actually made?

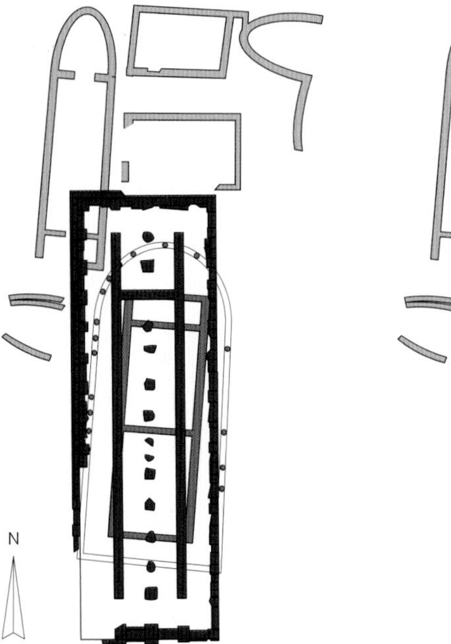

A

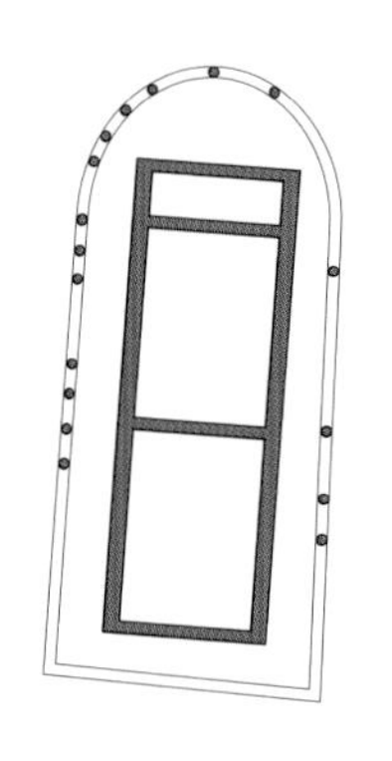

B

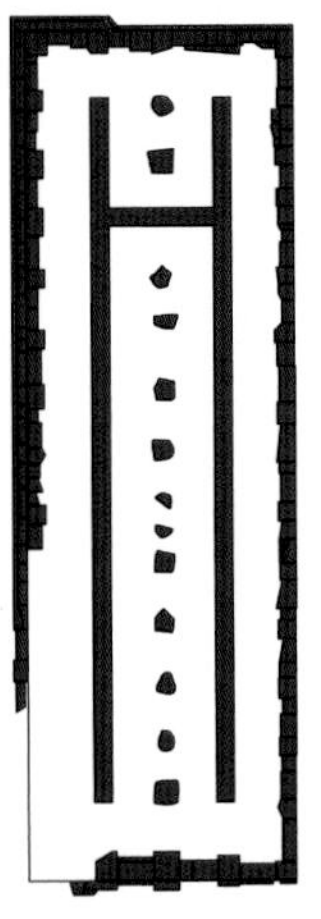

C

A criss-cross of Archaic buildings
Excavations of the early sanctuaries of Thermum, in Aetolia, north of the Gulf of Corinth, help us to follow the succession of sanctuaries between the ninth century and the late seventh century B.C. The plans are superimposed over a limited area:

- A The separated plans showing Temple I, at top left: an "apsidal" building with cob walls
- B Temple II with its rectangular *cella*, preceded by a vestibule and followed by the *opisthodomos;* a colonnade surrounds the "apsidal" chevet (eighth century B.C.)
- C Temple III, known as the Temple of Apollo and Megara, has a rectangular layout and a peripteral colonnade: a long *cella* with a row of posts which axially supported the thatched roof (late seventh century B.C.)

Funerary palace or temple?
At Lefkandi, on the island of Euboea, a remarkable building from the ninth–eighth centuries B.C. was unearthed in 1980. It is a *heroon* – a funerary sanctuary – whose "apsidal" plan, including a chamber with an axial colonnade, has divisions which had to do with a specific ritual. The interest of this large building, 45 m in length, lies in the "veranda" which surrounds it. This is an outer portico made with wooden shafts. Together with its "apsidal" chevet, this peristyle consisted of some fifty supports.
1 Apse
2 Passage between the ritual rooms
3 Ceremonial room
4 Ceremonial room
5 Axial colonnade
6 Burial-places
7 Vestibule
8 Porch

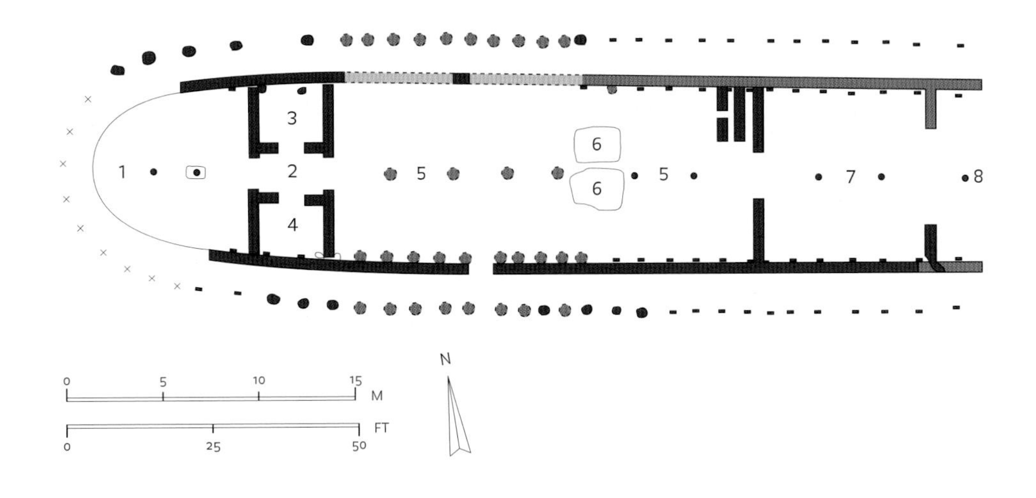

Archaeological Evidence

Recent excavations bearing on the oldest examples of sanctuaries, traces of which have been unearthed using very subtle archaeological techniques, concern various sites in continental Greece and the islands. The findings converge to a large degree and thus help to reconstruct the birth of these peripteral buildings. This is the case at Thermum, north of the Gulf of Corinth, at Lefkandi in Euboea, and at Eretria, also in Euboea, where there is evidence pointing back to the ninth and eighth centuries B.C.

What do we find at these sites? Among still primitive, round huts, there are mud constructions which are narrow in shape and set lengthwise, often to an east-west orientation. As if by analogy with the hut, these buildings have a rounded chevet, described as "apsidal". These structures therefore end in a semi-circular wall (which is more exactly semi-elliptical), and have interior divisions created by means of partitions with an axial corridor. These walls are set, on the one hand, between the entrance (vestibule) and the main room, and, on the other, at the opposite end between the *cella* and the apse (*opisthodomos*). Archaeologists have compared the arrangement of these areas with the *megaron* of the Mycenaean palaces.

A variety of developments influenced these early buildings, whose dimensions range from 10 to 12.5 m in width and 20 to 30 m in length. At Thermum, the Megaron A must have been covered with a timber frame and thatch, like the huts. At Eretria, a row of central posts supported the wooden roof. This building has been christened the "Palace of Apollo".

Before long, this early architecture with "apsidal" rooms was added to by a major additional feature. The building at Lefkandi, which the British School has been excavating since 1980, is surrounded by a series of posts forming a light outer portico, called a "veranda". This envelops the entire structure and turns the layout into an apsidal one. With a width of 10 m and an already considerable length of 45 m, the "Funerary Palace" or *heroon* of Lefkandi had some fifty wooden supports set 2 m apart from each other, forming a peripteral portico 2 m outside the building.

At Thermum, there is a smaller building, the Temple B, measuring 12.5 by 26 m, also with an outer portico. This sanctuary, with its "apsidal" plan, has a peristyle with a total of thirty-six posts. We should stress the fact that the plan used for the very elongated *cella* no longer includes the rounded feature of the chevet. It is rectangular (21.4 by 7.3 m) with a double interior division corresponding to those of the Lefkandi *cella*. Conversely, in keeping with the early plan, the portico retains the "apsidal" layout, whereas the *cella* takes on a more or less definitive parallelepiped appearance.

From the moment the two-sided roof appeared, whose gable dominates the entrance, situated on the narrow side of the "apsidal" building, the formula of the pediment that would characterize the Greek temple resulted in new carpentry and woodworking techniques. On the other hand, at the other end of the roof, the apse is surmounted by the rounded form of the semi-conical thatch roof. It was not until the disappearance of the "apsidal" plan that a symmetrical solution, with a double pediment, would come about.

This is the development which, from this embryonic peripteral sanctuary, would lead to the early prototype represented by the Temple C in the Sanctuary of Apollo. At the end of the seventh century B.C., this would be superimposed on the early wooden constructions which we have just described. This early temple at Thermum was built of stone, with a wooden peristyle, and a *cella* with a row of axial supports bearing the roof.

This is a building with five façade columns and fifteen lateral columns, originally made of timber, but before long replaced by stone shafts, with a décor of terracotta covering the woodwork in the upper parts. It has an *opisthodomos in antis* – in other words, a rear room set between the ends of two side walls, which form an extension of the side walls of the rectangular *cella*. This measures 100 feet in length (32 by 7 m), a feature which likens it to the so-called *hecatompedon*-sanctuary of Samos, which we shall discuss below.

So excavations, albeit still too infrequent, carried out at the so-called protogeometric and geometric levels referring to the corresponding pottery, help to make a schematic reconstruction of the origins of the peristyle in the earliest places of worship built by the Greeks in perishable materials.

The Significance of the Peristyle

The use of columns to support an awning which protects the entrance of a building, or, thanks to a hypostyle room, to create a very large roofed or covered area, represents a logical architectural next step. However, a specific concept lurks behind the idea of using a portico forming a peristyle to surround an enclosed *cella*, which is not accessible to the public. But this is less self-evident than might at first appear to an observer with preconceived cultural notions about the image of the Greek temple. What might be the significance of such a construction? And what kind of semiology was it founded upon?

As we have already pointed out, the first early buildings of the eighth and seventh centuries B.C. were made of timber. This fact will help us to grasp the essence of the portico. In the light of ancient writings and myths, it makes sense to link those early sanctuaries with agrarian forms of worship, in particular the worship of the tree, sacred wood and the forest. Roland Martin reminds us that "not far from the city of Samos, the effigy of Hera, brought by the Argonauts, was honoured beneath a baldachin, amidst clumps of sacred osier and altars erected in the open". Apollonius of Rhodes wrote that these same Argonauts stopped off at a small island and there "created, for Apollo, in a shady grove, a magnificent precinct and an altar made of piled stones".

The sacred tree of Athena, daughter of Zeus, was the olive (venerated in particular at the Erechtheum in the precinct called the Pandrosion). At Delphi, Apollo is associated with the laurel. At Eretria, the first Temple of Apollo is an "apsidal" building known as the "Hut of Laurel" or *daphnephorion*. At Dodona, Zeus took the place of a goddess of the tree, but he held on to the symbol – the oak, the famous oracular site.

What is more, the site of the oracles is often confused with a tree or wood. This is the case at Didyma, Claros, Gryneion, Alexandria in Troad (Troy), and Soura in Lycia. Asia, rich in Apollonian cults, boasted many sacred woods which served as sanctuaries. At Claros, Apollo found shelter among oaks. And up until the middle of the fourth century B.C., the sanctuary of Asclepius on Kos must have had just the one *temenos* formed by a cypress wood and an altar.

The old Temple of Hera at Olympia
Hera, the wife of Zeus, was the main object of worship at Olympia, in the north of the Peloponnese. A temple dedicated to her predated 600 B.C. This Heraion, which has six façade columns, enables us to follow the "petrification" of the outer portico, initially made of wood, with the shafts gradually being replaced by stone Doric columns.

The association between temple and sacred wood is thus a current one. So Strabo reckoned that "poets who embellish everything call any old sanctuary a 'sacred wood', even if the wood is treeless".

The fact remains that in Archaic buildings, where the columns are tree trunks, the analogy between temple and hallowed forest is obvious. It is in forests that the *xoana* are left – wooden statues representing a very rudimentary effigy of the deity. Pausanias even specified the plant species which are best suited to these consecrated woodlands: cypress, pine, plane, ash, oak, olive, and laurel.

As for Varro, who so often echoes Greek authors and traditions, he describes the inauguration of a sanctuary by emphasizing that "the temple is an area bordered by trees" (*On the Latin Language/De lingua latina*, VII,9). So the sanctuary was ritually bounded by the trees of the sacred wood. More specifically, these trees form the *peribolos*, the precinct of the divine realm which thus merges with its rustic setting.

From here to the admission that the peripteral colonnade is the reminder or recollection of this primordial forest, abode of the gods and goddesses in the Greek pantheon, it is just one short step. Architecture represents this pre-eminent place which contains the divine spirit (*numen inest*, to borrow the words of Ovid), where sacredness is concentrated. The outer colonnade or encircling portico is similar to vegetation, with stems and trunks bursting from the ground, and forms a sunny place where men and gods come together – a link between heaven and earth. So it is indeed this sacred wood which is embodied by the temple peristyle, and which sanctuaries keep the memory of, through the changes represented by the "petrification" phase of built structures, when the entire temple would be erected in stone – first, blocks of tufa, then in marble with its crystalline surfaces. In this way a kind

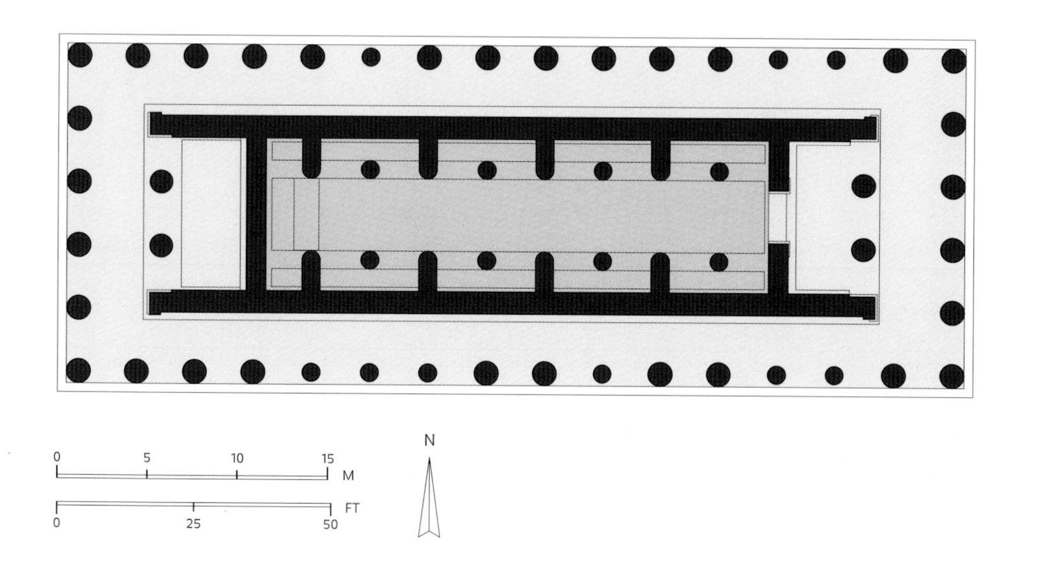

A *cella* lined with niches
The plan of the Temple of Hera at Olympia reveals the hesitation of the architect when he opted for two rows of inner columns instead of an axial colonnade. Every other shaft is replaced by a low salient wall – probably designed to deal with problems of statics. The *cella* is a *hecatompedon* – that is a structure, which measures a hundred feet in length.

of forest accompanied the sanctuary when this latter, leaving green groves and wild nature, would take up its place in the centre of cities.

The peristyle colonnade thus has a far-reaching significance which exceeds the mere aesthetic factor proposed by specialists. It is symbolic of the temple and its original context. It lends the building a crucial semiological value by linking it with the primitive sacred wood. Without this symbolic input, architecture might be reduced to a pointless act, stripped of meaning, whereas it clearly conveys the innermost intentions of its creators. Art for art's sake is a modern invention.

Columns and Materials

At Olympia, the Temple of Hera is a sanctuary erected in about 600 B.C., with six façade columns and sixteen lateral columns. It is a "hexastyle". We should note, in this respect, that constant use meant that the number of columns of a temple had to be established for the façade and for the long sides by taking the corner column into account each time. The *cella* has a *pronaos*, or vestibule, and, in accordance with the symmetrical number of the façade columns, does not have an axial colonnade. This Heraion of Olympia is in fact provided with two rows of inner columns. But these do not form three naves. Rather, they alternate with small perpendicular walls which, on either side of the central nave, create four niches with shafts rising up in the middle of them. This organization illustrates the hesitancy of those early builders in the way they would arrange the inner area of the *naos*.

At this stage of our study, the most interesting aspect of the Temple of Hera at Olympia lies in the way it came about. This helps us to follow up, in an active way, the material transformations made to the columns, by what is called "petrification". In effect, the outer portico had been built in timber. Little by little, however, the shafts were replaced by stone columns. It would seem that donors thus found an opportunity to display their munificence by making this kind of devout gesture. So the operation was carried out in various stages. The sanctuary with the wooden porticoes then turned into a stone temple.

This transformation affected not only the building technique itself, but also replaced a perishable material – timber – with stone, which is "eternal". In this sense, the sanctuary is part and parcel of a permanent prospect, unlike the cob dwelling, which is ephemeral. It can thus be all the better identified with the gods to whom it is consecrated.

In Syracuse, with the Temple of Apollo dating back to the early sixth century B.C., it is easy to follow this evolution marked by the erection of the first peripteral

Page 47
Squat columns
The Doric columns of the Temple of Hera at Olympia, which can be seen on the east façade of the temple, are distinctive for their large diameter (varying from 1 m to 1.28 m) in relation to their height.

building constructed entirely in stone: its monolithic columns accurately reproduce the squared trunks of wooden sanctuaries.

It is furthermore by analogy to the axe work on the surface of tree trunks that the flutes, which lend the column's surface its rhythm, came into being. This formula was probably "reinvented" by the Greeks, for it appeared in Egypt in *circa* 2650 B.C., in the funerary complex of Djoser, where back-to-back columns – they were not yet erected freely in space – present this characteristic which would later refine the shaft by making it "revolve" in the light that much better. Egypt reverted to the formula, once more between 2000 and 1500 B.C., with the polygonal, rather than fluted, columns of the buildings of the Middle and New Kingdoms. This style, which is described as "proto-Doric", preceded the Greek Doric style by more than 1 000 years. Even if it were to pass for a precursory sign of the architectural blossoming of the Greeks, it would be hard to find any influence – even remote – of Egypt over Greece.

The petrification process thus spread to all sanctuary structures, while at the same time conserving the forms that had been conceived in timber. The system of roofconstruction using timber frames was thus quite literally transposed into stone. The triglyphs of the frieze are the butt-ends of beams and joists, the crossbowmen are worked in stone, the ceiling coffers painstakingly reproduce joinery structures, and so on.

Things thus advanced based on a purely formal method, which did not take the properties of the material into due consideration. Just as a wooden beam is intended to have flexibility, so a stone lintel or platband, subjected to different situations and conditions, turned out to be inadequate. In the first place, the process of transposition was accompanied by a considerable increase in weight, which had to be taken into account in the construction plans. Further, stone hampered the use of wide intercolumniation and did not permit the creation of very large interior areas.

So petrification could, in some instances, culminate in nonsensical solutions, not to say technological aberrations. These results in no way disheartened the architects of the Greek world.

An Archaic Doric style
The oldest stone columns of the Heraion at Olympia have a broad capital with a jutting echinus, which seems to be as if compressed under the weight of the roof supported by the square abacus.

The Greek Orders

In the petrification process that resulted from the emergence of the peristyle, Greek architecture followed a twofold evolution and produced two styles. Authors of Antiquity themselves described these styles as Doric and Ionic. Before we broach our study of the orders, let us bear in mind that in the Archaic Age (beginning of the sixth century B.C.), the Aeolic capital had appeared on the north-west coast of Asia Minor. Its composition clearly reflected the role of the column, originating from the tree whose image it reproduced around the temple, so that the Aeolic capital, formed by two vertically salient volutes, unfailingly conjured up the image of a palm tree. With its long plant-like crockets, among which there blooms sometimes a palmette sometimes a crown of falling leaves, this Aeolic column, which is well represented at Larisa and Neandria, was probably influenced by the palm-decorated capitals of Phoenician architecture. Whatever the case may be, it merely bolsters the interpretation of the portico as an *analogon* of the sacred wood encircling the temple.

In dealing with the two great orders of Greece, we must also emphasize the "dictatorial" aspect which they have taken on in art schools. For a long time, the history of architecture has been focused on the features and variations offered by these stylistic elements, situated half-way between the realm of structure and the realm of decoration. Analysis of porticoes has galvanized all the energy of specialists, to the point where the study of the orders – for which, in the Renaissance, Serlio had provided a rigorous exposition in his treatise *L'Architettura* (1537–1547) – has become synonymous with the art of building.

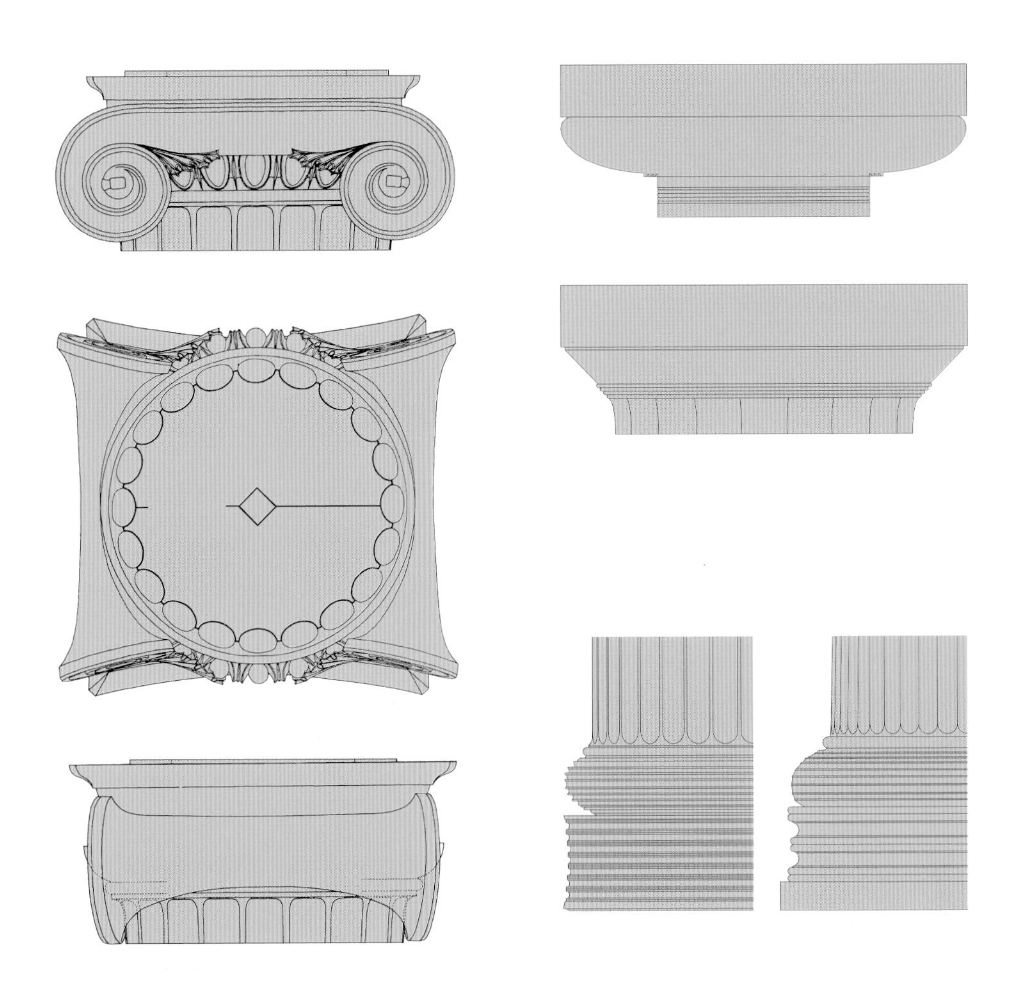

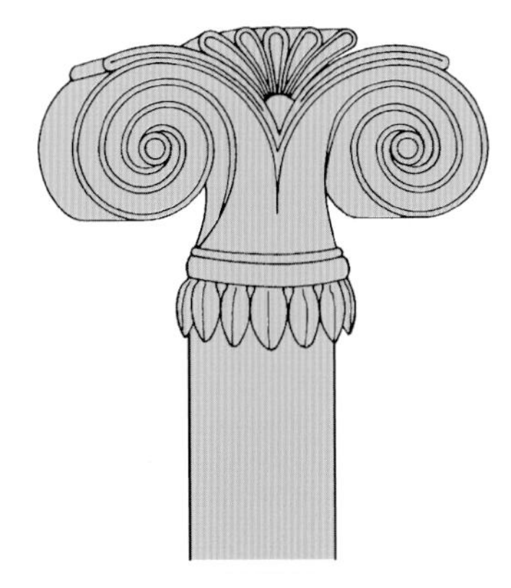

Capitals and bases
Left: Two Archaic capitals with Aeolic volutes. The one at top left comes from Larisa, in Aeolia, and the other, below it, was found at Neandria, a city in Troas. These Aeolic capitals, discovered in Asia Minor, date from *circa* 580 B.C. They foreshadow the vertical volutes of the columns of Persepolis.
Centre: An Ionic capital seen from the front, from below and in profile. The volutes now descend laterally and frame a row of ova.
Above right: Two profiles of Doric capitals, one Archaic, with a wide echinus, the other Classical, with a more elongated echinus.
Below right: Two types of bases of Ionic columns with a large number of *tori* and *scotias*.

The Doric order is essentially widespread in continental Greece and in Magna Graecia (southern Italy and Sicily), whereas the Ionic order, as its name suggests, is found on the shores of the Aegean and the islands.

We shall not go into any detailed description of these styles here, based, as it is, on an often specialized and off-putting vocabulary. If we adopt terms such as volute, echinus, abacus, gorgerin, drum, triglyph, metope, and the like, which are well-established by sheer use, we shall on the other hand only make passing reference to annulets, festoons, quarter rounds, mutules, dentils, cushions and springers, balusters, and astragals. We should not confuse the study of decoration with that of the building itself.

In his *Histoire de l'Architecture*, published at the very end of the nineteenth century, Auguste Choisy summed up as follows the qualities "of the two classic types of order: the Doric, male, squat, severe, and rough; the Ionic, rich, elegant, and light". The first style – the Doric – consists of columns which have no base, with the shaft tapering towards the top, surmounted by a geometric capital, with an echinus supporting a square abacus "whose conspicuous salience awakens the idea of a corbelled structure devised to reduce the span of the architrave".

A word is perhaps needed about the term echinus, which denotes the round part, in the form of a large moulding placed beneath the square abacus, the curvature of which, observed laterally, offers a more or less tight profile. In the Archaic Age, the echinus is full, with a generous spread, and can be likened to a flattened roll. In the Classical Age, it becomes straighter and more upright, before taking on a certain austerity in the Hellenistic-Roman world. The abacus is a square tablet set on top of the echinus. This element provides the transition with the upper sections. The whole structure of the capital thus forms an intermediary body between the

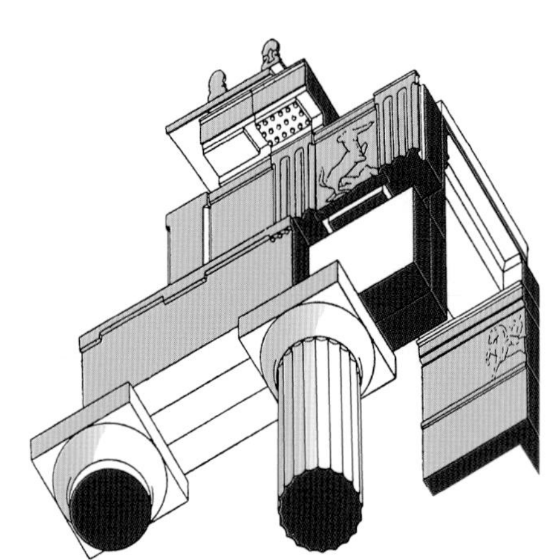

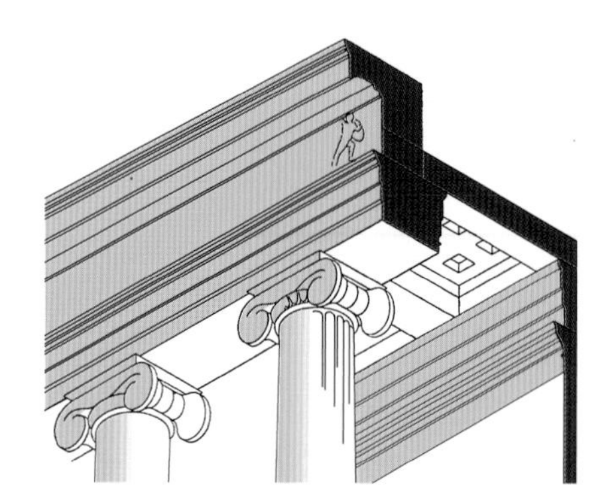

The Greek orders
The Doric structure and the Ionic structure at the level of the entablature.

The Doric, Ionic and Corinthian orders
Comparison between the Doric order (left), the Ionic order (centre) and the Corinthian order (right). The column becomes more slender and refined, and the entablature is accordingly lighter.

Page 51
The power of the Doric style in Sicily
Detail of a Doric capital in the so-called Temple of Concord at Agrigentum, dating from *circa* 430 B.C. The shift from the twenty grooves in the shaft to the Classical echinus, which is still fluid and noble, is achieved by means of the annulets of the gorgerin, which forms a tie-like feature between the vertical and horizontal elements.

vertical thrust of the column and the load represented by the horizontal structure of the entablature, made up of the architrave, the frieze and the cornice supporting the roof.

In the Doric order, the entablature of the building is given cadence by the alternating triglyphs each with three vertical grooves or flutes (more precisely two glyphs surrounded by two half-glyphs) and metopes, which are filler panels often bearing carved ornamentation. Lastly, the corners and the ridge of the building are decorated with acroteria which emphasize the pediment bearing the relief decoration.

The Ionic order developed later – in about 590 B.C. – and is characterized by the combination of a series of elements which already existed in the Asian world. The creations of Samos and Ephesus – today lost, but about which the writings of ancient authors and modern excavations help to give a fairly precise idea – reveal the main features: the column, considerably more slender than that of the Doric style, is narrow and not markedly tapered towards the top; it stands on a moulded base, sometimes bell-shaped, and has a capital with two lateral volutes, the spiral scroll-like motifs of which contain egg-and-dart patterns and palmettes. The architrave is lightened by staggered layers which suggest the superposition of three beams; the frieze which runs around the building is not interrupted by the regular presence of triglyphs, and so lends itself to a continuous decorative motif; the cornice, which is not very salient, sometimes has a row of dentils showing the ends of joists inherited from wooden architecture. All this petrified woodwork is nevertheless treated in a lighter way than in the Doric order. For the prime quality of the Ionic order resides in its refinement, its femininity, and in the wealth of its ornamentation.

We should add here that the two orders – Doric and Ionic – are not confined to their respective areas of origin. Ionic temples were erected in Sicily and on the

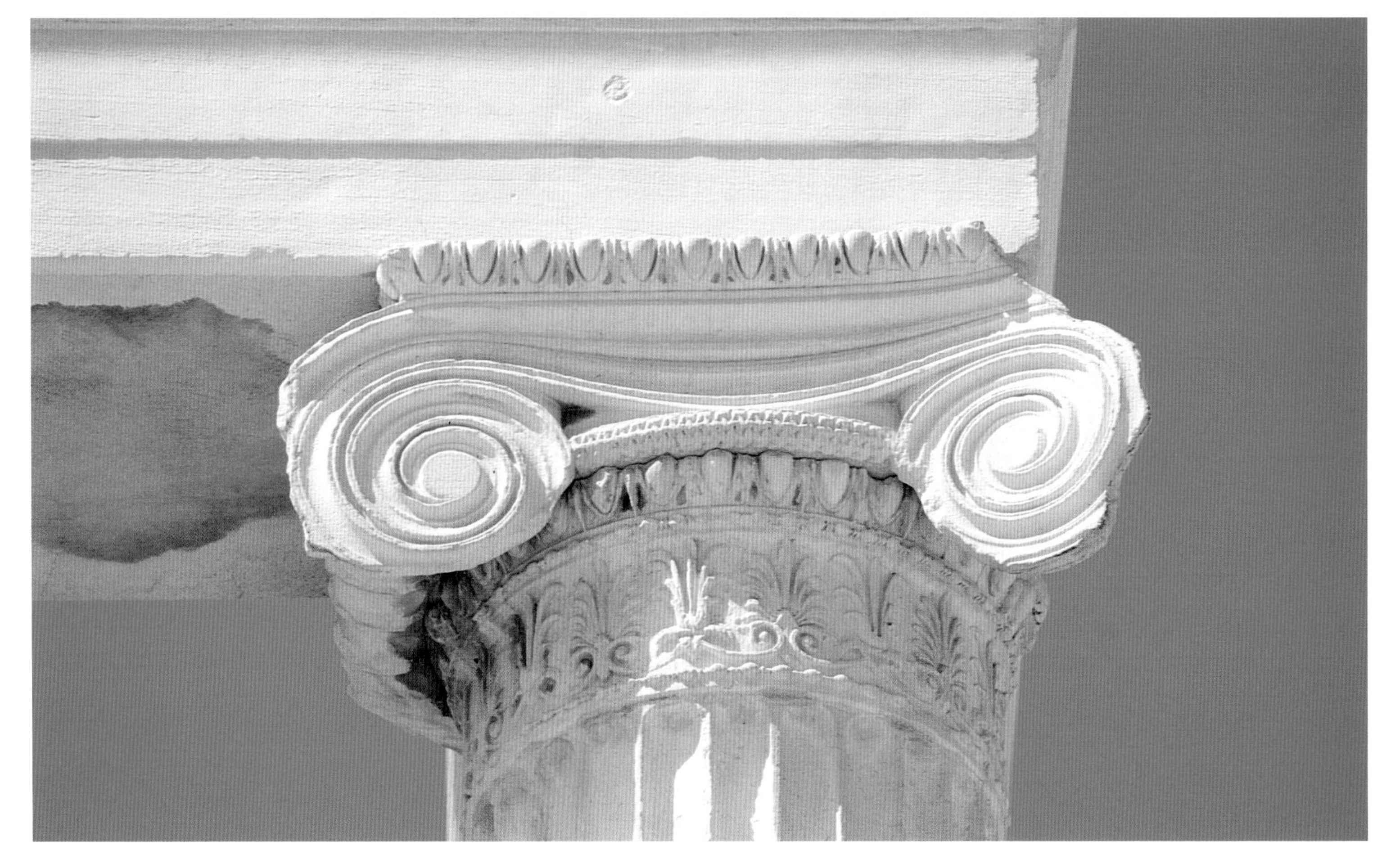

Ionic subtlety in the Erechtheum
The colonnade forming the east façade of the Erechtheum, on the Athenian Acropolis, includes an Ionic capital made with marble from Paros, where the corner volute is off-centre, and out of line. This is the solution adopted to accentuate the ends of the portico.

The elegance of the Corinthian style
The basket formed by the Corinthian capital – the last of the Greek orders to make its appearance – is based on the decorative element represented by the acanthus leaf. This leaf bursts forth in superimposed rows beneath the four corner volutes supporting the abacus. Tradition has it that the Athenian sculptor Callimachus designed this floral capital after seeing a bunch of flowers embellishing a tomb in Corinth. Capital from the Tholos of Polyclitus the Younger, at Epidaurus. (Epidaurus, Museum)

Acropolis in Athens. Doric sanctuaries in Greece and Italy have an internal organization that is handled in the Ionic style, as is well illustrated by the Temple of Apollo at Bassae and the Temple of Athena at Paestum. The association of these two inspired styles which fuel Greek architecture greatly enhanced forms of plastic expression. It shows the remarkable creativity of the Greek builders, free of all manner of "sectarianism".

The Role of Sculpted Decoration

In the Greek temple, sculpture is not restricted to a secondary role involving mere ornamentation. It adds a broader significance to the monument and lends a specific spiritual dimension to its role of sanctuary. The set of bas-reliefs places the building in a cosmological and religious system: the connotations of the outer portico closely link the temple with the natural sources of pantheist rites and worship. In addition to the obvious allusion to trees and sacred woods represented by columns arranged in peristyle form, its decorative embellishments and motifs endow it with another interpretative key, based on the themes expressed in sculpted pediments and friezes.

The study of this architectural ornamentation certainly reveals a world in which man rubs shoulders with gods and monsters alike. A whole hieratic bestiary looms up on the tympana of the sanctuary, enlivening the friezes and metopes which run all round the building. Gorgons and Medusas, Centaurs and Cyclopes, Harpies and Erinyes, Chimaeras and Sirens, male and female Sphinxes and Sphinges, all confront human beings under the eye of the gods.

Mighty battles of giants and bloody battles of Amazons, the duels of Achilles against Penthesilea (queen of the Amazons) and the Centaurs against the Lapiths

A winged sphinx from the Acropolis
This sculpture, dating from the mid-sixth century B.C., was discovered at the end of the ninteenth century. It illustrates the apotropaic, or evil-averting, role of the monsters and figures gracing the Greek temple. (Athens, Acropolis Museum)

A fiery steed
Dating from the late sixth or early fifth century B.C., this handsome horse made with marble from Paros was one of the sculptures that were buried as a result of the destruction wrought by the Persians when they sacked Athens in 480 B.C. (Athens, Acropolis Museum)

The lions of Delos
These Archaic lions, sculpted in Naxian marble, stand on the island of Delos, on a terrace dedicated to Apollo. They date from the end of the seventh century B.C., and line the processional route leading to the sacred lake.

illustrate the eternal struggle between good and evil, and man's fight against immoderation and the irrational.

Everywhere, on the front of temples, the heroic feats of Heracles slaying the lion, the stag, and the Cretan bull, bearing off the Cercopes and wrestling Triton, Theseus thwarting the wiles of the Minotaur, and, in turn, doing battle with the Centaurs, are so many vivid and graphic illustrations of the great myths. Here we have a mixture of primordial terror, primitive violence, and *hubris*, that excess and that driving force of the dramas which put rhythm into the elegant verses of the Greek tragedians.

For Greek art, as it is proclaimed by the embellishments of sanctuaries, is not just a hymn to beauty. It also highlights terrifying and salutary images of monsters: the savage smile of the Gorgons, and the petrifying stare of the Medusas, that turned everything to stone.

It was in the Archaic Age, for the most part – as if to conjure up chthonian powers and their evil spells – that formal expression was given to such themes. They lend the sanctuary its cautionary character, for the lions of the gutters and the griffins of the acroterias are symbolic, apotropaic depictions which are designed to enable people to thwart the forces of evil. Victory also puts in an appearance, by way of paradigm, in this iconography, when Perseus cuts Medusa's throat, on a metope at Selinus, or when the lions of Cybele, mother-goddess of Anatolia, devour the giants, in the Treasury of Siphnos.

But the repertory of the sculptors who decorated the temple with its figurative ornamentation was not limited just to clashes symbolizing war, and terrors triggering the vicissitudes and anxieties of life. It not only included the statue of the god in all his majesty, the "idol", in his comforting power and beauty, but also offered a

The "Calf-bearer" of the Acropolis
Discovered in 1865, this statue of the "Calf-bearer", which dates from the mid-sixth century B.C., conveys the desire for humanity which is expressed in Archaic sculpture. The artist underscores both the virile strength of the figure and his gentle attentiveness to the person portrayed.
(Athens, Acropolis Museum)

radiant image of Man – the statues of the *korai* and *kouroi*, those young people who express a quiet hope in life, play the role of offerings in sanctuaries. In their motionless and serene poses, they attain their greatest perfection in the collection of sixth-century sculptures which was hastily buried by the fleeing Athenians when the Persians arrived to occupy and destroy the Acropolis in 480 B.C., on the eve of the battles of Salamis and Plataea.

These works, which adorned the first Parthenon, and which were recovered during excavations undertaken in 1865, are among the most impressive examples of the irrepressible faith in Man that Greece has ever offered up. The beautiful and solemn girls, in their most precious attire, with its drapery frozen in Archaic folds, and the athletic young men, immobile in their primordial nakedness, glorify the Greek people.

Between the grandiose and inaccessible effigy of the god, in the splendid solitude of his *naos*, and the grimacing sphinxes repelling harmful forces, and the fearsome giants which symbolize the barbarian world, these radiant images of a new civilization turn the Greek temple into a peerless place of balance and moderation.

The enigmatic smile of a *kore*
This beautiful Archaic statue of a *kore*, dating from around 520–510 B.C., combines a concern for the details of clothing and an austere stylization. The vestiges of polychromy help us to imagine the original appearance of this statue which was designed to embellish the Sanctuary of Athena.
(Athens, Acropolis Museum)

It stands, like a reassuring point of reference, between the macrocosm of the astronomers and the microcosm of the physicists, those two chasms explored by the pre-Socratic philosophers.

The "Peplos kore"
Made in 530 B.C., this statue, which is clad in the strict Doric *peplos,* is among the discoveries made at the Athenian Acropolis. It retains the somewhat stiff quality of the primitive *xoana*. The red head of hair tumbles in long curls over the garment, which shows no folds. (Athens, Acropolis Museum)

A rapid development
Between the monsters on the pediment of the original Temple of Athena, in Athens, dating from 560 B.C., and the handsome head of the "Blond Boy", of 480, less than a century elapsed – and sculpture had reached its full maturity. (Athens, Acropolis Museum)

The Role and Function of the Greek Temple

The Greek "idol"
It is thus that the learned world was introduced, in 1815, to the "Minerva of the Parthenon" on her throne, according to a print taken from the *Olympian Jupiter* by Quatremère de Quincy.

In a polytheistic Greek religion with a whole host of deities, where mythology tells of their powers, attributes and behavior towards human beings, temples play a specifically collective role. The temple is the abode of a god – Apollo, Zeus, Hera, Aphrodite, Athena, and the like. Inside the sanctuary the deity appears in the form of an "idol" – the statue of the god is represented with anthropomorphic features. Originally an unsophisticated wooden effigy, the god was subsequently depicted in the form of a stone sculpture, then a bronze one, until he – or she – finally turned into a precious "icon", whose face and hands were made of ivory, with gold finery, thus forming what is known as a chryselephantine statue – made of ivory and gold.

This hallowed statue – standing or seated – which gave the deity a hieratic and impressive image, held solitary sway in the *naos*, occupying the centre of the *cella* of the temple. It was the sign of the immanent presence of the sacred power within the city.

This Greek deity addressed the group in particular. It only dealt with individuals in exceptional circumstances, in the secrecy of the sanctuary, for personal devotions. The temple was devised as the centre of a series of rites and the clergy alone was permitted access to it to perform the services required by the particular cult. In this sense, the temple, which was not designed to receive the congregation of faithful souls in its *naos,* was an instrument which attracted and focused on processions and festivals, and received offerings and libations. The (outside) altar was used for lavish sacrifices of thoroughbred animals, both for holocausts (sacrifices usually involving destruction by fire) and for the most symbolic and specific of gifts required by the service of the god. The temple treasure was thus made up of precious fabrics to clothe the god, and the utensils (dishes and so on) used in services of worship.

Statues were also dedicated to the god: *korai* and *kouroi* were offered as proof of a person's piety and of the devoutness of members of societies expressing their thanks for wishes granted. Sculptures played the part of *ex votos*, exalting the glory conferred by victories won. Likewise, in the great pan-Hellenic sanctuaries, cities erected symbolic columns to commemorate a happy event, for which the divine powers were duly thanked.

Above all else, worship called for acts of purification, lustrations (cleansing ceremonies) and fumigations. Prayers then rose up from the whole congregation gathered before the sanctuary. They beseeched the higher forces to be benevolent and associated the deity with the decisions of the society for which it acted as guardian. It was the god who ensured abundance in agrarian rites, as well as the fertility of the herds and flocks. It was the god who guaranteed the success of undertakings which he steered towards an assured future.

In all these activities the temple played the role of a catalyst: it embodied that preeminent function of holy setting or *temenos*, forming the transition, by way of its porticoes, between omnipresent Nature and the divine world. It embodied the *cosmos*, or universal order, as a place where man and god met, emphasizing even more the omnipotence of the Olympian gods. It was the place of *religio*, to use the Latin term which underlines the god's role as intermediary of the sacred.

Sanctuaries of Magna Graecia

From Archaism to Classicism

Page 61
Delicately sketched
The small ceramic bottles containing perfume were called *alabastra*, because they were originally made from a hollowed-out and turned block of alabaster. On this white-ground vase, dating from *circa* 470 B.C., the skilfully rendered scene depicts a young woman at her toilet. The burial places of Magna Graecia – like those of the Etruscans – housed valuable imported Attic pieces. (Geneva, Museum of Art and History)

The Greek West, otherwise known as Magna Graecia, has one obvious advantage over continental Greece and Asia Minor for today's observer: it did not suffer from the ravages of the Persian Wars. No cities were destroyed, as they were after the revolt of Ionia against the Achaemenids, no monuments were levelled, as they were in Athens at Darius' command. In Sicily and southern Italy the hiatus caused by the catastrophic events of the decade from 490–480 B.C. simply did not exist.

Nowhere do so many sanctuaries exist in such a relatively good state of conservation. In Magna Graecia, there are no less than six great temples whose porticoes are still standing, dating back to the sixth and fifth centuries. So the vagaries of history have not robbed us of such early – Archaic – creations, which have often vanished elsewhere.

It is thus possible to trace the development of architecture from these early examples – with buildings such as the "Basilica" of Paestum (*circa* 540 B.C.), up to the Classical monuments erected a century later at Agrigentum and Segesta, where work on the unfinished Temple of the Elymians came to a halt in around 425.

Colonization and Development

At a very early stage, Greek colonization spread throughout the Mediterranean basin. This expansion, which began in the eighth century B.C., occurred at the same time as the appearance of the temple, complete with its peripteral colonnade – that characteristic feature of the sanctuary dedicated to a cluster of city deities. Greek colonization had two main foci: on the one hand, the creation of trading posts set up to serve Greek vessels plying the Mediterranean, and, on the other, the establishment of colonial settlements which made farming possible – and the surplus farm production could be profitably traded with the mother country.

Authors of Antiquity looked for the reasons and causes behind this expatriation toward far horizons, as opted for by certain denizens of the city. They attributed it to a chronic shortfall of workable land. Certainly, this same shortage of agricultural resources still afflicts Greece today. At the outset, the Greeks laid the blame at the feet of the inheritance system which split estates up among all the male heirs. The parcelling of land brought about by this custom very soon made it impossible to farm any property in a profitable way. Peasants and smallholders were driven to sell their paltry patches of land. The result was the formation of huge estates belonging to wealthy landowners. These properties simply grew and grew in size. Their owners forced their farm labourers to set out in search of fortune to other shores, where they might find their place in the sun, even if by force of arms. Cities fitted out vessels on which settlers-to-be then embarked, adventurously heading, with their whole families, for the great unknown. In the eyes of modern observers, however, the essential cause of this colonial phenomenon lies rather in a continual growth in population, resulting from a better use of natural resources.

In its very earliest phase, Greek expansion dates back to the Mycenaean age and the taking of Troy, that key to the Hellespont (the strait now known as the

On the tympanum of the temple of Marasa
One of the Dioscuri – the Sons of Zeus – with his horse, supported by a triton. This marble sculpture, 126 cm high, dates from the end of the fifth century B.C. With its spare elegance, it once adorned the pediment of the Ionic sanctuary of Marasa, at Locri. (Reggio di Calabria, National Museum)

Dardanelles), which barred access for Greek mariners to the world of the Scythians. In no time it had crept eastward to the shores of the Sea of Marmara, then to the Black Sea as far as the Crimea, and the mysterious Colchis region, south of the Caucasus. In Asia Minor, the Greeks occupied the shores of Pamphylia. In Syria, in about 800 B.C., they set up a trading post (*emporion*) at Al-Mina. To the south, Cyrenaica was colonized in 631 by settlers from Thera.

It was to the west, however, in the direction of Magna Graecia (southern Italy and Sicily), that the movement was busiest. Indeed, there are echoes of it in the mythical voyage of Odysseus. Cumae, just north of Naples, was a Greek outpost founded in 757 on Italian soil. Naxos, near Taormina, and Catania were founded in the same period. Zancle (present-day Messina) dates back to 740, Rhegium (modern Reggio), in Calabria, to 735, and Megara Hyblaea in Sicily to 727. The site of Syracuse, together with the small island of Ortygia, was occupied by Corinth in 733. Sybaris was established in 720, Tarentum (modern Taranto) in about 710, Metapontum in about 690, and Gela in 688. Selinus and Posidonia (Paestum) date back to 650, Himera to 648, Acragas (Agrigentum) to 580, and so on.

The creation of these cities was not achieved without struggles against the Phoenicians, who had gained a firm foothold in the west. Battles also had to be fought against the indigenous people. There were noteworthy clashes with the Elymians in Sicily and with the Etruscans who held the northern part of the Italian peninsula, from south of Rome upward.

The settlers' spirit of enterprise, coupled with the richness of the land they then farmed, very quickly turned these western Greek possessions into thriving cities. The arts and sciences flourished, while innovative political systems were worked out – in particular, strong powers based on the personal authority of a tyrant.

By way of example, we should mention Dionysius I and his son Dionysius II of Syracuse, as well as their relative, Dion, who summoned the philosopher Plato. We should also mention Gelon, tyrant of Gela, Theron of Acragas (Agrigentum), and Gelon's brother Hieron, patron and protector of the poets Aeschylus, Pindar and Simonides. But we should make special mention of the role of one particular and enlightened despot: Archytas of Tarentum (*circa* 430–350), friend of Plato, strategist, engineer and astronomer, who was also an outstanding Pythagorean philosopher.

The great thinker and mathematician Pythagoras, born in Samos in Ionia in about 570, had emigrated to Croton (modern Crotone) in Calabria in 530, where he had founded his school. He was eventually driven out of this city under pressure from democratic – not to say demagogic – movements, and died in Metapontum in about 480 B.C. He bequeathed not only a corpus of work of paramount importance in the field of the theory of proportions and whole numbers, but, among his disciples, he also passed for a thaumaturge – a miracle-worker – and a genius (*daimon*).

Pythagoras played a role that greatly resembled that of the founder of a religion. With his motto "All things are numbers" as a point of departure, he would develop a sort of rational mysticism which was to have a considerable influence in the artistic arena.

Aesthetics and Numbers

For us, today, it seems self-evident that Greek architecture is beautiful, and that the ancient temples fulfil an aesthetic need. We tacitly admit that Classical monuments were designed to give concrete expression to an aspect of the Beautiful, so better to honour the gods. But these concepts of beauty and aesthetics never feature in the sadly rare writings of Antiquity which discuss architecture.

When philosophers – and Plato and Aristotle in particular – worked out theories dealing with aesthetics, these theories were applied to very different subjects. In addition to the physical beauty of the human being – which leads to attraction (*eros*)

Page 65
The "Basilica" at Paestum
The first Temple of Hera, at Posidonia (Paestum), dating from 540 B.C., has nine Archaic columns on its façade. The distinctive features of this building, miraculously preserved, are its powerful colonnade with curved shafts, and the Doric capitals with their flattened echinus.

Greek expansion in Italy
The foundation of colonies often clashed with local peoples who put up stiff resistance to the establishment of Greek trading-posts. The result was a series of conflicts in which cavalry and infantry both took part. This base of an Attic bowl, attributed to the vase painter Euphronius (about 500 B.C.), shows a horseman armed with a lance. (Rome, Villa Giulia Museum)

The warriors of Riace (Calabria)
These two classical Greek bronzes, discovered in 1972 on the Calabrian coast, were a phenomenal find in the field of submarine archaeology. Originating from Attica, they date respectively from 460 B.C. for Warrior A (on the left), and 430 B.C. for Warrior B (detail, on the right). These pieces were made using the lost-wax technique, and are a good illustration of the Classical zenith of Greek art. (Reggio di Calabria, National Museum)

– aesthetics related (and still relates) to the arts, and to sculpture and painting in particular. In these areas, the criteria for judgement are consequently the true, the good, and the right. The best sculpture is thus the one that is truest and bears the closest likeness (*mimesis*); the most beautiful painting is the one that comes closest to nature. And the ancient authors would mention the famous Grapes of Apelles (fourth century B.C.) which – or so the celebrated anecdote has it – were so lifelike that "birds would come and peck at their seeds".

In relation to architecture, there could be no question of attraction, resemblance or naturalism, any more than of truth or the philosophical good, for the very structures of architecture are not figurative. It stems from neither *eros* nor *mimesis*. This is why works dealing with the aesthetics of monuments are wanting. It would seem, in reality, that architecture, in the mind and spirit of the Greeks, was based on other criteria.

The first author of Antiquity to draw up a treatise on architecture was Vitruvius, with his *De architectura,* a work in ten books, written in Latin in the first century B.C. The interest of this work, for our purposes, is that it makes constant reference to Greek writings. Vitruvius in fact mentions texts which, on the whole, have not sur-

An Archaic metope at Paestum
Coming from the Heraion at the mouth of the Silarus (about 530 B.C.), this sculpted metope depicts two young female dancers clad in the *chiton,* decorating this small treasury close to Paestum. These are the first monumental sculptures which make up the Doric decoration. (Paestum, National Museum)

vived to this day, but which do share one basic thing in common: they are commentaries in which architects explain their work.

Thus Theodorus wrote about the Temple of Hera on Samos, Chersiphron of Crete and his son Metagenes wrote on the Temple of Artemis (the Artemision) at Ephesus, Pythius of Priene on the Temple of Athena at that site, Philon of Eleusis about the arsenal on the Piraeus, Ictinus on the Parthenon, and so on. So these writings did not form a general theory of architecture. Rather, they confined themselves to imparting the intentions of the builders concerned.

Vitruvius, however, also cites one or two theoretical treatises – by Silenos, a *De symmetriis doricorum* ("On Symmetry in the Doric"), and by Arcesias a *De symmetriis corinthiis* ("On Symmetry in the Corinthian"). Philon, likewise, is purported to have published a *De aedium sacrarum symmetriis* ("On Symmetry in Sacred Temples"). In all these works, the term "symmetry" should be understood in its accepted meaning peculiar to the Greeks, which does not tally with ours. It is this meaning which concerns us here.

Vitruvius himself included the notion of symmetry within a system of proportions. Through a series of correspondences, these latter tend to subject the composition of a work of art to a set of relations based on reciprocity and balance, which produce harmony. These relations, or proportions, are conveyed by numerical values. They are expressed by means of single numbers. This interplay within governs the monument and forms a kind of network which obeys arithmetic and geometric rules. It is these proportions which form the "symmetry" in the meaning used by Greek authors. And the "mathematical" construction subsequently represented by a building is based on numerical factors.

The entire significance of this system lies in the value which the Pythagoreans invested in numbers. For Pythagoras, numbers are the expression of a fundamental language and vocabulary which link men and gods. Number is the principle behind all things. It represents the eternal character of reality. "Number pre-exists in the mind of god." And this "divine number" lies at the root of rhythm and harmony, which depend on the ratios of proportions. It is they which imbue a work with its beauty and perfection.

In the minds of the ancients, numbers thus represented the *numen* (power, force, majesty) of the divine. For Plato – who was greatly influenced by Pythagoras – "numbers are the highest degree of knowledge", and the neo-Pythagorean Nicomachus of Gerasa, declared that "everything is ordered by numbers". Numbers were thus studied as units which express an eternal Truth.

As the outcome of a set of calculated and quantified proportions and ratios which are applied as much to the ground plan as to the elevation of a building, the Greek sanctuary forms a "model" designed to express pure ideas and set down the essential principles of divine "thought". It rendered tangible the Word (*logos*), in the meaning given to it by the architect in his material construction, governed by mathematical rules.

In order to gain a meaningful grasp of the real nature of this approach, which turns the temple into a harmonious three-dimensional arrangement, based on *symmetria*, we must refer to the combinations which are made possible by whole numbers in Pythagorean thought. These numbers each have their own value, within a reference system which is part of a coherent body of thought. They express a semiology that is loaded with meaning. For these numbers can be squared or cubed; their root can be deduced; they can be set down in an arithmetical or geometric series, and the like. They are accordingly part of a mathematical syntax. These relations imbue them with their meaning in an interplay of proportions, as well as in a symbolic system.

With regard to this Law of Number, which governed both musical chords and the architecture of the universe long before it came to control the architecture of

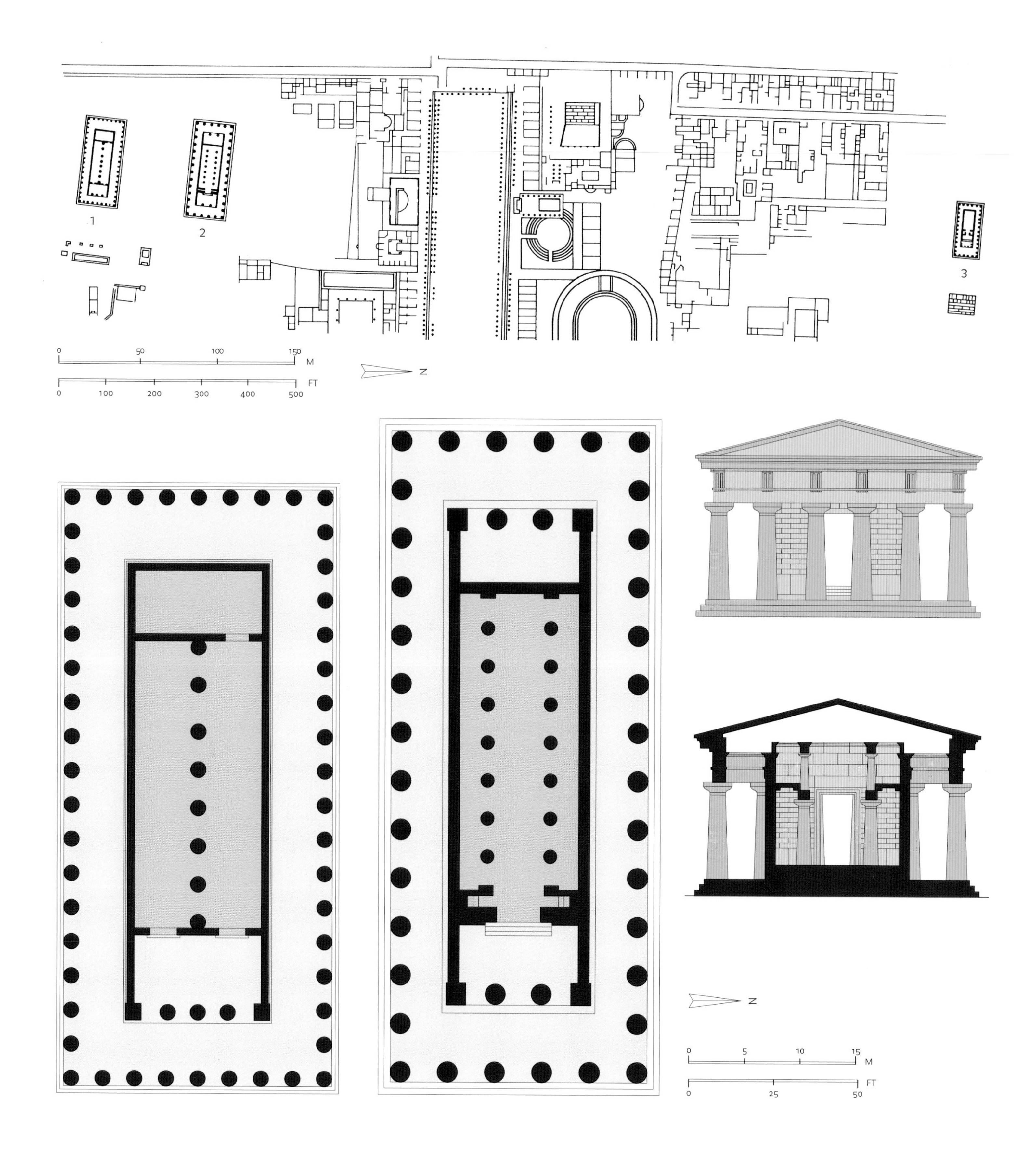

The plans and site of Paestum

The Greek city of Posidonia, south of Naples, shows a regular layout with its main avenue lined with three Doric temples:

1 First Temple of Hera, known as "Basilica"
2 Second Temple of Hera
3 Temple of Athena

Below: Plan of the "Basilica" and plan of the second Temple of Hera, with elevation of the façade and section.

Paestum: a museum of Doric art
The coastal plain of Posidonia is the site of admirably preserved Greek monuments in wild natural surroundings. In the foreground, the Archaic temple known as the "Basilica", behind which stands the Classical Sanctuary of Hera, dating from 460–440 B.C., contemporary with the Parthenon in Athens.

sanctuaries, we should mention one or two properties of the proportions applied by Greek builders. Thus we have the famous right-angled or so-called Pythagorean triangle which is based on the numbers 3, 4 and 5 and their respective squares (9 and 16 which equal 25), from which stem a whole set of essential ratios; likewise, the arithmetical and geometric sequences of whole numbers, like the Fibonacci Sequence, come into this calculated transcription of reality. Lastly, a mention of the Golden Section, also known as the "Divine Proportion", the formula for which goes thus: "Division of a line into mean and extreme ratio". This abstract formula can be more simply translated as the "division of a given line so that the ratio of the whole line to the larger interval equals the ratio of the larger interval to the smaller".

For the Pythagoreans, numbers were conceived as surfaces, shapes and points. These constructions based on points set at regular intervals, forming homogeneous groups, were formulated with the help of the *gnomon*, that is, the set square. This instrument – or, more precisely, this tool – which makes it possible to draw shapes or figures, reveals the profound connection between architects and Pythagorean mathematicians. For the set square is the very symbol of the master-builder.

The mathematical approach leads to the use of a constant: a module. It is the module – appropriate to each and every building – that makes it possible to attain *eurhythmia*, that harmonious organization stemming from an *ordinatio*, or a common measurement of the different parts of the work. Numbers and proportions are thus the proper language of the architect. In expressing a higher reality, they turn the temple into the material realization of divine Truth.

The Role of Magna Graecia

The bulk of Pythagoras' work saw the light of day in Magna Graecia. It was at Croton and Metapontum that the great Ionian philosopher instructed and taught his followers, assembled in a school of active, if frequently persecuted, "zealots". So it is a good idea to embark on the study of Greek sanctuaries by considering the buildings of southern Italy and Sicily.

Our illustration of these overall principles and philosophical-*cum*-religious and numerical concepts which govern architectural expression may well involve just the standard example of the Parthenon of Athens, culmination of the quantified abstraction of Greek art, but Magna Graecia nonetheless offers the possibility of tracing the development of architectural forms, because of the numerous temples still standing there.

By studying the buildings that have come down to us, often admirably preserved, the way the building of these sanctuaries was approached helps to grasp the *techne* – the art of building – of the Greeks. These temples are among the earliest endeavours to construct monuments between the last third of the sixth century and the end of the fifth, the period which marks the pinnacle of classical architecture. The Greek cities of Sicily and southern Italy – among which we should mention, in particular, Posidonia (Paestum), Syracuse, Acragas (Agrigentum), Selinus and Segesta – form, in effect, a museum of buildings which spans more than a century. Unlike many sanctuaries in Greece and Ionia, the buildings created in Magna Graecia were not built of marble, because that material of choice was not available. They were built of local stone which, in most cases, was nothing more than rather rough tufa. It is because of this feature, moreover, that these buildings escaped the fate of many other ancient monuments destroyed by lime-burners to make mortar.

One of the capitals of the "Basilica"
Broadly flattened beneath the square abacus, the Doric capital of the first Temple of Hera shows a decorative motif formed by lotus-flower leaves around the gorgerin, where the shaft meets the base of the echinus.

Page 71
A perspective view of the Archaic portico
The energy of the first Temple of Hera at Paestum is expressed by powerfully fluted grooves which underscore the accentuated curve of the early Doric style.

An Archaic Example: the "Basilica" of Paestum

The site of Posidonia (Paestum), south of Naples, miraculously survived the Middle Ages, forgotten as it was in the marshy plain at the mouth of the river Silarus (modern Sele). From the end of the imperial Roman period, and in particular in the immediate wake of the great invasions, the marshes created by the river's spates and bursting aqueducts which continued to convey mountain waters, turned the city, in effect, into an insalubrious area. Flooded land turned into coppices in this malodorous delta, hiding from view all the temples there, which consequently sank into oblivion, while the city itself was abandoned.

In the eighteenth century, when the ancient city was rediscovered with its walls and three sanctuaries virtually intact, Europe started to develop a keen interest in Antiquity. This was when the excavations at Pompeii and Herculaneum began.

The oldest of the three temples at Paestum, the so-called "Basilica", a sanctuary dedicated to Hera, dates back to *circa* 540 B.C. Its portico has fifty columns (nine widthwise and eighteen lengthwise). The fluted shafts are conspicuously curved and have beautiful capitals with an elegant echinus in the form of a rounded loaf beneath a square abacus. A gorgerin or small frieze of leaves marks the link with the shaft itself. Above the portico, only the blocks of the architrave have been preserved. The entire frieze, decorative work and superstructures have all vanished.

Because the shorter sides have an uneven number of columns (nine), the organization of the sanctuary is governed by an axial colonnade. In this sense, the "Basilica" is a copy of Archaic models, such as the Temple C in the Sanctuary of Apollo at Thermum, discussed in the previous chapter, and the first Heraion of Samos, dating back to the eighth century B.C., which is a *hecatompedon* (a temple that is 100 feet in length). At Paestum, this inner portico which divides the *naos* into two equal naves has eight columns, with those at the ends set against the inside walls which delimit the smaller sides of the hall. The antepenultimate intercolumniation is wider

The first Temple of Hera
Taken from the work published in 1791 by de Lagardette and entitled *Les Ruines de Paestum ou Posidonia*, this inner view of the Basilica shows the organization based on the axial colonnade which governs the symmetrical structure of the building, dominated by a nine-shaft façade – a survivor of the Archaic formulae.

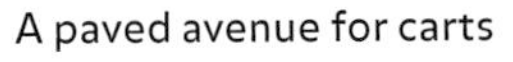

A paved avenue for carts
The main thoroughfare which linked the sanctuaries of Paestum still exists in the form of a straight road, evidence of a form of town-planning that has features which relate it to the Hippodamian plan.

than the others, so that it can accommodate the statue of the goddess. The "Basilica" has a vestibule or *pronaos* with three columns between the *antae,* and a treasury chamber which is entered through the *naos*.

To illustrate the system of proportions characteristic of the design of this temple, we should point out that the dimensions of the ground plan are 24.5 by 54.3 m, and that the length of the stylobate (the basal area on which the columns stand) corresponds to 100 Ionic cubits. The layout corresponds to the 4:9 proportion that we find in the Parthenon. On the four sides of the temple, the surrounding gallery measures one unit and this determines the proportion of the very elongated *cella* which recurs in all the early sanctuaries.

This *cella* is based on the 2:7 proportion (that is, 4–2 = 2 and 9–2 = 7). Without counting either the *pronaos* or the treasury chamber forming a sort of *adytum*, which each measure one unit of depth, the *naos* fits the 2:5 proportion.

So the interplay of *symmetria*, based on whole numbers, is strictly observed in the "Basilica" of Paestum, which was erected precisely at the time when Pytha-

A temple dedicated to Athena
Situated chronologically between the "Basilica" and the second Temple of Hera, the sanctuary of the daughter of Zeus, at Paestum includes typically Archaic features – conspicuously curved shafts and broad Doric capitals. It also has an entablature on the lofty pediments, with somewhat cumbersome triglyphs and metopes.

Page 75
The majestic façade of the Temple of Athena
The hexastyle marks a lightening of the columns when compared with the broader shafts of the "Basilica". But everything here conveys the Severe style of the contemporary sculpture on metopes.

goras was teaching at Croton, less than 200 miles from Posidonia. The fact that the first Temple of Hera is based on a length of 100 Ionic cubits supports the hypothesis of the influence of the philosopher-mathematician from Samos. What is more, the ground plan itself, with its broad galleries surrounding the *cella*, attests to a "concept of space that is more Ionic than Doric" (Roland Martin).

The Temple of Athena

The influence of Ionic architecture is clearly visible in the Temple of Athena at Paestum. Built shortly after the "Basilica", this temple – long known as the Temple of Ceres – dates from the end of the sixth century. It is a hexastyle (six façade columns) with thirteen columns at the sides. It measures 14.54 by 32.88 m (that is 40 feet in width and 96 in length), and is set in a 5:12 rectangle, which tallies exactly with the number of intercolumniations (after Gottfried Gruben).

The interest of this temple lies in the eight inner columns (four in front of the *pronaos* and two on either side of the back of the corner, with the second up against the end of the anta wall); for, unlike the portico of the outer peristyle in the Archaic Doric style, the inner organization is purely Ionic, with volute capitals. The proportions of the *naos* correspond to the simple 1:2 ratio (two adjacent squares).

This inner portico, which precedes the entrance to the *naos*, shows a determination to bring together, in a well-balanced whole, the two major stylistic trends – the Ionic order and the Doric – peculiar to Greek architecture. This experiment was undertaken several times over, in particular for the temple at Bassae in the Peloponnese attributed to Ictinus.

The entrance of the *naos*, which has neither treasury nor *opisthodomos*, is framed by two stair wells giving access to the upper parts of the building. It would seem that this distinctive feature, which recurs in several temples at Agrigentum (Temples of Heracles and Hera Lacinia and the so-called Temple of Concord), shows oriental origins. We know that Syrian-Lebanese sanctuaries included access ways to a hypaethral (or roofless) terrace designed for fire rituals calling for the provision of pyres and similar to those later unearthed at Baalbek and Palmyra. Do these symmetrical stairwells – the one for going up, the other down – derive from this oriental custom?

A mixture of styles at Paestum
If the peripteral colonnade is purely Doric, the Temple of Athena at Paestum – showing the influence of the architecture of Asia Minor – offers one of the earliest examples of a blend of Doric and Ionic styles. In fact it adopts an Ionic organization for the eight shafts of the inner portico. In this way, four columns of the *pronaos*, plus two corner columns and two columns set so as to abut the *antae* walls, are more slender, and surmounted by capitals with volutes.

Classical power

Although the second Temple of Hera at Posidonia (Paestum) was contemporary with the Parthenon in Athens, it still retains a certain Archaic austerity at the moment of full Classicism. The Doric columns have not completely shed a heavy quality that has a certain power. Built in about 460–440 B.C., this sanctuary, once attributed to Poseidon, stands, as do its neighboring buildings, on three steps which raise it above the level of the plain.

The pure Doric style

The capitals of the second Temple of Hera, at Paestum, have lost the floral decoration which characterized the join between the shaft and the echinus in the Archaic examples. From this point on, a row of annulets "ties" the top of the grooves together.

Page 78
Two levels of columns
Among the solutions henceforth adopted, the superposition of the two storeys, which is a feature of the inner colonnades in the Doric style, is a distinctive aspect of the Temple of Hera at Paestum. These inner porticos form three naves in the *naos*.

A sober rhythm
The line of Doric capitals in the Temple of Hera at Paestum has a generous quality which has not yet been stifled by the austerity of the late Doric style.

To the east of the main façade of the Temple of Athena at Paestum stands the large altar, 14.54 m wide (like the temple), which was used for solemn sacrificial ceremonies. Its purpose was to concentrate the ceremonial of worship around the slaughter of animals dedicated to the gods.

The second Temple of Hera

The second Temple of Hera, which replaced the old sanctuary known as the "Basilica", was formerly given to Poseidon, whereas it was actually consecrated to Hera Argiva (protectress of those navigators, the Argonauts). It dates from *circa* 460–440 B.C. and is therefore contemporary with the Parthenon, but it expresses an aesthetic concept that is in quite a different style. This building has survived to this day in a remarkable state of preservation and enables us to perceive the architect's intentions. Its majestic, if slightly cumbersome, perfection with its thirty-six columns with powerful capitals expresses a bold and vigorous Greekness. It marries power and stability. At once dense and determined, its outline plays with the mystery of shadows.

When we contemplate it, we realize the authority of this Classicism raised to the level of the obvious and the sober moderation sought by those Greek builders. The interior of the *cella* reveals a double colonnade with two superposed porticoes, like those in the Temple of Aphaia on the island of Aegina, built some fifty years earlier. So was the building dedicated to Hera perhaps affectedly Archaic?

This is a peripteral hexastyle, with fourteen columns lengthwise; the dimensions of the stylobate are 24.31 by 59.93 m, that is 72 by 180 feet. The result is a proportion of 2:5. Again, whole numbers, which relate back to the teaching of Pythagoras. The *cella*, too, suggests a certain Archaic quality. It is very elongated, and includes a *pronaos*, a *naos* with three naves delimited by two porticoes with seven columns on each side and an *opisthodomos*.

In order to get an idea of the original appearance of this grand architecture in tufa (conchitic or shell-rich limestone), whose rustic surfaces seem out of place today, we must imagine the beautiful white stucco rendering that once covered the entire structure. The polished surfaces then played with polychromatic features, where blues and reds alternated on the frieze and triglyphs.

Greek painted tombs in southern Italy
One special contribution made by southern Italy is its examples of splendid tombs with paintings. This ritual funereal dance, from Tomb II at Ruvo in Apulia, dates from the latter half of the fifth century B.C. Its style differs conspicuously from the decoration of Greek vases. (Naples, National Museum)

The Painted Tombs at Paestum

It was in 1969 that several Greek tombs were unearthed at Paestum. They were made of large dressed rectangular blocks surmounted by two slabs arranged like a saddle-roof. This type of burial place, more Italiot than Greek, held a big surprise in store: the interior panels were covered in magnificent paintings. For the very first time, pictorial Greek works could be said to have come down to us, helping to evoke a whole area of Greek art that was still little known.

The oldest of these tombs, which archaeologists have managed to date at around 480 B.C., thus go back to the beginning of the Classical period. One of the burial places is particularly eye-catching. This is the tomb known as the "Tomb of the Diver". On the two side panels there are elaborate and vivid banquet scenes, with the guests lounging languidly on couches designed for the *symposion*. The laurel-wreathed participants, holding wine goblets or lyres, are gently reclining and conversing. On the end panels, figures of fluteplayers and cupbearers enliven the scene. We know that the *symposion* always started with libations to the gods, so it had a religious character.

But it is the scene on one particular roof panel which reveals the paramount iconographic interest of this painting by bringing us back again to the figure of Pythagoras. Here we see, in a pared down setting symbolized by two austerely drawn trees, a diver who plunges from the top of a building into the water below. By analogy with the "leap of Leucas" (the poetess Sappho hurled herself into the sea off this Ionian island to rejoin the world of pure ideas), the Pythagoreans adopted this image as a symbol of the passage of the soul into the eternal universe. As an image of resurrection, this plunge into the waters of the primordial Ocean illustrates the return to the heavenly homeland that souls smitten by god go through after their death, as demonstrated by Jérôme Carcopino. We are thus in the presence of an illustration of the symbols of Pythagorean mysticism, the themes of which would be borrowed once more in the Roman era (in the Basilica of the Porta Maggiore in Rome).

Other later tombs at Paestum show a Lucanian influence and date back to around 340 B.C. They offer superb funeral scenes, chariot races, boxing and wrestling fights (the *pancratium*), flute-players, and more. Their style, at once loose and flexible, conjures up life with great lightness and a remarkable economy of means.

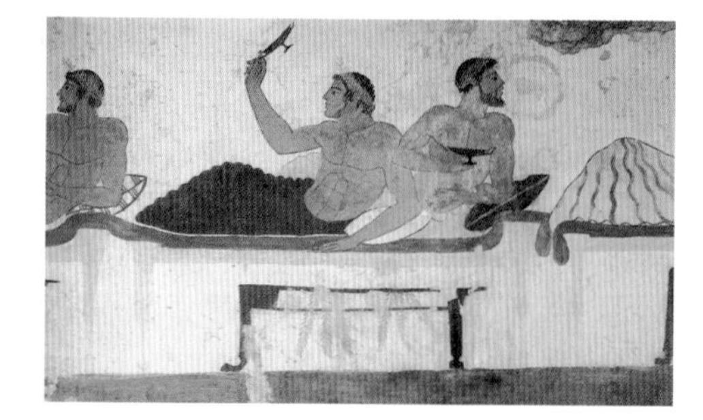

The tombs of Paestum
Above: A banquet scene from a tomb discovered in 1969 at Paestum. These sepulchral paintings, dating from around 480 B.C., decorate the inner surface of large erect slabs which form an area covered by a saddle-roof.
Below: From another tomb at Paestum, and dating from around 340 B.C., a winged figure presides over the fate beyond the grave and shows Lucanian influence. (Paestum, National Museum)

A *biga* (two-horse chariot) race
Among the funerary scenes of the painted tombs of Paestum, chariot-races often symbolize the vagaries of human life. This light vehicle preparing to negotiate the column on the racetrack dates from the fourth century B.C. (Paestum, National Museum)

The "Tomb of the Diver"
This scene depicting a diver at the very moment when he is plunging from a tall structure into the waves illustrates a symbol of resurrection of which Pythagoras was fond. The image decorates one of the slabs of the saddle-roof of a tomb at Paestum dating from 480 B.C. In southern Italy, where the philosopher had taken refuge, Pythagorean ideas had gained a firm footing. (Paestum, National Museum)

An Archaic colonnade at Selinunte
Only a portico has survived in the Sanctuary of the Spring, otherwise known as Temple C, at Selinus in southern Sicily. It shows the features of the Archaic style dating from the early sixth century B.C. The line of columns proudly towers above the sea below.

The Temples of Selinus

Situated on the south coast of Sicily, the city of Selinus (now Selinunte) was built by settlers from Megara in about 650. The oldest part of the city stands on a plateau facing the sea and hemmed in by two watercourses, the river Selinus to the west – after which the city is named – and the Cotone to the east. The Acropolis dominating the shore would soon be used to accommodate a series of temples (known by the letters C and D, as well as A and O). Selinus has its prosperity to thank for the blossoming of monuments that occurred between 550 and 460.

The success of the city was so dazzling that the city-plan itself had a dazzling effect. New neighborhoods had to spread beyond the walls and occupy the hills situated to the west and even more to the east. To the east stands a new religious centre, with temples which – since we do not always know for sure to which gods they were dedicated – we have taken to calling by the names Temple G, Temple F, Temple E, and so on. In its heyday, Selinus had a total of seven large peripteral temples, the earliest of which dates back to the middle of the sixth century B.C.

Openness and light at Selinunte
In Temple E at Selinus – a Classical Heraion – the Doric structures have a quality of lightness which is conveyed by the proportions of the shafts and the scale of the intercolumniation.

All these great buildings fell victim to a terrible catastrophe – they were all razed to the ground and totally destroyed. The city itself was sacked in 409 by the Carthaginians, but it managed to come back to life. Then a second destruction by the Carthaginian armies in 250 destroyed it once and for all. Today, looking at the huge piles of toppled drums and capitals which litter the ground, archaeologists are unable to explain the calamity which struck Selinus. Some attribute its total ruin to a very local earthquake (which affected neither Agrigentum nor Segesta). Others believe that the Carthaginians had developed a technique of destruction which enabled them to "flatten" the largest of buildings using a system of hoists and levers. Whatever the case may be, just one temple (E) has been re-erected and now stands for all to see. Another (C) has had just one portico reconstructed.

The Acropolis of Selinus has been restored thanks to powerful supporting walls. It forms a vast *temenos* measuring about 200 by 150 m. This is where we find Temples C and D. The oldest, Temple C, whose peristyle colonnade now stands upright once more, is a hexastyle with seventeen shafts on the sides. The stylobate measures 64 by 23 m. A double portico used to rise up to the east, behind which a large gallery encircled a very long, narrow *cella*. It measured 10.4 by 41.55 m, that is 20 by 80 cubits (G. Gruben). So its proportion is 1:4. The *naos* is preceded by a *pronaos* and followed by an *adytum* which is only accessible by way of the cultroom. Like the "Basilica" of Paestum, the columns are very curved and surmounted by large capitals with a very flattened echinus.

The largest temple at Selinus stood on the eastern hill. Built between 510 and 470, it is known as Temple G and is identified as the Temple of Apollo. It is a truly colossal edifice in whose ground plan we can make out a vast pseudo-dipteros. Its

Classicism at Selinus
In about 465–450 B.C., after a series of buildings signalling the development of the Doric style, the architecture of Selinus achieved the Classical formulation with Temple E, dedicated to the goddess Hera. The rebuilt sanctuary, which underwent a thorough process of *anastylosis*, is a hexastyle that measures almost 68 m in length.

Lighter structures
The north-east corner of Temple E at Selinus shows, on its lofty stylobate with tiered steps, the aspiration to elegance – which is further heightened at Acragas (Agrigentum), with the so-called Temple of Concord.

Stucco and polychromy at Selinus
The somewhat rough Sicilian tufa of Selinus was disguised by the application of a thick layer of stucco, which was polished to look like marble. Some of the shafts lying on the ground – and thus protected for centuries from bad weather – still show this white cladding today. The polychrome decoration was applied to this layer of stucco.

Giants struck by lightning at Agrigentum
All that now remains of the huge Olympieion of Agrigentum, which measures 113.5 m in length and was never completed, is a field of colossal ruins. Among them we find one of the atlantes (or *telamones*) which used to hold up the entablature of the roof. Dating from the first half of the fifth century B.C., these sculptures measure all of 8 m in height.

vast proportions clearly show the influence of the major Ionian sanctuaries (Samos, Ephesus). It measures no less than 50.7 by 110.12 m. So its length is almost twice that of the second Temple of Hera at Paestum. Its octostyle façade, with seventeen columns lengthwise (like the future Parthenon) rose to a height of 22.5 m at the cornice and 26 m at the top of the pediment.

The width of its peripheral gallery (which exceeds 10 m and covers two intercolumniations) must have called for enormous blocks of stone, whose arrangement formed a veritable stone "frame". Like the colossal structures in Ionia, this Doric temple at Selinus represents an amazing mastery of technology. In front of its *cella*, the *pronaos* is preceded by a four-columned portico, with one angle shaft on each side. The holy of holies is accessible through a triple entrance-way leading to three naves, separated by two small colonnades with ten shafts each. The central nave led to a kind of inner *naïskos* (or chapel) which must have housed the statue of the god. At the end of the *cella* there was an *opisthodomos* with two columns.

Temples F and E are located to the south of this building. The latter, dedicated to Hera, has been completely surveyed by archaeologists. It displays the elegance of a remarkably light Doric portico. Built between 465 and 450, this peripteral hexastyle, with fifteen columns on the sides, shows similarities with the second Temple of Hera at Paestum. It measures 25.32 by 67.74 m at the stylobate, but there is no inner colonnade in its narrow *cella*. On the other hand, the *naos* is preceded by a two-columned *pronaos in antis*, and followed by a treasury with access from the hall. Behind this *adytum*, the *opisthodomos* is also situated between the *antae* walls, preceded by two columns, as at the other end of the *cella*. Because the columns were left flat on the ground for a long period, their stucco covering has survived in many places and helps us to understand the appearance that these temples of Magna Graecia must have had when the surface of tufa or shelly limestone was hidden.

Despite the ruin that overtook Selinus, we can easily understand how the opulence of this city made it possible to carry out various architectural experiments and research projects. We can trace here an ongoing evolution leading from Archaism to Classicism, with an amazing impetus and enthusiasm instilled by the desire to rival the huge sanctuaries of Asia. We can also make out surprising elements surviving from the middle of the fifth century, in particular in the formula of the somewhat narrow *cella* that did not require any internal support (Temple E).

Agrigentum encircled by temples
On the crag which runs south of the city of Acragas (Agrigentum), a series of sanctuaries seems to be on guard duty. Temple D, known as the Temple of Juno Lacinia and built 450 B.C., crowns the lofty promontory.

The romanticism of ruins
A temple at Agrigentum, as depicted by the painter Nicolas Houel, in his *Voyage pittoresque des isles de Sicile, de Malte et de Lipari* (1782–1789).

The Temple of Concord on its rock at Agrigentum
The main façade of the temple known by the name of "Concord" – in more prosaic terms, Temple F at Agrigentum – was built in about 430 B.C., and is a fine example of Greek Classicism. The building is contemporary with the Parthenon in Athens.

The Buildings of Agrigentum

Agrigentum, known as Acragas in Antiquity, is situated half-way along Sicily's southern shore, in a position that is relatively easy to defend. Like Selinus, it is bounded to the east and west by two watercourses (the Hypsas and the Acragas), and protected by a sheer cliff beside which stand the temples: from west to east, the Temple of Hephaestus, Temple L, the Temple of Zeus or Olympieion, and the Temples of Heracles, "Concord" and Hera Lacinia. So the visitor arriving in the city is greeted by a veritable ring of sanctuaries, and the city itself is perched like a stronghold, from where the view stretches out to sea.

The ruined Temple of Heracles, which has only one remaining colonnade, was built in about 500 B.C. It had a *cella* of about 12 by 30 m, that is 36 by 90 feet, which is equivalent to a proportion of 2:5. The inner width of the *naos* reaches more than 11 m, without the portico (as in Temple E at Selinus). It must have been covered by huge lintels or a wooden frame. The stairs on either side of the entrance, behind the *pronaos*, are typical of a style in which access to the upper parts of the building possibly attests to oriental influences.

Like the Temple of Apollo at Selinus, the Olympieion of Agrigentum is no more than a huge heap of rubble. The immoderate, arrogant nature (*hubris*) of the people of Agrigentum, who were keen to surpass the achievement of their western neighbors and be on a par with the Ionians, led them to design this strange building which was intended to be the largest Doric temple ever constructed. This Temple of Zeus (B) measured 56.30 by 113.45 m. With the sights set squarely on the grandiose, the monument only attained its goal by completely altering the rules of the game.

A lofty silhouette
The Classical style of the so-called Temple of Concord is reinforced by the width of the intercolumniation and the uncurved shafts. The south-east corner dominating the rock at Agrigentum is a prime example of elegant architecture which is not harsh. In comparison with Selinus (Temple E, see page 86), it has an even lighter effect.

The untried formula did away with the portico, and replaced it by half-columns, almost 20 m high and 4.5 m in diameter, set against an impressive peripteral wall, which was totally blind. The ground plan included seven façade supports and fourteen supports running lengthwise. Between the Doric half-columns, atlantes – or *telamones* – seem to hold up the entablature.

Most of the details of the spatial arrangement of this never-completed building escape us. In fact, we do not know either what the *cella* looked like, with its spans exceeding 12.5 m and which can only have been covered by a wooden ceiling, or what the dark *naos* of this sanctuary contained. Was it actually roofed, or, as in Ionia, was the courtyard open to the sky?

This colossal undertaking, executed by thousands of Carthaginians taken prisoner after the battle of Himera in 480, was intended to glorify the victory not only of Theron, but also of Zeus over the barbarians. Diodorus records that the 2.5 m frieze, that crowned the building, depicted the Olympians vanquishing the giants.

Agrigentum: a Classical hexastyle façade
The so-called Temple of Concord, at Agrigentum, lends the Greek temple a perfect balance and a real harmony. But the local Sicilian tufa never achieves the quality of marble with its luminous effect.

The Temples of Hera Lacinia and "Concord"

Rather than looking at razed buildings, let us take a look at temples that have survived: the Temple of Hera Lacinia (said to have been erected by the hero Lacinius) has retained a large part of its peristyle. Built in about 450, it adopted clearly more "Classical" dimensions: with its stylobate measuring 16.91 by 38.10 m, it is, as G. Gruben notes, almost nine times smaller than the Olympieion.

This hexastyle, which has thirteen side columns, rises up on a lofty base in front of which, to the east, are the traces of a large sacrificial altar. At the eastern end of the series of Agrigentan temples, it dominates the tall cliff which forms the city's natural defensive bulwark.

But when we think of Agrigentum we think, above all, of the so-called Temple of Concord. For this building, built twenty years after the Temple of Hera, is one of the best preserved examples of Greek architecture. It has similar measurements (16.92 by 39.42 m) and the same number of columns (six by thirteen).

The Temple of Concord was turned into a church in 597, but has undergone only a few alterations (the addition of vaulted doors in the side walls of the *cella* and removal of the wall separating the *naos* from the *opisthodomos*, for example). Like the other temples at Agrigentum, between the *pronaos* and the *naos*, the building has stairways providing access from both sides to the upper parts of the structure.

The elegance of its portico, the lightness of the pediments, the subtle rhythm of the triglyphs, the perfection of the liaison between the fluting of the columns and the capitals by incorporating annulets, and the tension of the echinus, all create a harmony and a balance which fully respond to the goal of Greek art at the height of its mastery.

Measured rigor
Above: Beneath the cornice of the so-called Temple of Concord, at Agrigentum, the dripstone and its "petrified" drops, and the triglyphs of the entablature.
Below: Surmounting the architrave, the arrangement of the Doric capital with its carefully shaped echinus. The triglyphs are accentuated by the so-called *regula* motif which echoes the drops of the dripstone.

Page 93
View along the portico
The south peripteral gallery of the Temple of Concord, at Agrigentum. This sanctuary, which was turned into a church in the latter stages of Antiquity, is one of the rare ones still to have its *cella*.

A dynamic arrangement
Although the temple at Segesta – where the columns have no fluting – is purely Classical in style, it retains an almost rustic look with its spare elegance.

Page 94
A marooned temple in the land of the Elymians
The unfinished temple at Segesta, in north-western Sicily, stands in a harsh landscape, where its colonnade incorporates the Greek order in an almost incongruous way. Built at the end of the fifth century B.C., between 425 and 416, it was never roofed, and it never had a *cella*.

Segesta, an Unfinished Masterpiece

In the mountains of north-west Sicily, in the heart of the land of the Elymians, the unfinished temple at Segesta (Egesta) is one of the most moving testimonies to the penetration of the Greek spirit into an indigenous western society. The threat represented by the dynamism of Selinus caused the inhabitants of Segesta to appeal to their ally, Athens, whose own unsuccessful expedition against Syracuse in 415, to gain a foothold in Sicily, marked a downward turn. After that, the construction of the temple embarked upon in about 425 came to a standstill. The successful campaigns of Hannibal, who landed on the island in 409, were not to help Segesta regain its independence while its foes – Selinus and Acragas (Agrigentum) – were from then on ravaged by Carthaginian troops.

In wild land off the beaten track, the temple of Segesta is a peripteral hexastyle with fourteen columns on the sides, measuring at the stylobate 23.13 by 58.03 m (giving a proportion of 2:5). Its handsome Doric columns were never fluted, and the planned *cella* never got beyond the foundation stage, which has recently been unearthed by archaeologists.

At the highest point of the site of Segesta, on Mount Barbaro (altitude 415 m), the shell-like form of a small Hellenistic theatre opens onto the plain, offering a splendid view over the land of the Elymians. Its twenty stone tiers attain a diameter of 63 m. In this late period (third century), the function of the semicircular auditoria was no longer limited to stage representations. Theatres were also often used as public meeting places, where citizens could discuss issues concerning the city area.

Refinement and power at Segesta
Above: The huge area that is encircled by the peripteral colonnade of the temple at Segesta must at one time have contained a *cella*, as has been shown by recent excavations.
Below: A perspective view of the stylobate of the temple at Segesta shows its curvature, where the stone blocks still have the salient tenons which were used to help set them in place.

Page 97
Austere harmony
The raw material of the columns of Segesta, and the power of the way they thrust upwards, make this unfinished temple a good example of the slightly coarse Classicism which characterizes Magna Graecia.

A theatre like a crow's nest at Segesta

The late *cavea* of the theatre at Segesta, placed not unlike a balcony or dress circle surveying the surrounding Sicilian countryside, clearly shows the importance attached to cultural facilities by the Hellenized people known as the Elymians.

Recently Unearthed Meeting Places

Magna Graecia: places where the people were consulted
Politics was a crucial factor of Greek culture. Even if Magna Graecia was not a hub of democracy, the presence of an *ecclesiasterion* – recently unearthed both at Paestum (left) and in the market-place (*agora*) at Metapontum (right) – is clear evidence that the people were consulted. These round, open-air edifices were designed for discussion and exchanging opinions, a function that would be later assumed by the *bouleuterion*.

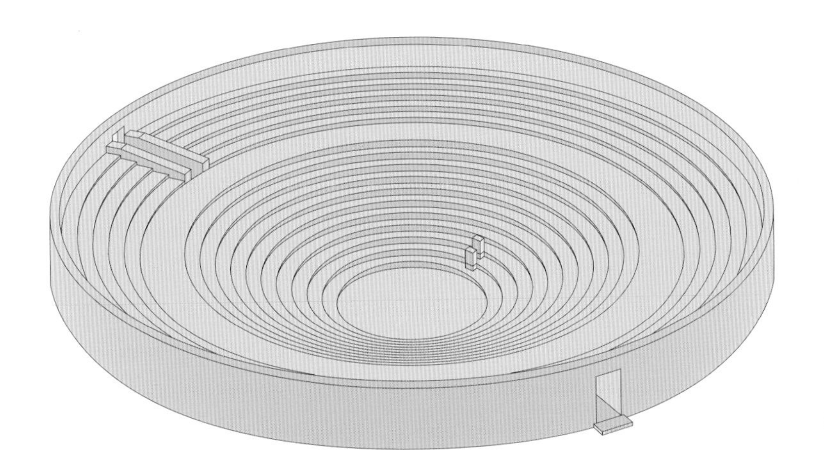

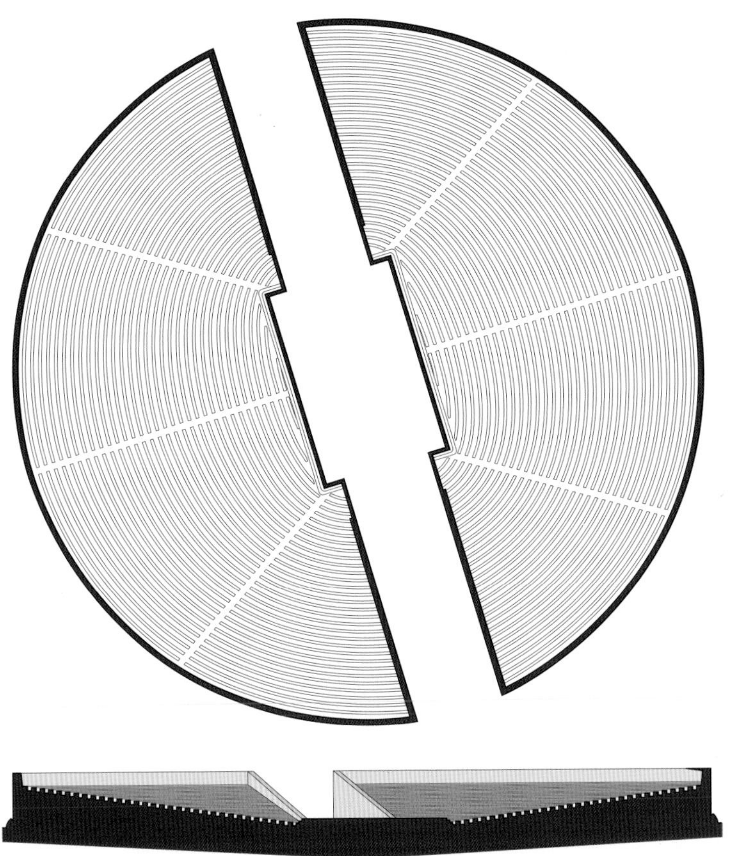

In Magna Graecia there is very early evidence of the existence of buildings designed for gatherings of citizens and their representatives. Here, a special type of building came into being: the *ecclesiasterion*. These are round buildings, designed for meetings of the *ecclesia*, which assembled all the citizens. They were secular public buildings – as opposed to sacred temples – which seem to have appeared from the middle of the sixth century B.C. onward. Looking like a shell, a form which symbolically conveys the function of the building, they have tiered rows and call to mind a small amphitheatre – a building which would not make its appearance until several centuries later in the Roman period.

There is a particularly good example in the *agora* of Metapontum, where a structure with concentric rows has been discovered, whose seats encircle a kind of central podium. In fact, this *ecclesiasterion* was formed by two semicircular auditoria set face to face, each having the shape of an odeum (or roofed theatre), even if the gradient of the tiers was not nearly so steep. This *ecclesiasterion* at Metapontum, built in the first quarter of the fifth century B.C. (when Pythagoras was in the city), could accommodate some 8 000 citizens for their deliberations.

The building at Paestum, built in the same period, has recently been located on the site. It is also a round structure, but is not divided into two opposed halves. The existence of these civic buildings shows that the presence of tyrannical systems in the Greek west did not exclude the participation of citizens in the administration of the city *(polis)*. So these discoveries prompt us to reconsider the political machinery governing the development of several cities in Magna Graecia in the Classical period. And whereas the rule of the tyrants was marked by the *hubris* of grand designs, such as the Olympieion of Agrigentum and the Temple of Apollo at Selinus, the authority of one single man could still not stifle the aspirations of the people keen to express their democratic ideas.

The Role of Greek Asia Minor

The Art of Ionia and the Achaemenids

Page 101
A ritual vase used in the cult of Dionysos
This sumptuous silver *rhyton* in the form of a horn, with a *protome* or forepart of a horse, is a Greek piece that was discovered in a princely tomb in northern Bulgaria, near the Danube. An inscription indicates that it was the work of a silversmith called Etebus, probably from Asia Minor, working for King Cotys (383–360 B.C.). This wealthy sovereign, who reigned in Thrace in the fourth century B.C., did business with the Greek cities, trading wheat and horses for works of art and pieces of jewellery made to order. This *rhyton* was designed for use in the ritual of the Dionysian mysteries, which were very widespread at the court of the Thracian kings. (Roussé Museum, Treasury of Borovo)

Ionia is the cradle of the language of Homer, which would become the tongue of all Greeks. It was in Ionia that the Greek script, so vital to the transmission of knowledge, took form. The rich cities on the shores of Asia Minor were also the home of philosophy and of the Presocratics. The proximity to and contacts with the Near East and Egypt encouraged cosmological and scientific research. The Milesian school established there shone with the dazzling and remarkable minds of those whom we call the "natural Philosophers": Thales (*circa* 625–547), the astronomer, mathematician and traveller, for whom water was the first principle from which the universe was fashioned; Anaximander (*circa* 610–547), the geographer who observed the oblique nature of the ecliptic and built a system based on opposites; and Anaximenes (*circa* 585–525) who based his cosmology on air. Ephesus, an Athenian colony, prided itself for its part in having given shelter to Heraclitus (*circa* 550–480), who considered that everything was movement, and that "everything is in a state of flux" *(panta rhei)* – the universe is in a state of constant transformation and change. This aristocratic philosopher for whom "war has engendered the world and reigns over the universe" was a realist: he was in touch with the Persian King Darius I, a stance which clearly conveys the opportunism which would steer the whole political attitude of the Ephesians.

It was in this region that the Ionic style, so typical of Greek architecture in all its various forms and manifestations in Asia, took shape. But Ionia was not limited to its coastal cities: it also included the offshore islands, and Samos in particular, where the sanctuary to the goddess Hera was of great importance in the creation of the peripteral temple.

The Gradual Birth of the Heraion of Samos

It is worth remembering that, in the sixth century, Samos was renowned both for its Heraion and for its man-made pier, two *stadia* in length (about 350 m), which protected the harbor, but even more so for the famous tunnel built by the engineer and architect Eupalinus in around 530 B.C. to accommodate a 1035 m long water pipe for the city's supply.

The Heraion of Samos is the sanctuary which best enables us to trace the development from the worship of the tree to the worship of Hera. The process got under way in the tenth century B.C. with the stone altar that was erected beside the sacred tree. Via several phases, this led to the colossal Temple of Polycrates, built in 540–530. Here we see the appearance, step by step, of the baldachin forming the awning for the venerated statue which had first been placed outdoors. In about 800 B.C., the Samians erected a long hall for the "idol", measuring just 6.5 m in width, but with a length of 32.86 m, that is 100 feet by 20 (5:1). This was thus the first temple described as a *hecatompedon*. Cob walls and a central line of thirteen wooden posts on stone bases supported the roof. At the entrance, three pillars divided the corridor into four. The statue of the deity stood at the back of the building, half hidden by the pillars.

A *kore* or an Archaic Hera?
This sculpture, coming from Claros, north-west of Ephesus, and dating from around 580–570 B.C., is a good example of the purity of early Ionian art. It is of a type known as a *xoanon*, in other words an "idol", still close to the barely carved wooden sculptures which were placed in the holy of holies of the sanctuary. (Izmir, Archaeological Museum)

Towards the end of the eighth century, this *cella* was provided with a "veranda" surrounding it: wooden columns (seven for the façade and seventeen on the sides) held up the roof. The peripteral concept was born. The development that followed is similar to that earlier described for the "apsidal" temple of Thermum, and for the Heroon of Lefkandi (Euboea).

In around 650, this first temple of Samos, made of perishable materials, was replaced by a new building. The *cella* (30.66 by 6.80 m) was transformed by doing away with the axial colonnade and replacing it with fourteen pillars set on either side along the walls. The view of the sacred effigy was thus no longer blocked. At the entrance, two columns divided access to this *naos* into three. The 37.7 m long peripteral portico consisted of six façade columns and eighteen lateral columns. In addition it was doubled at the entrance, foreshadowing the development towards the dipteral formula typical of Ionic architecture.

It was in *circa* 570–560 that the Samians summoned the very first architects whose names have come down to us; Rhoecus and Theodorus. Their task was to construct, according to the new politics of prestige, a fantastic temple in stone with a double peripteral colonnade. It would measure 52.5 by 105 m (the proportion of two equal squares, that is 1:2, representing 100 by 200 Samian feet). These dimensions had nothing in common with the measurements of previous temples. It was at this point that the Ionic style and the dipteral building came into their own.

This temple built by Rhoecus, with its double row of columns that has earned it the name of the "labyrinth of Samos", has eight façade columns and twenty-one on either side. Its *cella* measured 52.5 by 25 m. The inner area was divided into three naves by two colonnades each with nineteen columns. The Heraion of Samos thus boasts a total of 104 stone columns of almost 18 m in height.

Is it possible to claim that in the mid-sixth century B.C. the "petrification" of buildings on Samos had already spread as far as the roof, and in particular to the trusses forming the frame? We can answer this question by citing the example of the Oikos of the Naxians at Delos (580), with three columns *in antis*, eight of which were inside, placed along the central axis supporting marble beams – "a fundamental edifice" in the words of G. Gruben. But we should bear in mind that the dimensions of these two constructions were in no way comparable. The span of the lintels straddling the intercolumniations in the temple built by Rhoecus was huge. This

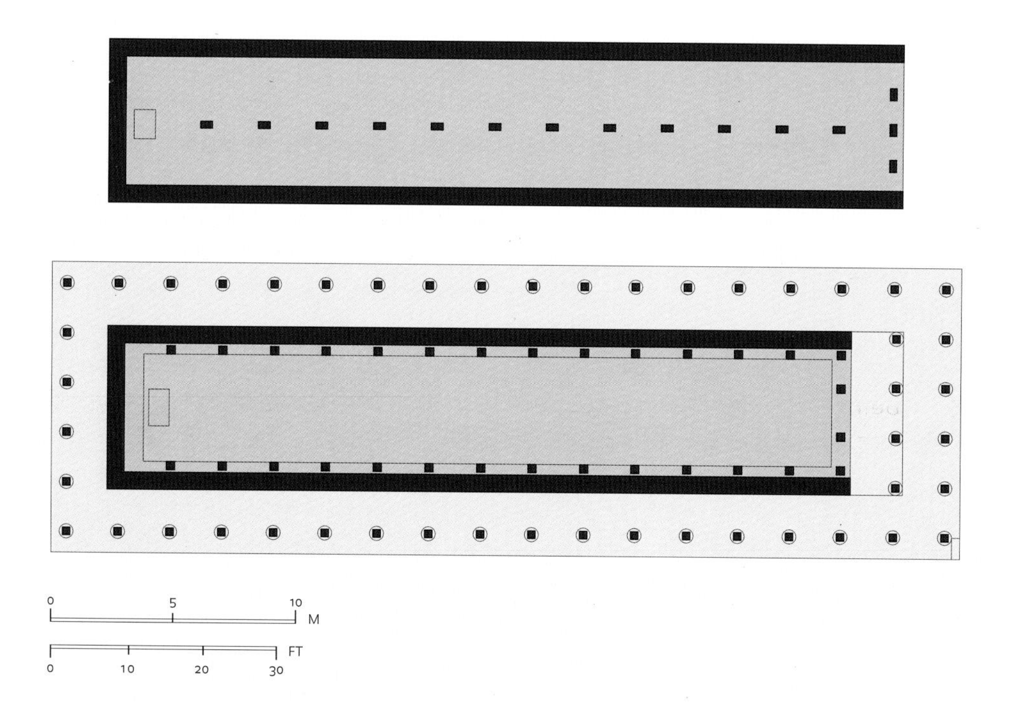

The Hecatompedon of Samos
The Sanctuary of Hera at Samos started out modestly enough. Originally, its *cella* was only 100 Samian feet in length, equivalent to 32.86 m.
Above: In about 800 B.C., it was a narrow building (6.5 m wide) constructed with stonework and rough bricks, in which a wooden colonnade supporting the roof filled the longitudinal axis, partly concealing the cult statue.
Below: In about 650, a gallery, or outer surrounding portico, was built around the *cella*. The axial pillars were pushed up against the sides of the *cella*, which is itself preceded by a double portico on the smaller side, with a hexastyle façade.

A colossal Heraion at Samos
In the sixth century B.C., the Temple of Hera at Samos was of immense proportions. Under the orders of the tyrant Polycrates (538–522), and following the collapse of an earlier temple built in about 560 by Rhoecus, the Samians embarked on the construction of an impressive sanctuary measuring 52.5 x 105 m, realized in marble by the architect Theodorus. The elevation of the façade, with its eight columns, 18.5 m high, clearly shows what the formula of the Ionic temple had accomplished. The plan shows a dipteros, consisting of three rows of shafts along the façade and at the chevet, and a double colonnade in the vestibule and the *cella*.

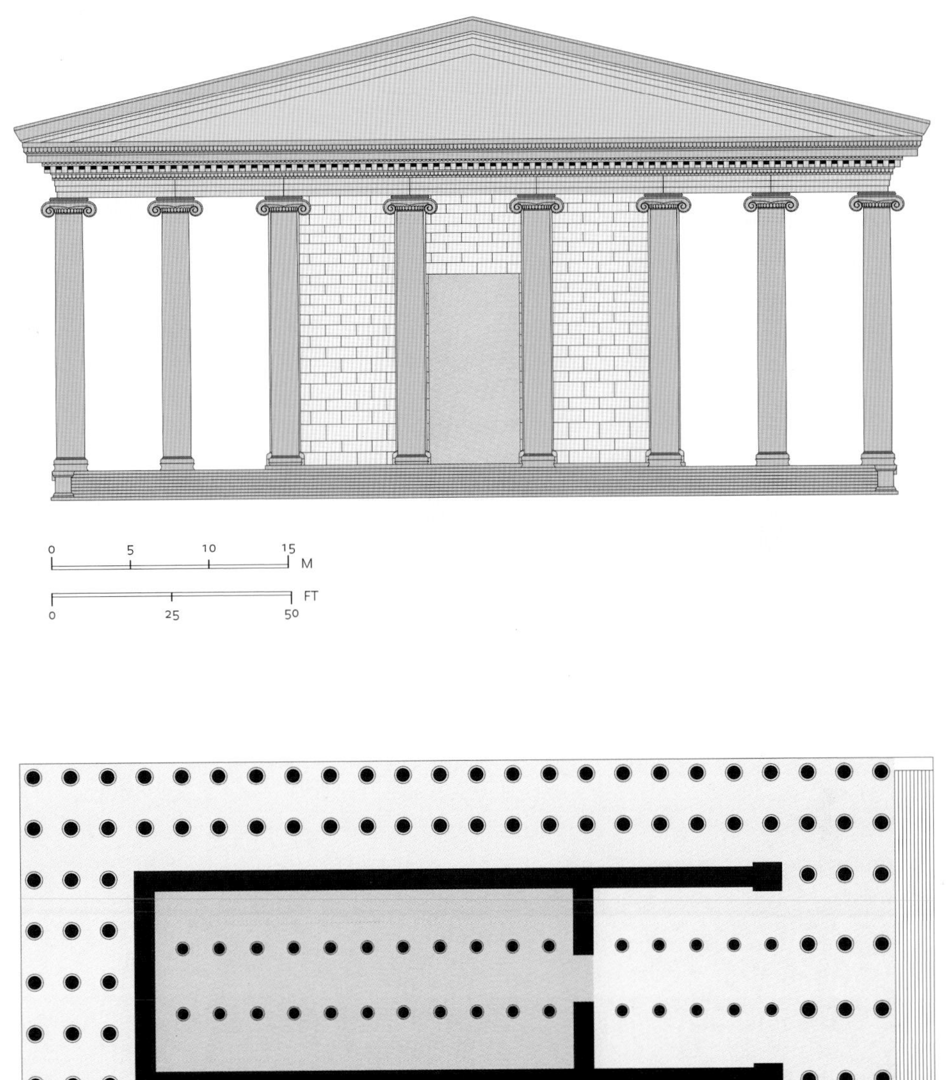

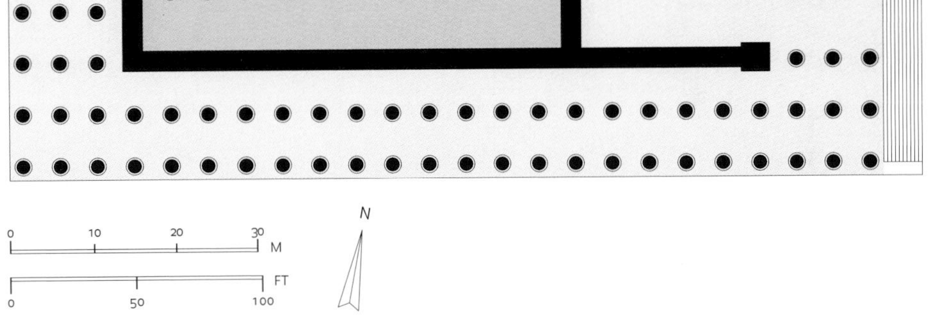

is why it is not improbable that the roof of this Heraion would still have been constructed out of timber.

The building was not, however, destroyed by fire, as has been claimed. The most recent excavations have shown that it simply collapsed because its foundations were set on marshy ground and were not stable enough. This collapse led to the temple being abandoned in about 540. It was subsequently demolished and rebuilt from top to bottom.

It was the tyrant Polycrates of Samos who undertook the construction of a sanctuary even larger and more perfect than the Heraion. This second dipteral structure, which aptly expressed the thriving economy of the island, was to be made entirely of marble, probably by Eupalinus, the architect of the tunnel, the construction of which had represented a wager at the impossible, in so much as the labourers had started to dig it out simultaneously from each end.

After moving the site of the new Heraion 40 m westward to find more solid ground, the architect re-used some of the materials of the old building as foundations for the future one. The temple of Polycrates, measuring 108.63 by 52.45 m, had 137 columns, and in particular nine shafts at the chevet, while the façade – to accommodate the axial access – only had eight, 18.5 m in height, which meant that there were variable intercolumniations with a wider axial passage. At the two ends, the façades presented three rows of columns which apparently justified its description as a "forest of columns". Sadly, all that now remains of this great building are unremarkable ruins.

By this stage, Ionic architecture had attained its greatest dimensions. The dipteral temple can be likened to the most colossal of the hypostyle halls of Egypt. This Heraion covered a total area of 5700 m^2, while the huge inner area of the hypostyle room of the Temple of Amon at Karnak covered 6800. There was just the slight difference that, in the Pharaonic building, the supports were situated within an enclosed area. The columns of the temple of Samos, for their part, were visible from all sides and, in full daylight, formed a much lighter peristyle. At Karnak, there were 134 columns some 20 m in height and more than 3 m thick, while in the masterpiece of Polycrates, the diameter of the 137 columns did not exceed 2 m. The intercolumniations at Karnak were set on average at 3.4 m, and at most at 6 m (in the central row), while at Samos they reached 8.5 m.

The creation of such an outstanding and revolutionary building on the island of Samos was bound to attract the attention of sovereigns close at hand and far afield alike. In fact, prestige prompted tyrants and kings to order symbolic buildings to be constructed, each more extraordinary than the last, the splendor of which reflected on their entire reign. It has been observed that, in Sicily, tyrants embarked on buildings of similar dimensions, in particular the Olympieion of Acragas (Agrigentum) and the Temple of Apollo at Selinus.

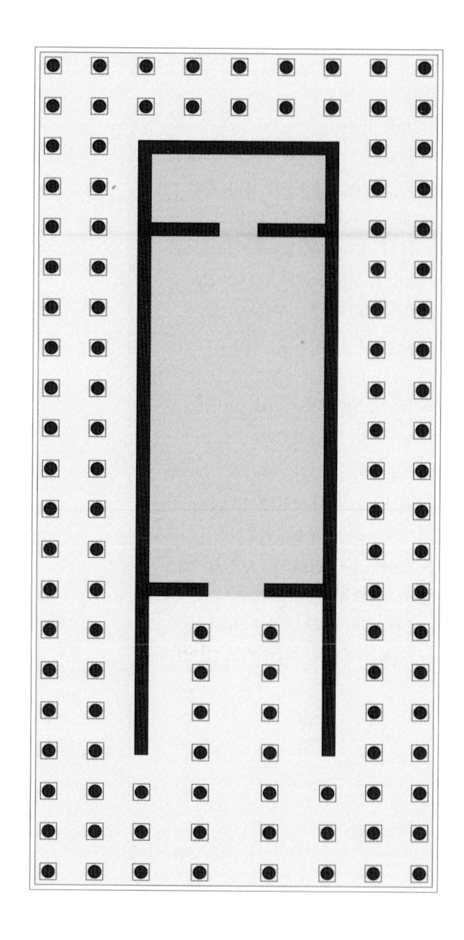

The Artemision of Croesus at Ephesus

At almost the same time as the construction of the Heraion of Rhoecus on Samos, Croesus (561–547), the last sovereign of Lydia, compelled to compete, chose Ephesus as the site for the construction of a gigantic temple dedicated to the goddess Artemis. It was in the form of Cybele, venerated in Asia Minor, that this Phrygian deity, known from the time of the *Iliad*, appeared to Greek settlers when they arrived in Ionia. During the Trojan War, she came to Priam's aid. Artemis ruled wild animals and the growth of plants. In the Artemision of Ephesus stood the statue or *xoanon*, originally made of wood, which would replace the disquieting sacred image of the goddess known as "polymastic", that is, with many breasts.

In the seventh century there was an original "apsidal" temple (as at Thermum and Lefkandi) on the site of Ephesus, which was followed by a *hecatompedon*, which burnt down in the sixth century. In about 560, Croesus entrusted the architect Chersiphron together with his son Metagenes, later joined by Theodorus, once he had finished his building on Samos, with the task of constructing a sumptuous dipteral temple in marble. Like its Samian model, this first Artemision was colossal: 115.14 by 55.1 m, with 114 columns (eight on the façade, twenty-one on each side, and nine at the chevet), all 18.9 m in height. These extremely elegant shafts, which were unusually bold in their design, had a diameter of 1.57 m, so they were twelve times as high as they were wide. This is the perfect example of the graceful elegance of the Ionic style.

It should be noted that the building does not have an enclosed *naos*, but rather a hypaethral courtyard (open to the sky), set slightly sunken, in which there must have been a *naïskos*, or "tabernacle" containing the statue of the goddess.

In addition to the magnificent volutes of the Ionic capitals, unearthed traces of this temple show quite clearly that, on the lower drums surmounting the bases of the superimposed tori, the foot of the columns bore sculpted reliefs depicting

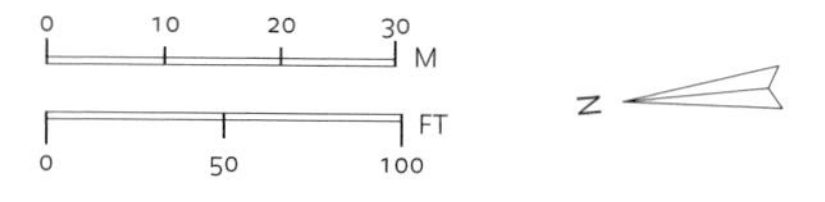

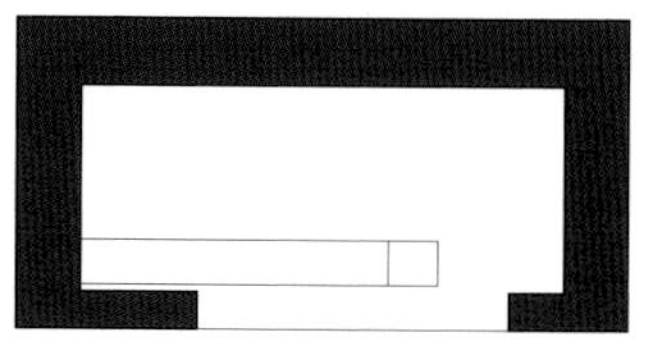

The first Artemision of Ephesus
Similar in size to the Temple of Hera at Samos, the sanctuary dedicated to the goddess Artemis at Ephesus was built in the reign of Croesus, the last king of Lydia (*circa* 560). Its dimensions (55.1 by 115.14 m) show that the architects Chersiphron, Metagenes and Theodorus of Samos worked in a spirit of competitive rivalry. But in the place of a *cella*, the sanctuary at Ephesus had a huge open-air courtyard. It was preceded by an enormous sacrificial altar.

figures on a heroic scale (greater than life-size, in other words). This décor of unprecedented magnificence was further enhanced at the top of the architrave with the continuous frieze, peculiar to the Ionic style, illustrating the myth of Artemis.

The building was set within a sacred area forming a vast park planted with trees and including wild animals in honor of Artemis. Are these gardens, which call to mind the "paradises" of Achaemenid Persia, contemporary with Croesus, or were they created after the victory of Cyrus?

At Ephesus, as in Samos, all that remain are ground-level traces of these fantastic creations peculiar to the art of Ionia in the sixth century.

Enamelled brick at Susa
The decoration of the palace of Darius I (521–486) at Susa, which points to Assyrian influence, was made with enamelled brick. This frieze of archers, typical of the Achaemenid style, would be transposed, at Persepolis, into a delicately carved bas-relief largely executed by Ionian and Lydian sculptors. (Tehran, Archaeological Museum)

An Oracular Temple at Didyma

Throughout the region great Ionic sanctuaries increased in number – though they never attained such vast proportions. Thus, at Didyma, near Miletus, a temple dedicated to Apollo was built in the middle of the sixth century. In its initial state, the Didymaion already measured 87 m in length by 42 in width. This oracular sanctuary also had a courtyard containing a sacred spring in a laurel grove (laurel being the symbol of the god) as well as a *naïskos* measuring 24 m by 10. The small inner temple in the form of a tabernacle housed a famous statue in bronze by the sculptor Canachus of Sicyon (*circa* 500), which was borne off by the Persians to Ecbatana, and not returned until 295 B.C., by Seleucus I.

This first Didymaion had received major donations from Croesus. Like most of the Greek creations in Ionia, it was destroyed by the Persians in 493 after the Ionian revolt. It was not until Alexander arrived that this prestigious centre of pilgrimage was revived (a topic which will be dealt with in greater detail in the book on eastern Graeco-Roman architecture).

It will suffice to know that, once more, this was a giant undertaking. Its dimensions are close to those of the Artemision of Ephesus: 109.34 by 51.13 m (the stylobate of 340 by 170 feet), with a *cella* of 300 by 100 feet encircling an open-air courtyard. The Hellenistic building, which offers us some beautiful ruins, is a decastyle consisting of a total of 122 columns, 20 m in height with a diameter of 2 m. It culminated in a cornice 27 m from the ground.

From Cyrus to the Persian Wars

During the reign of Croesus, the Hellenized sovereign of Lydia, whose capital was the city of Sardis in the Hermos basin, the kingdom enjoyed a proverbial prosperity – do we not, after all, talk about being "as rich as Croesus"? However, the king who came to the throne in 561 would be the last sovereign of independent Lydia. He reigned over the Greek cities of Ionia who paid him tribute in exchange for their security. But Persia, the power on the rise in the Near East, would put an end to this lavish reign.

In 546, in their clash with Cyrus II, the Lydians were beaten, Sardis taken, and the Achaemenid sovereign extended his authority over the whole of Anatolia. The Ionian cities put up stout resistance, apart from Ephesus which had sided with the conqueror. After the surrender of Miletus, Priene and Magnesia were sacked. In 542, the Achaemenid programme of unification was accomplished. From then on, the Ionians had to provide contingents for Harpagus, commander of the coastal regions in the name of Cyrus, and pay tributes to the Persians. Sardis, on the 2500 km thoroughfare linking Susa and Ephesus, became the seat of the satrap, or Persian governor. As for Croesus, he spent two decades at the court of the Persian sovereigns, undoubtedly proffering them wise artistic counsel.

For decades there have been discussions about the connections between Greek and Achaemenid architecture – with extraordinary examples of the latter at Pasargadae, Susa, Persepolis and Nakh-e Rustam. It may be interesting to reconsider this issue in the light of new observations. For analysis nowadays leaves us no

The tomb of Cyrus at Pasargadae In the plain of Pasargadae, the burial-place of Cyrus II (sixth century B.C.) stands on a pedestal in the form of a stepped pyramid. Its shape is akin to that of Lycian tombs in southern Asia Minor.

option but to admit the preponderant role of the Ionians and the Lydians in the blossoming of the Persian palaces. This is why it was vital to include Achaemenid buildings – though the Achaemenids were the implacable foes of the Greeks – in the history of Greek architecture. It is a paradoxical position, given the destruction brought on by the Persian Wars, and the designation "barbarians", with which the Greeks (and Aeschylus in particular) saddled the Persians.

Cyrus II, who was the true founder of the Persian Empire, came to the throne in 559 and reigned until 529. He chalked up a long list of great conquests: in 549, he took Ecbatana from the Median King Astyages; in 546 he annexed Lydia under Croesus; in 539, he gained possession of Babylon and Mesopotamia. His son, Cambyses II (530–522) occupied Egypt in 525. The Achaemenid Empire stretched from the Persian Gulf to the Nile Valley.

Upheavals led to the usurpation of Darius I (521–486), who married Atossa, daughter of Cyrus II, to legitimize his authority. Darius reinstated the power of the Achaemenids, who flourished under his rule. In Asia Minor, he seized Samos, the city which Cambyses had attempted to lay his hands on by dispatching to it the Persian Oroetes, governor of Sardis, whose task was to negotiate with Polycrates the re-alliance of the island. He fought campaigns in Thrace, then conquered the East as far as the river Indus.

From then on all peoples from the banks of the Indus to the Sudan and the Dardanelles were forced to pay the tribute imposed on subjects of the Great King. But Persian domination over the Ionian cities does not seem to have been too heavy-handed. The Greeks, however, were reluctant subjects. In 499, the major cities of Ionia – apart from Ephesus – rose up against the Persian yoke. Aristagoras of Miletus – who had abolished the tyranny – refused to pay the tribute. He was backed by Athens and Eretria. The rebels marched against Sardis, and set fire to the city and its temple in 498. The Persians retaliated with ruthless repression, which lasted from 497 to 493, the year when Darius had Miletus razed to the ground. The Persian sovereign sent his son-in-law Mardonius to Ionia, his mission being to take possession of Macedonia. In 490, the Great King decided to attack Athens and Eretria, to punish them for the support that they had lent to the rebels. Thus was triggered the first Persian War. The Persians were beaten on land at Marathon and grew thirsty for revenge. It was Xerxes (486–465), successor of Darius, who embarked on the second Persian War in 481, by launching an onslaught against Greece. The

The Persian tombs at Nakh-e Rustam
Hewn in the cliff-face, the burial-places of the Achaemenid sovereigns look like tall cross-shaped compositions which imitate the façade of a palace where the columns frame the entrance.
Below: The decoration which surmounts them shows a bas-relief symbolizing the might wielded by the King of Kings over the nations of the empire.

Achaemenid ruler, who had emerged the victor at Thermopylae, let loose his armies on Attica, seized Athens, which he duly sacked, and tore down the buildings of the Acropolis. But at sea he suffered a disastrous defeat at Salamis in 480. The defeat of his troops at Plataea, followed by the total destruction of his fleet at Mycale, completed the Persian rout when confronted by the Greek cities. So this chapter came to a close with a new wave of uprisings in the Ionian cities in 478.

Despite the Greek victory, the toll of this clash was catastrophic: in addition to the devastated Ionian cities, the great temples razed – with the exception of Ephesus – and the grand monuments of Athens sacked, life was seriously disrupted and slowed down throughout the Greek settlements in Asia until the conquests of Alexander from 334.

In terms of architecture, there is a huge hiatus, not unlike a gaping wound, in the cities of Ionia. The progress of the great Ionic style came to a shuddering stand still there for almost 150 years. The few exceptions include the Mausoleum of Halicarnassus, for which we have a Hellenized satrap of the Great King to thank.

The Monuments of the Achaemenids

In contrast to the stagnation that afflicted Ionia, there was considerable activity in Persia, with grand buildings being erected everywhere. Here we shall simply list these buildings and discuss them in more detail at a later stage. They include, essentially, the palaces of Pasargadae, dating from the reign of Cyrus, as well as his pyramidal tomb, erected in the immediate vicinity. Then, under Darius, there was the palace of Susa, in Elam, whose full scale and scope have been revealed by excavations, with its hypostyle hall or *apadana*, and lastly the vast complex of Persepolis, not far from Pasargadae, with its covered esplanade of hypostyle rooms and apartments, monumental gates and doors, stairways and thoroughfares, its

A gold founding inscription at Persepolis
On a solid gold plaque, the founding text of the Apadana of Persepolis (late sixth century B.C.) is written in cuneiform characters in Old Persian, in Babylonian and in Elamite. (Tehran, Archaeological Museum)

arsenal, its warehouses and its treasury. Not far from Persepolis are the great rock tombs of Nakh-e Rustam, as well as the tower dedicated to the worship of fire.

This architecture, at once utilitarian, ritual and symbolic, is based on a characteristic style, which conveys an original inspiration, even if many of the details hark back to obvious precursors: Egyptian cornices, Babylonian bas-reliefs in enamelled brick, Assyrian orthostats and doors with winged bulls, columns whose base and shaft call to mind the Ionic style, capitals in the form of griffons with hooked beaks resembling Greek monsters, and so on.

These monuments were all erected within the period between about 540 and 350. They are thus strictly contemporary with the Greek temples and the Archaic and Classical architecture of the Greek world.

The Greeks and Persian Architecture

We have mentioned the fact that, from 542, the Ionians provided the Persians with contingents. These were soldiers enlisted in the army of the Great King and specialists and craftsmen whose work formed part of the tribute. Even before the Persian Wars, Greek subjects were thus in the service of the Achaemenids. We know, for example, that Darius' physician was a certain Democedes, and that other Greek physicians were employed at the court. The same must have been the case with architects. But there is less evidence about these latter.

After admiring the great Ionic diptera of Samos, Ephesus and Didyma, which surpassed all contemporary architectural production in Asia and the Near East, the Persian sovereigns quite naturally – just as the tyrants had done before them – appointed Greek designers to accomplish their symbolic and dynastic works. So Greek architects, artists, technicians, sculptors and craftsmen were all enlisted to work on the construction of the Achaemenid palaces. We also know that there were teams of itinerant builders. Because of the Persian presence in Asia Minor, it was logical enough that these teams should be called upon to undertake the grand designs with which the Great Kings wanted to stamp their reigns.

These facts are confirmed by the foundation charter discovered in the palace of Susa. The text, which probably dates from 520–510, mentioned the country of origin of different elements earmarked for the building of the palace. The entire Empire was called upon to contribute. In this charter we read in particular that "cedar beams were brought from a mountain known as Lebanon. Syrians transported them as far as Babylon, and from Babylon the Carians and the Ionians took them to Susa. ... The decoration of the walls of the terrace came from Ionia. ... The stone for the columns which were worked on the spot were imported from the region of Apitarus, in Elam. The craftsmen who cut and dressed them were Ionians and Sardians."

It is clear that the Greeks were much called upon to construct the buildings of the

Page 111 below
Like ancient griffins
Inspired by the Archaic Greek griffin, like this bronze in the museum at Delphi dating from the seventh century B.C. (left), the capital at Persepolis in the form of the forepart or protome of a griffin leaves very little doubt about the Greek influence seen in the palace architecture of the Achaemenids (right).

Achaemenid court. In his recent *Histoire de l'Empire perse* (1996), Pierre Briant writes: "There can be no doubt that, to complete his building programme at Pasargadae, Cyrus called upon craftsmen from Lydia and Ionia." They built the columns which – it should be noted – form the key element of this architecture. According to Diodorus, Cambyses was also in the habit of taking with him craftsmen who were entrusted with the construction of his royal palaces. In the text in question Egyptians were involved, but the fact is that whole teams were appointed for the building sites of the Great Kings. Greek graffiti found in a quarry close to Persepolis also name the quarrymen Pytharcus and Nicias.

In the Susa charter, the reference to the decoration suggests that Greeks also worked on the sculpted reliefs. We know, thanks to Pliny, that a sculptor by the name of Telephanes of Phocis came to Persepolis.

The Genesis of the Persian Palaces

Originally, the Persians were a pastoral and semi-nomadic people. At the dawn of the sixth century B.C., they thus had no technical and artistic "baggage". The suc-

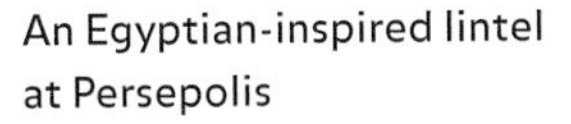

An Egyptian-inspired lintel at Persepolis

The gates of the palaces of Persepolis are surmounted by Egyptian grooving, as seen in the Pharaonic temples. The art of the Achaemenids was the product of a broad syncretic phenomenon which conveyed the diversity of the empire.

From Samos to Persepolis
The comparison between two Ionic columns in the temple of Polycrates at Samos (left), and – on the same scale – a column from the Apadana of Persepolis, clearly shows the single origin of these structures, which are characterized both by their similar proportions between diameter and height and by the execution of the fluting.

Page 113
The irresistible thrust of the shafts of the Apadana at Persepolis
The public audience-chamber of the palace of Persepolis, built in the reign of Darius I in about 520–510 B.C., had thirty-six columns, 23.15 m in height including their capitals, and thirty-six other columns forming the three entrance porticoes. The technique of the drum shafts, complete with fluted grooves and surmounting an ornate base, is typically Ionian.

Power and elegance at Persepolis
Behind the frieze of Median and Persian warriors who guard the stairways of the Apadana, the columns of Persepolis rise up today just as they did 2500 years ago.

Persepolis at dawn
Here stood the most monumental hall designed for ceremonial rituals in Persia: the Apadana of Darius I. It was during the fire lit after the victory of Alexander the Great over Darius III to avenge the destruction of the Acropolis by the troops of Xerxes I, in 480, that this sumptuous building, roofed with timber frames made of cedar of Lebanon, was destroyed in 330 B.C.

At the top of the columns of the Apadana
The capitals of the audience-chamber at Persepolis included large *protomai* of bulls symbolizing the imperial might of Persia. Like Greek temples, the Achaemenid buildings were decorated with apotropaic figures, designed to ward off evil.

cess of their weaponry helped them to draw from the heritage of the countries they subjugated: Medes, Elamites, Urartians, Babylonians, Assyrians, Egyptians, Phoenicians, and Greeks from Ionia, Caria, and Lydia. For the Persian monuments were an original creation resulting from the combination of elements issuing from different civilizations. In no way did they constitute a hybrid style, but rather a fruitful merger of varied sources reflecting the different parts of the Empire.

What are the indigenous "models" which had an influence on the spatial and functional design of Persian buildings? In particular, what are the origins of the great hypostyle rooms, the best examples of which are offered by Persepolis, after Pasargadae and Susa? If we go back to the thirteenth century B.C., we find Palace D of the Hittites of Bogazkoy, on the Acropolis of Büyükkale, with its twenty-five columns supporting the ceiling of a square room. This is not so much a paradigm as an archetype. We should also mention the palace of Hasanlou, south of Lake Urmia, dating from the ninth century, with its eight columns in a room measuring 25 m by 19 m, as well as the palace of Erebouni, in Urartu (Turkey), dating from the eighth century B.C. (if the existence of its thirty columns is not a revision of the Persian era). In the seventh century another Urartian palace, built at Altintepe, included a fine hypostyle room measuring 44 by 25.30 m, with eighteen columns (in three rows of six). Last of all, we should mention, in the same period, the Median palace of Godin Tepe in present-day Iranian Kurdistan, which also boasts a hypostyle room. It is evident that the principle of inner space created by wooden supports is widely attested to in the Near East before the arrival of the Persians.

When the Achaemenid sovereigns decided to build rooms designed for their official ceremonies and rituals, it was their wish to create buildings as impressive as those they had seen in Ionia. So it is not surprising that they should turn to Greek architects to work out a programme that would be in keeping with the requirements of public audiences and royal banquets alike.

Because of the considerable advances which the Greeks of Asia had made with their large dipteral temples during the three decades leading up to the surrender of Ionia to the Persians, they would occupy a vital place in the design and construction as well as in the embellishment of Achaemenid seats of power. A study of the buildings provides ample proof of this. As we have emphasized, the distinctive feature of the Persian palace resides in the great hypostyle rooms or *apadana*. It is here that stone columns would play their leading role, based on their function in a traditional Fars house with its veranda made with wooden posts. So it was this "petrified" sup-

The heart of the Palace of the Achaemenids at Persepolis
In front of the Apadana, the Hall of the Hundred Columns, or Throne Room, there is a huge hypostyle area, access to which is gained through several gates.

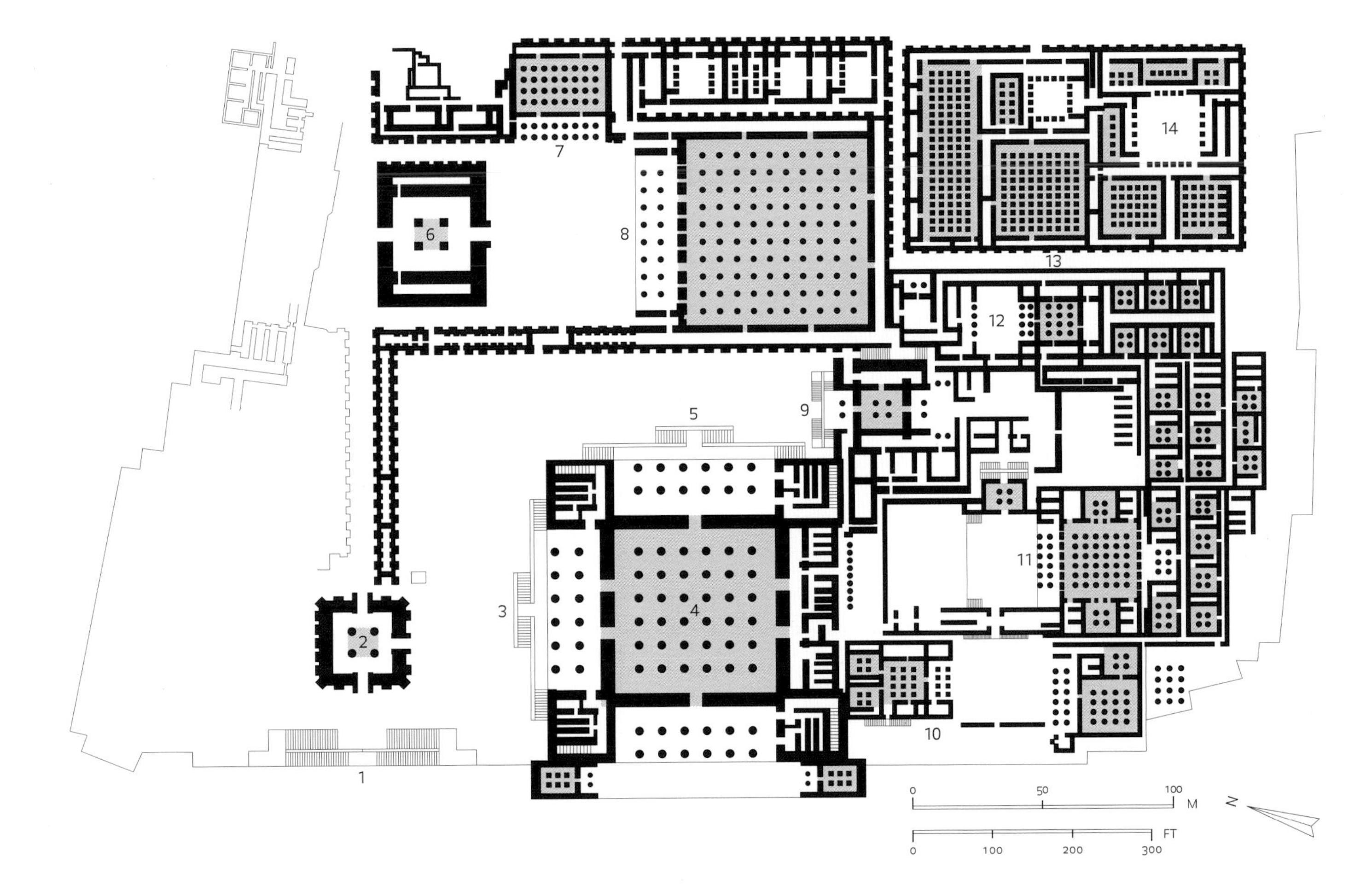

Plan of the palaces of Persepolis
Constructed on a vast esplanade, partly man-made and lined with terraces supported by tall walls, the Persepolis complex consists of ceremonial buildings, buildings earmarked for courtly rituals, and apartments for the sovereign and his retinue:

1 Stairways to the esplanade
2 Xerxes Gate
3 North stairs of the Apadana
4 Hypostyle chamber of the Apadana with thirty-six columns
5 East stairs of the Apadana
6 Unfinished gate
7 The Hall of the Thirty-two Columns
8 The Hall of the Hundred Columns
9 Stairs to the Tripylon
10 Palace of Darius
11 Palace of Xerxes
12 Palace
13 Wall of the Treasury
14 Treasury

The monumental entrance at Persepolis
Access to the upper part of the terrace at Persepolis is gained by way of a double stairway with two flights of opposing steps which lead to the Gate of All the Nations built by Xerxes (486–465).

The Xerxes Gate
One of the great winged and lion-tailed bulls of the Propylaea or monumental gateways of Xerxes I. This is an adaptation of those Assyrio-Babylonian monsters which combine the beings of the tetramorph: bull's body, eagle's wings, human face, and lion's mane and tail. These supernatural creatures stood guard in front of emblematic buildings (temples or palaces).

The "fortress" of power
At the top of these skilfully built walls, which rise to a height of some 20 m, the palaces of Persepolis survey the surrounding plain.

port which emerged as the major new feature of Achaemenid architecture, both in its dimensions and in the perfection of its construction.

The columns which bore the lofty ceilings of Persian assembly halls suggest a purely Ionic style. The bases, with their *tori,* like the shafts with their refined fluting, fit into the research carried out in the sanctuaries of Samos and Ephesus. The columns of the Apadana of Persepolis were 23.15 m in height, with capitals with double protomes of bulls, lions or griffons, but measured only 1.9 m in diameter.

In the late sixth century B.C., the Ionians were the only people capable of erecting stone shafts higher than 20 m and made of drums whose diameter was less than one tenth the height. They were also experts in the technique of fluting. These columns were the extraordinarily elegant and daring instrument which created those vast inner areas in the palaces then covered with roofs of cedar.

Inner Areas

The palaces of Pasargadae built by Cyrus II in 540 B.C. consist essentially of huge hypostyle rooms. The *apadana* of the most recent building on the site measures 36 by 28 m. Its roof was supported by five rows of six columns (thirty stone shafts). The most intriguing aspect of this palace lies in the two porticoes which – like Greek *stoai* – flanked the room on its long sides. These double colonnades, which projected from both sides of the room, gave the building an H-shaped layout. The south-east portico had two rows of twenty columns; the one situated to the north-east had two rows of twelve columns, with a chamber at each end, to brace the structure. These showy porticoes, which had sixty-four columns in all and respectively measured 90 m and 78 m call to mind not only the *stoai* which had appeared at Samos, but also the lateral colonnades of the dipteral buildings of Ionia.

This type of plan, with its jutting wings, was nevertheless unsatisfactory. That is why, at Susa as at Persepolis, the *apadana* would take on a more coherent and rigorous appearance. The actual room was now part of a square and, in both instances, had thirty-six tall columns in six rows. The inner area of Persepolis measured 60 m per side. The distances between the axes reached 8.9 m across, and the space between two columns was 7 m. The end result was an appearance of great lightness, contrasting with the hypostyle rooms of Egyptian temples. Compared with Karnak, where the proportion between the diameter of the columns and the "void" between two shaft bases was about 1:1.2, this ratio attained 1:3.6 in Persepolis.

Pages 120–121
Under the watchful eye of the "Immortals"
The east stairways leading to the terrace of the Apadana and the audience-chamber are lined with three levels of bas-relief friezes. Here, the imperial guard watched over the King of Kings. The guard-rails are lined with typical staggered merlons. It was in this palatine area that the royal procession took place, which preceded the *agapes* or meals of fellowship in a kind of *symposion*, which was an official banquet designed to sign and seal the unity of the nation.

The stairways of the Tripylon
The double flight of steps that leads to the three portals of the palace is lined with friezes, depicting the Median and Persian delegations – identifiable respectively by their round and vertically pleated headgear – attending the reception given by the sovereign. Here, too, the guard-rails are surmounted by staggered merlons.

The Persian guards of the Apadana
The "Immortals", armed with spear, bow and quiver, and in some cases with a round shield, formed the imperial guard of the Achaemenid sovereign. The strict order of the warriors contrasts with the liveliness generally visible in Greek bas-reliefs, where an essential feature is the attempt to convey movement.

This lightening was due not only to the fact that the Egyptian supports bore stone slabs instead of a wooden ceiling, but also to the "Ionic" style applied by the Persians, where the *apadana* resembled the great diptera of Samos and Ephesus.

With its 23.15 m stone columns bearing the cedar roof trusses, the volume of Darius' audience chamber was 90000 m^3. "Never in Antiquity had art shown such daring", wrote the Iranian history specialist Roman Ghirshman.

This Apadana was itself flanked on three sides by double porticoes with two rows of six columns (thirty-six columns in all), while at the corners of the structure stood four square "towers", whose sides measured 15 m each. These corner features provided the bracing of the building, which was part of a square with sides 110 m in length and covering a total area of 12000 m^2.

Lastly, to the north and east, wide staircases with double symmetrical flights, edged with staggered merlons, formed entrances to this stunning room which Darius built in 513 B.C. For the entire building stood on a socle 3.7 m high, flanked by steps with converging flights. On the sides of the socle, bas-reliefs were carved in the manner of Assyrian orthostats. Here we find, in long horizontal registers, the army of the Immortals, forming the guard of the Great King, and the Procession of the Tributaries, where all the peoples of the Empire paraded past during the Mazdaic feast of Now Ruz, symbolizing the Iranian New Year. With their processional narrative these sculptures call to mind the continuous friezes of Ionic architecture.

At Persepolis the vast palace complex covered a colossal man-made esplanade measuring 450 by 300 m (13.5 hectares), bordered, on the lowland side, by high walls resembling bastions with two large double spiral staircases whose flights, first diverging then converging, led to the only entrance to the palatial site: the Gate of Nations, or Gate of Xerxes.

The complex contained various other hypostyle rooms, in particular Xerxes' Throne room (*circa* 480), which was situated within a square layout, 70 m each side, and numbered 100 columns (10 by 10). A double portico flanked it to the north forming the entrance. Various areas were columned. Here there were 100 (20 by 5), there 99 (9 by 11), there again 32 (8 by 4) and 16 (4 by 4), and so on.

It is clear to see that the basic supporting feature of Ionic architecture found a remarkable application in the hypostyle areas of the Achaemenid *apadana* and throne rooms. But we must not overlook what it is that separates these Persian spaces, on the one hand, and those of Greek buildings on the other. If the techniques of Greek architects form the basis of the accomplishments of Persepolis, the two cultures merge in differing customs. Unlike Greek temples, where the *cella* is not designed to accommodate masses of people, the reception rooms of the Achaemenids are assembly halls, areas designed for grand courtly rituals, where the pomp and circumstance of the Empire could be displayed. In this sense, Persian architecture represented a revolution in the spatial concepts of Antiquity.

Lastly, we should stress the fact that the synergy between Greeks and Persians was not limited to the use of columns; it was also applied to the sources of ornamental forms. From the seventh and sixth centuries on, in fact, there existed in the Median region certain strange "Ionic" capitals with volutes, embellishing the rock tomb of Kizkapan, in present-day Iraqi Kurdistan. In the same period, the rock tomb (of Cambyses I) at Da-u Duktar, in Khuzistan, also contains examples of early "Ionic" capitals, proof that scroll-type motifs, present at Persepolis as well, were already widespread in the early period.

So there is a great deal of convergence in Asian regions, and those bitter foes, Greeks and Persians, often drew from a shared aesthetic source. This is especially noteworthy in the goldsmith's craft, where *rhytons,* bracelets and rings all presented similar decorative motifs. It is also the case with the fierce lions which, on the bas-reliefs of Persepolis, attack bulls, and which we also find in the Ionian decoration of the Treasury of Siphnos (525) at Delphi, carved several decades earlier.

Pasargadae and its paradise gardens

Above: When Cyrus II (559–529) embarked on the construction of the first major palatine complex of the Achaemenid dynasty at Polycratese, on the upland plateau of Persia, he designed a reception-building flanked by two porticoes *(stoai)* with a double colonnade, between which stood a hypostyle hall with thirty tall stone shafts (5 by 6).

Below: The palace buildings were arranged in a huge park – a "paradise" – traversed by irrigation channels, the geometric layout of which formed a garden on a human scale. It was this type of garden that the Persians would introduce at Sardis, in Lydia, the western capital of the empire, from where their influence would extend to the Hellenistic parks *(paradeisoi)* under the Attalids.

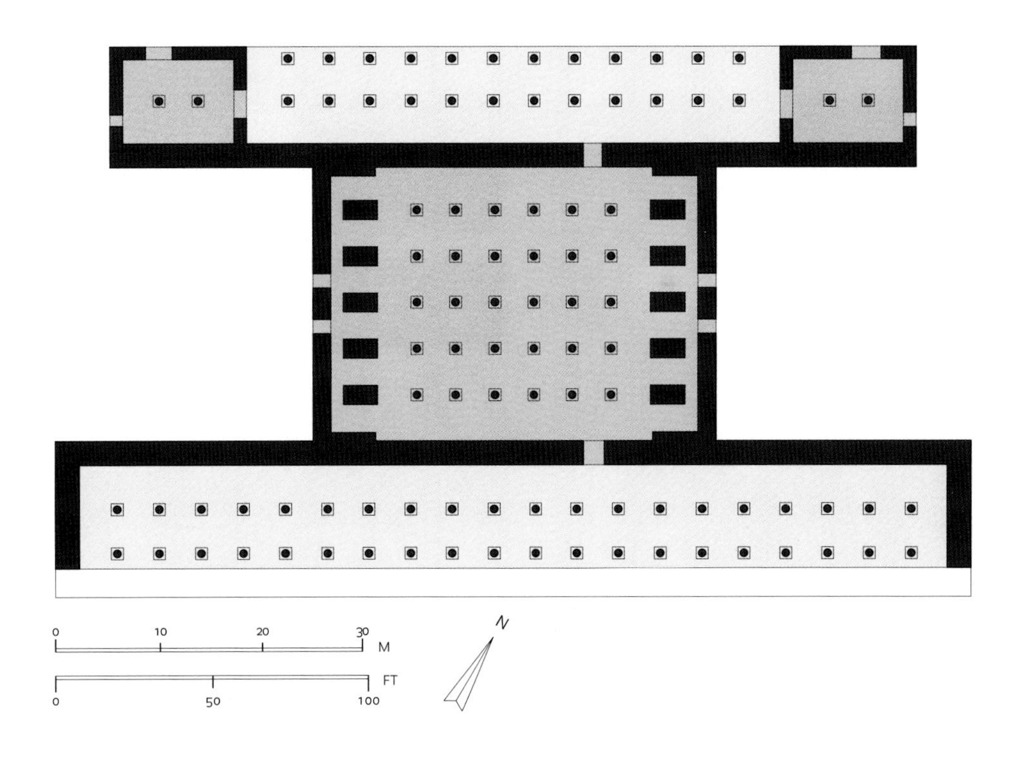

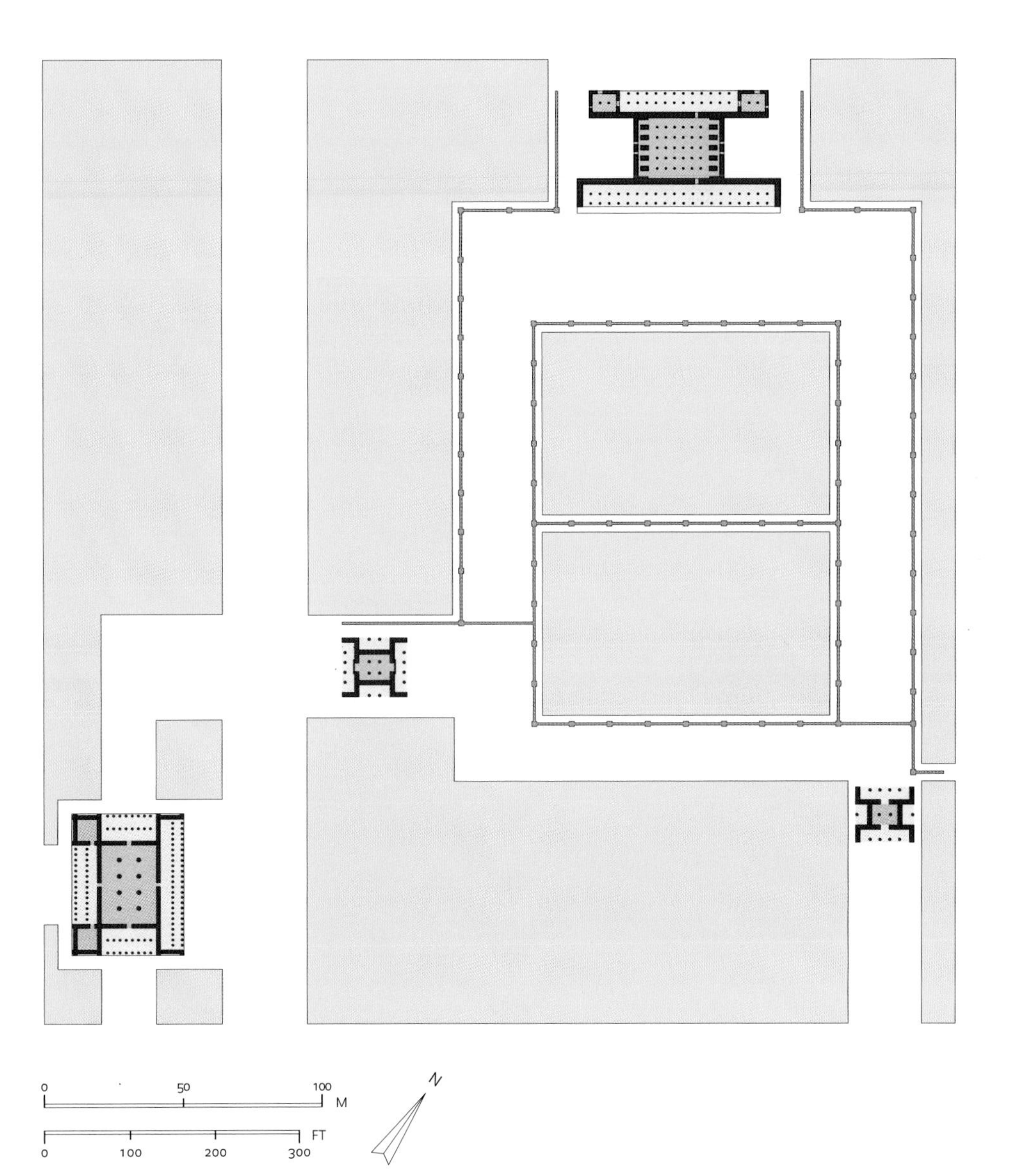

The similarity of the symbols of power

The palace of Persepolis and the Treasury of Siphnos, at Delphi – which are contemporary (*circa* 525 B.C.) – both include the theme of the lion, guardian *par excellence* by virtue of its fierceness. Note the similarity between the two representations, with the animal portrayed head on, in the same position, in both cases. *Above*: An Achaemenid lion (*in situ*) striking down a wild bull. *Below*: A lion in Dionysus' team, attacking a giant. (Delphi, Archaeological Museum)

The Telesterion of Eleusis – a Room for Initiation into the Mysteries

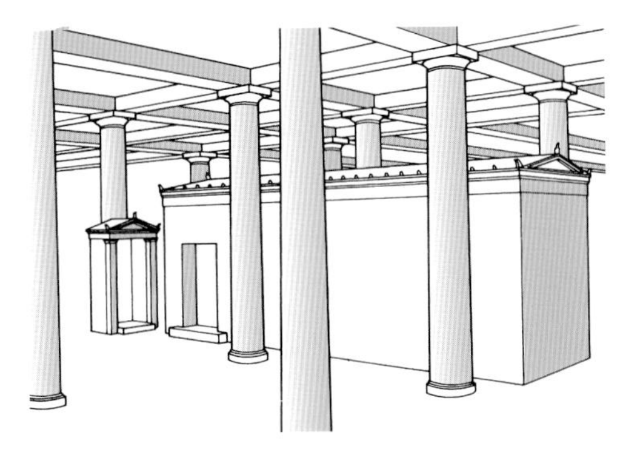

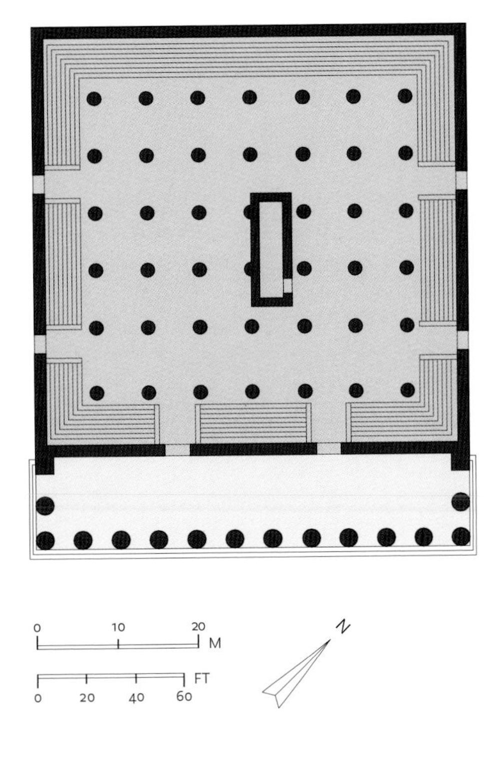

Greek hypostyle halls
If Persia developed columned halls and chambers in its palaces, Greece also had square meeting-places, where the roof or ceiling was supported by rows of shafts. Good examples include the Odeon of Pericles, the Thersilion of Megalopolis and especially the Telesterion of Eleusis, designed for religious assemblies attending initiatory mysteries. The reconstructed view of the area of the *naïskos*, or holy of holies, suggests that there was a complex timber frame, supported by Doric columns.
Right: Plan of the Telesterion of Eleusis, built in the fourth century B.C., with its surrounding tiers of steps and its forty-two shafts and entrance portico.

In Greece, near Athens, at the initiatory site of Eleusis, dedicated to the mysteries of Demeter and Persephone, there was a fine example of a Greek hypostyle room. In its last state – towards 440 B.C. – this space resembled the *apadana* built by the Achaemenids. The Telesterion of Eleusis, which accommodated meetings of initiates and *mystae,* was in fact in the form of a square building measuring 51.20 by 51.55 m, bordered on all four sides by tiers, where those attending the rituals sat.

The building had forty-two columns in six rows of seven shafts. Compared with the "Ionic" columns of Persepolis, those of Eleusis are quite modest, measuring just 11.65 m in height, with a diameter of 1.97 m, and culminating in a Doric capital. We have no precise knowledge about the actual roof, which was made of timber. It may well have consisted of a structure with trusses, forming a sort of lantern tower at the centre which provided lighting for the inside space whose total area covered some 2600 m^2.

The Telesterion of Eleusis went through many stages of building, starting from a small structure dating back to the Mycenaean age. In the reign of the tyrant Pisistratus (525), it was already square in form, with twenty-two columns. Later, under Cimon (*circa* 470), it was enlarged, but remained unfinished. Then Ictinus – the architect of the Parthenon – undertook the planning for the construction of a square room with twenty columns, arranged in two concentric rows (fourteen in front of the peripheral tiers and six in the middle), which flanked the holy of holies or *anaktoron*, in the form of a *naïskos*.

This project was abandoned in favour of the layout already mentioned, with its six rows of seven shafts, as designed by the architect Coroebus, who built it up to the height of the architraves. The work was subsequently finished by Metagenes and Xenocles. Some time later, in about 330, the building would be given an entrance portico consisting of twelve Doric columns on the south-east façade, with two angle columns. As a result of this gallery, designed by the architect Philon, the Telesterion assumed its full majesty.

At Eleusis, with all the proportions respected, the function was just the same as that of an *apadana*. This meant providing a large public with an area permitting a participatory ceremony – sometimes for Greek mysteries, at others, holy Persian banquets.

The Tent of Xerxes, abandoned by the Achaemenids after his defeat at Plataea, had fallen into the hands of the Greek troops. It also had an influence on Greek architecture. Various assembly sites, such as the Odeon of Pericles in Athens, and the Thersilion of Megalopolis in Arcadia, which were square hypostyle buildings like the Telesterion of Eleusis, reveal similarities with the rooms of the *apadana*. For this Tent of Xerxes, which was a veritable moveable palace, probably reproduced the appearance of permanent banqueting rooms, as was the case with the tent of the Symposion of Ptolemy II Philadelphus (third century B.C.). The shape of this temporary structure, with its fifty columns, would in any event explain the presence of a pyramidal roof, with a lantern at the top, in Greek assembly buildings.

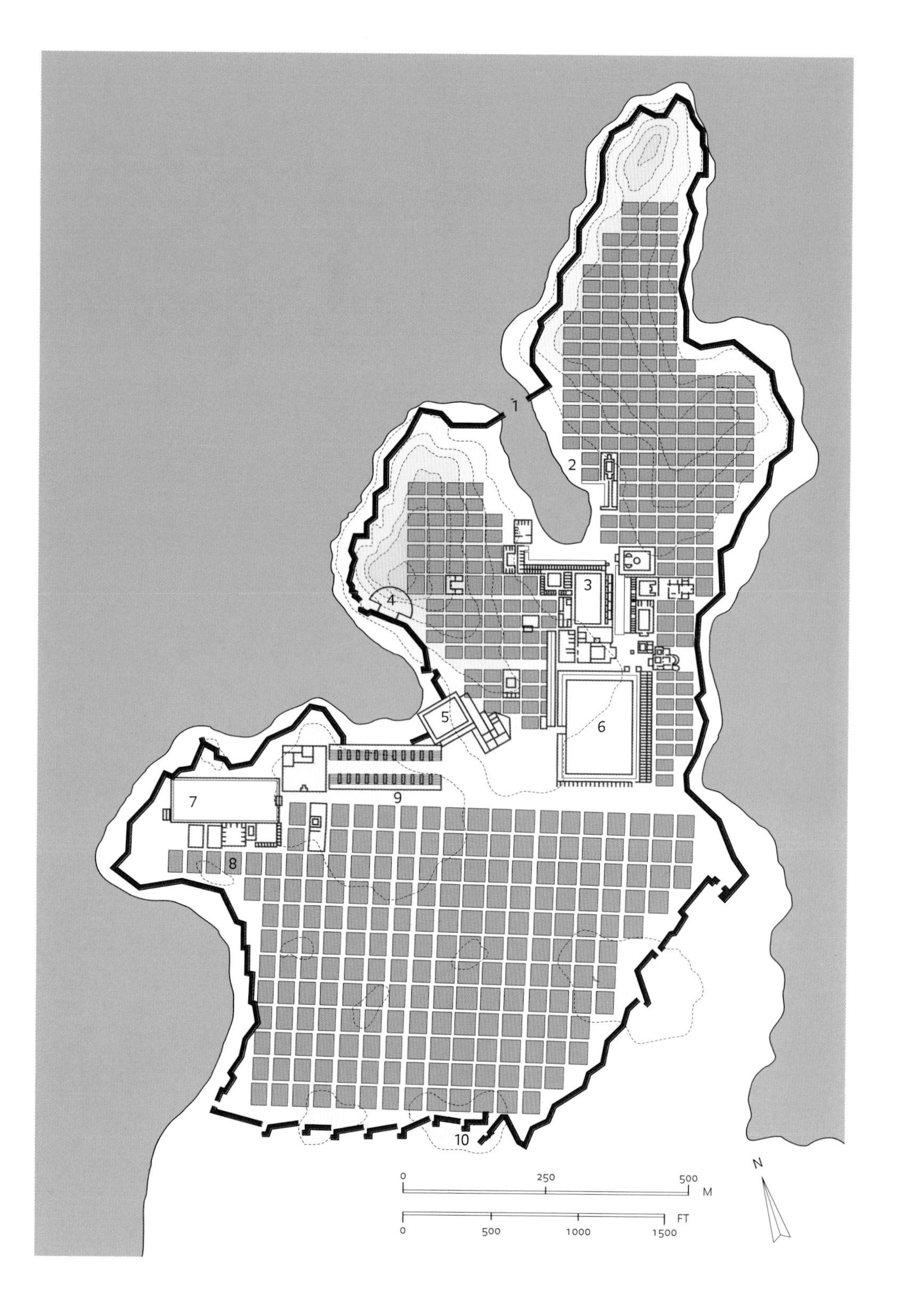

The Hippodamian plan at Miletus
Designed by the father of classical town-planning, Hippodamus of Miletus, the plan of the great Ionian city, rebuilt after 479 B.C., shows the application of the grid or chessboard layout, with its right-angled streets, designed by the architect and theoretician of Greek society. Whatever the configuration of the coast, the rectilinear system is applied to the spatial arrangement as developed on flat ground.

1 Lion Gate
2 Roman baths
3 North *agora*
4 Theatre
5 Palaestra
6 South *agora*
7 West *agora*
8 Temple of Athena
9 Stadium
10 Sacred gate

Asian Greece after the Persian Wars

The city of Miletus had suffered more than others from the Ionian Revolt. It was razed to the ground, and all its inhabitants had been hauled off in captivity to Mesopotamia. Everything had to be rebuilt from scratch. Before its harbours were invaded by the flood-waters of the Maeander, which have now left Miletus land-locked, the city was situated on a long and very rugged bar which jutted 1800 m into the Latmic gulf, in the lee of the island of Lade.

Following its liberation in 479, the decision was taken to put the Greek city back on its feet. It was Hippodamus, a citizen of Miletus, who was given the task of drawing up the plans for the city. Though reckoned to be the inventor of the orthogonal plan loosely referred to as Hippodamian, and regarded as an architect, Hippodamus was in reality a geometrician and a land-surveyor – a theoretician rather than a

A rigorous arrangement at Priene
It was also in Ionia, at Priene, that the application of the Hippodamian plan would reach its limits. To calculate the layout of the streets, the architect overlaid his right-angled plan on an area of land that was at once very hilly and steep, and cambered. This done, certain north-south streets were transformed into stairways and steps, in a site where the city-wall rose more than 350 m, between the low-lying stadium and the top of the Acropolis. The slope is interrupted by long porticoes *(stoai)*.

1 Acropolis dominating the Hippodamian city
2 Temple of Demeter
3 Theatre
4 Temple of Athena
5 *Bouleuterion*
6 *Stoa*
7 *Agora* and Temple of Zeus
8 Gymnasium
9 Stadium

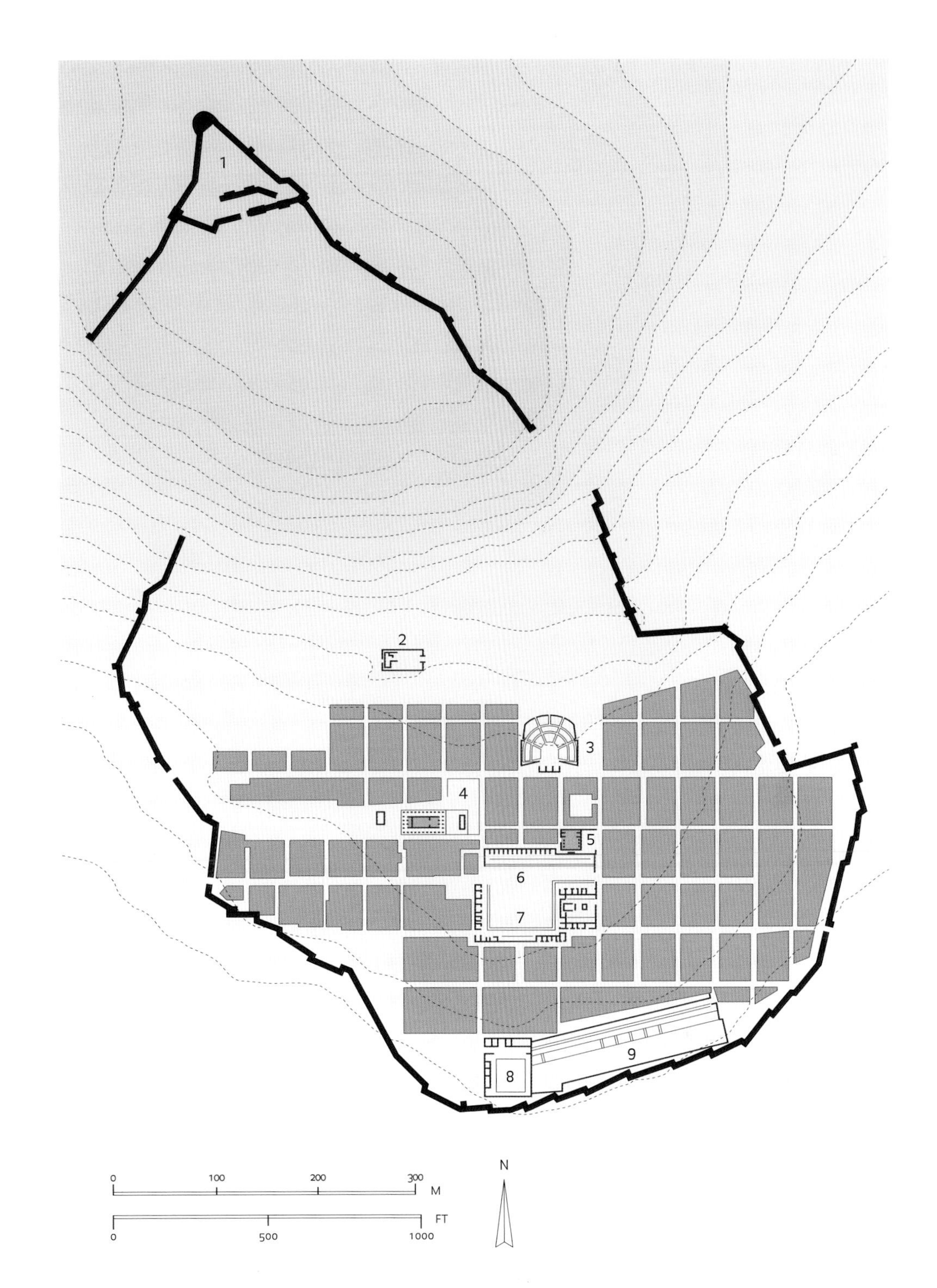

builder. For the plan of the grid-like chessboard cities, with their straight and right-angled streets existed before the advent of Hippodamus. Without going back to the necropolises of the Pharaohs, with their aligned *mastaba,* or to the city founded in 1350 by Akhenaton and called Akhet Aton, we can mention a whole series of Etruscan foundations (Marzabotto, Spina) and, more particularly, numerous Greek colonies from the eighth to the sixth centuries (Megara Hyblaea, Syracuse, Naxos, Senus, Acragas, Camarina, and so on), all based on strict outline, with the parallel thoroughfares forming a regular checkerboard.

So what part did Hippodamus play in the creation of a new concept of town-planning with which his name is associated – the Hippodamian plan? We must set the work within the concept of its period and imagine the concerns of the citizens of those times: following their subjugation by the Persians, after a phase in which the

The monumental terrace of the Temple of Athena at Priene
The slope is so steep at Priene that it was necessary to construct enormous supporting walls with regular blocks of stone, forming a rusticated masonry-work punctuated by horizontal courses. On these infrastructures, the architect Pythius would erect the sanctuary of Athena Polias during the latter half of the fourth century B.C., on the eve of the Macedonian conquest.

Page 131
A famous masterpiece of Antiquity
The Temple of Athena is a building in the Ionic style which had a Classical hexastyle façade. It was the work of Pythius, the architect of the Mausoleum of Halicarnassus. Today, five of the temple's columns have been re-erected on the terrace at Priene. But this *anastylosis,* where there is a missing drum in each column, does not really do justice to the elegance of the original building.

early constitutions heralding a movement towards democratic trends were followed by tyrannical regimes, it was the political principle of *isonomia* that was imposed. Isonomia, which means the equality of all before the law, is a theoretical concept which is tempered by the creation – in a spirit which foreshadows the Aristotelian categories – of social classes corresponding to urban zones of activity.

The interest of the work of Hippodamus is that it gave a socio-political content to a simple layout. The various "neighborhoods" were earmarked for precise purposes, jobs and tasks were shared out on a topological basis, and the mass of the inhabitants was divided up into orders and classes. The city was planned and designed in a coherent way, at once functional and rational. So it was this isonomic scheme – to which a "moral" value was attached – which would govern the plan. This formed the law, the *nomos*, combining politics and geometry.

Greek authors tell us that Hippodamus was a "meteorologist" as well, in other words, based on the accepted meaning of the term at the time, an astronomer, concerned with the organization of the cosmos. The way in which he mapped out and planned the city – the *polis* – had to be part of the order of the world. Within the

A theatre which is married to its surroundings
At Priene, the theatre – which was built during the fifth and fourth centuries B.C. – is integral to the landscape. Its *cavea* backs up against the mountainside (above) and the rows of concentric seats form a shell-like basin (below). From here, the view stretches over the plain traversed by the river Maeander. The circle of the *orchestra* comes closes to the edge of the *proscenium*, where the structures in front of the stage-buildings can be made out.

Page 133
Honorary seats for councillors
Luxurious stone chairs – whose design heralds the Empire style! – were provided at the edge of the *orchestra* of the theatre at Priene for the eminent members of the *boule*, or city council.

city, space and time – to borrow the words of J.-P. Vernant – "quite naturally become the reflection of sidereal realities, in such a way that they involve the microcosm of the city in the macrocosm of the universe".

On a practical level, Hippodamus planned the northern districts or "neighborhoods" of Miletus on the basis of a network made up of blocks measuring 70 by 60 feet (20.75 by 17.70 m). When the city was enlarged in a southerly direction, in the Hellenistic-Roman period, the huge new district, which doubled the urban area, was planned on a larger chessboard layout measuring 175 by 100 feet.

This topographic principle ordering the city on the basis of *isonomia* and the reforms imposed by Cleisthenes of Sicyon, in the sixth century B.C., took on a symbolic value in relation to the protection of people's rights. It was used, like a "talisman", to assert a political idea: town-planning became the expression of political choice.

This semiological content thenceforth espoused by the Hippodamian plan ended up being misappropriated, sometimes to an absurd degree. The city of Priene (in modern Turkey) is a striking example of this. For while the Hippodamian formula was easy to adapt to flat terrain, it was difficult to adapt it to a jagged terrain. At Priene, built in the middle of the fourth century on the edge of the plain of the river Maeander, the city occupied a spherical rocky escarpment with sheer sides. The gradient was very steep: the foot of the encircling wall was at an altitude of 30 m, while the top of the acropolis stood at 381 m. The *agora*, the Temple of Athena Polias, the *bouleuterion* and the theatre all stood on a ledge half-way up, which was partly man-made and supported by sturdy retaining walls with large rustic work.

Over the entire zone covered by the Hippodamian plan, streets turned into stairways at their ends. Movement within the city was chaotic. Nevertheless, for reasons

A ritual banqueting hall at Labranda
The building which bears the name of Andron A at Labranda, an eyrie-like site in the mountains of Caria, was the setting for the *symposion*, or sacred meal with libations to the gods. Designed for use by members of the royal family and the college of priests, this building, dating from the mid-fourth century B.C., accommodated these gatherings in a vast *megaron*-like hall, lit by windows on either side of the large door situated behind the colonnade.

which defy all rational analysis, the plan was applied with all the meticulousness compatible with the ups and downs of the land. Each lot formed a block of 160 by 120 feet (47.20 by 35.40 m), strictly oriented north-south.

Work started on the Temple of Athena in about 340 B.C., supervised by Pythius, who had just completed the tomb of the satrap Mausolus at Halicarnassus. This was an Ionian hexastyle with eleven columns at the sides, and two columns *in antis* at each end of the *cella*. The measurement of the stylobate represented 60 by 120 Attic feet (1 to 2), and the *cella* covered 40 by 100 feet (2 to 5).

The *cavea* of the theatre, set hard against the slope, merged with the landscape and formed not only a place designed for spectacles, but also a place where the city population (*ecclesia*) could gather for meetings, until Priene, in about 150 B.C., acquired a handsome *bouleuterion*, in the Hellenistic style, which is in a very good state of conservation. But this does not fall within our brief in this study.

To the south-east of Ionia, the city of Labranda, in Caria, was built to a great extent by the Hecatomnids, satraps under the Persian rule, during the fourth century B.C. The founder of this dynasty, Hecatomnos, who died in 377, was the father of Mausolus. Before Mausolus left his Carian mountains for Halicarnassus, the capital of this little Hellenized kingdom was situated in this wild site of Labranda. There is an interesting banqueting hall here, built by the satrap Idreus, brother of Mausolus. Behind a pair of Ionic columns *in antis*, a large door with two windows on either side gave access to the inner area which had a wooden roof. It was here that sacred banquets were held by the members of the royal family and the college of priests. The building thus had a function similar to that of the Persian *apadana*.

From the early Homeric period on, the Greeks practiced cremation on pyres, then laid the deceased's ashes in the grave, alongside votive urns. But at time the scarcity of wood caused them to prefer burial (see the Ceramicus Cemetery in Athens).

Like the Persians, the Carians had themselves buried. Sovereigns built impressive tombs, and thus we have inherited funerary monuments, the most impressive of which must have been the Mausoleum of Halicarnassus, which we shall come back to. At Labranda, in any event, a fine (royal?) tomb marks the recourse to the use of the roofing system which would become widespread during the Hellenistic period: the vaulted chamber. The chamber, whose roof consisted of just six enormous arch-stones – without any keystone! – contained three stone sarcophagi arranged like the beds of a *triclinium*, or rather of a *symposion*.

A vaulted funerary chamber
This tomb at Labranda, which dates from the fourth century B.C., is one of the oldest Greek vaulted buildings. The funerary chamber, lined with three sarcophagi arranged in a U-shape, is characterized by most impressive stone-cutting – stereotomy – involving large blocks jointed with great precision.

Situated in the centre of the city of Halicarnassus, the Mausoleum which the satrap Mausolus, along with his sister (and wife) Artemisia, had constructed in 353 B.C., was a great monument described by numerous authors, including Vitruvius and Pliny the Elder. The building was visible from a long way out at sea. It attested to the autonomy enjoyed by the satrap in relation to the Great King. For even if Mausolus himself had conceived of the project, he had it built by Greeks: the architects Pythius and Satyrus, and the sculptors Scopas, Leochares, Timotheus, and Bryaxis.

Based on this tradition and the findings of archaeological excavations undertaken on several different occasions since 1791, when the British examined the ruins and sent fragments of friezes back to the British Museum in 1846 and 1851, various hypotheses began to shed some light on the descriptions. The excavators attempted several reconstructions to try to visualize the original appearance of the building. The most recent works of the Danes (and of Jeppesen in particular) were published in 1958, 1971 and 1976. They help us to establish certain missing links and unanswered questions relating to this building, which was still intact in the twelfth century A.D., when it was destroyed by an earthquake and then served as a quarry for the Knights of St. John Hospitaller, when they built their castle in 1506.

The dimensions referred to by Pliny are impressive: the height exceeded 140 feet (41 m) and the length of the podium was 440 feet (130 m), along which were the friezes depicting the battles of the Amazons and Centaurs. At the base of the podium was the opening to the underground funerary crypt. The building which surmounted the tomb itself was surrounded by a peripteral Ionic colonnade of nine columns by eleven (measuring 33 by 38 m). Inside the *cella*, bounded by the porticoes, there was a third frieze illustrating a chariot race. This massive structure in the form of a tower was crowned by a pyramidal roof. At the top stood an immense quadriga sculpted by Pythius. In it, the sovereign and his wife were depicted, it would appear, on a colossal scale on a ceremonial chariot.

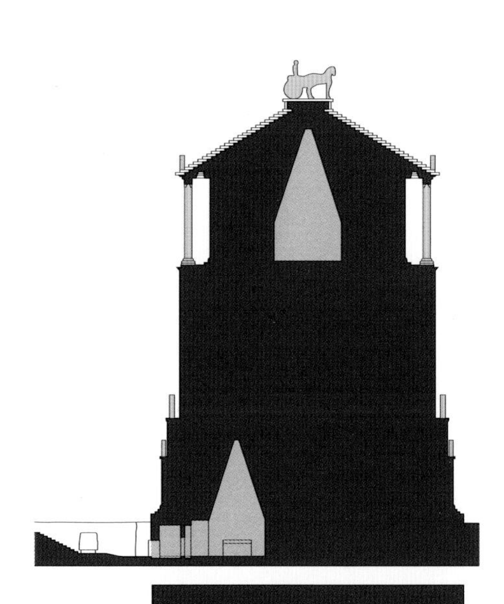

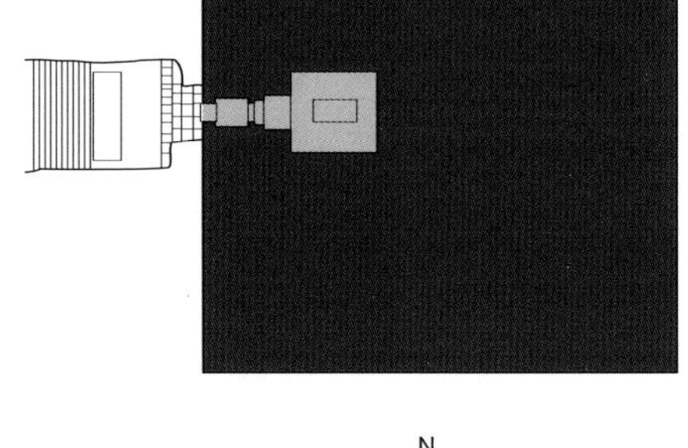

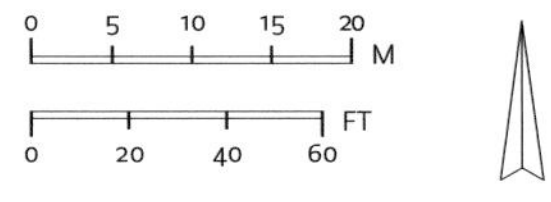

In many respects the Mausoleum of Halicarnassus would seem to be part of a Lycian tradition, of which the Nereid Monument at Xanthus possibly formed one of the milestones. Built in about 420 B.C., at the height of the Classical period when the city was freed from its Persian dependence, this small Ionic temple – today reconstructed in the British Museum – was a funerary building probably dedicated

Page 136 above
The Battle of the Amazons at Halicarnassus
From 353 B.C. onwards, the most famous classical artists set to work on the celebrated Mausoleum – the tomb of the (Persian) satrap Mausolus – of which only a few traces remain in evidence to this day. But various writings, in particular those of Pliny the Elder and Vitruvius, have unanimously showered praise on this monumental work. The bas-relief friezes, and especially the fight against the Amazons, glorify movement with tumultuous dynamism. (London, British Museum)

An Ionic marvel at Xanthus
The Nereid monument, erected in about 420 B.C., has been reconstructed from evidence discovered at the site of Xanthus, in southern Lycia. It is a funerary building (a *heroon*) which has a distinctive elegance in its façade, with large openings punctuated by slender Ionic columns. Between these supports stand graceful statues of dancing women – the Nereids – responsible for accompanying the soul of the deceased in the hereafter. The stylobate is covered with superimposed friezes in the Ionian style.

Page 136 below
A hypothetical building
The reconstructed section and plan of the Mausoleum of Halicarnassus attempt to bring together the findings of recent excavations with information supplied by the authors of Antiquity. But many features are still shrouded in mystery in this building with its unusual shape.

to a Lycian king. This *heroon* with four façade columns, surmounted by a pediment with dentils, had a frieze with hunting scenes on its architrave. The lower part presented very lively reliefs illustrating battles and kidnapping scenes. Lastly, between the columns there stood elegant life-size statues representing young women skipping and dancing with a lightness and exquisiteness of movement, and making gestures of a rare elegance. These are the Nereids, who accompanied the soul of the deceased to the hereafter, with the wind billowing their garments.

Compared to the severe style of the Doric buildings of Magna Graecia, we can see that, despite the sombre periods ushered in by the Persian Wars, Ionia brought an outstanding sense of freedom, imagination and grace, as well as a powerful and original inspiration. Just as philosophical thinking and cosmology had done, so architecture enjoyed considerable advances here. The effects of this profoundly innovative character and this technological daring can be seen in the far-flung dissemination of Greek concepts. Persia benefited from them in the structuring and building of its immense assembly halls designed for the receptions and sacred banquets of the Great Kings who ruled over the Greeks of Ionia for a long time. Thus Pasargadae, Sardis and Persepolis are the remote echo of the activities of Greek builders, and they reflect the influence of the great dipteral buildings which today have vanished from Samos and Ephesus.

Monuments of Classical Greece

ΚΑΛΟΣ

The Flowering of Temples and Fortresses

Page 139
Oedipus and the Sphinx
This vase, which was made in about 440 B.C., is called a *pelike*. It is 26 cm in height, and decorated with red figures on a black ground, in the style of the "Pasithea painter". It shows the meeting between Oedipus and the Sphinx, according to ancient legend. (Geneva, Museum of Art and History)

Now that we have discussed Magna Graecia, Ionia and their repercussions in Persia, it is time to look at the buildings which saw the light of day in Greece proper, away from, or following the Persian wars, the ravages of which created a resounding break in the history of the Greek world.

One monument which escaped the destruction – resulting from the never-ending antagonism between Athens and the island of Aegina, in the Saronic Gulf – was the temple dedicated to Athena Aphaia, the Invisible. The temple at Aegina, in a magnificent setting, surveying the sea in all directions and surrounded by pine forests, is the finest example of Greek architecture from the islands.

This hexastyle Doric building, which only has twelve columns on the sides, was erected in about 495, on the eve of the Classical age. It is contemporary with the first Parthenon of the Pisistratids. Despite its smallish size, this Temple of Athena Aphaia is remarkably well balanced and harmonious. It measures 13.77 by 28.81 m. Its columns, 16 Doric feet (1 Doric foot = 0.328 m) high, rise to 5.25 m. There are 5 feet between the columns. The *cella* has both a *pronaos* and an *opisthodomos*, both preceded by two columns *in antis*. The *naos* is divided into three naves, by means of two porticoes of five Doric columns each on two storeys (as in the Temple of Hera at Paestum). But the inner area is limited, because the nave is no more than 3 m wide.

The Invention of Architectural Polychromy

The temple of Aegina, which has been outstandingly restored, was formerly stuccoed to conceal the unevenness of the shelly limestone of which it had been built. This is one of those ancient monuments which stirred up much lively controversy in the celebrated "polychromy debate" which raged on throughout the eighteenth and nineteenth centuries and, for many a decade, exercised the world of archaeologists and art historians in France, Germany and Great Britain.

In their monumental publication dedicated to the *Expédition scientifique de Morée*, which appeared 1831–1838, the draughtsmen A. Blouet and F. Trézel stressed the chromatic features seen on the ruins of the Temple of Aphaia. They were not the only people to have made such findings. In fact, the sanctuaries of Magna Graecia and the Acropolis of Athens have also revealed the presence of colored touch-ups and highlights in the architecture and sculpture of ancient Greece. These discoveries have in turn released much impassioned argument.

Since the work by J. Stuart and N. Revett, *The Antiquities of Athens*, appeared in 1762, it has provoked "frenzied enthusiasm and bitter controversy in Europe" (to borrow the words of Marie-Françoise Billot, in the catalogue of the exhibition *Paris – Rome – Athènes*, held in 1982). Specialists such as Dodwell, Stackelberg, Bröndsted, Labrouste and Quatremère de Quincy hurled themselves into the fray. In France, the extreme position of J.I. Hittorff, originally from Cologne, but who studied in Paris, attracted the most inflammatory writings. In 1823, the author visited Sicily, noting that the upper parts of Doric architecture are polychrome. His views were finally backed up. In 1835, the excavations of the Acropolis showed –

Painted architectural decoration from the Acropolis in Athens
Examples of painted scenes discovered in ancient monuments are rare. This plaque from the Acropolis, which depicts a running hoplite, dates from about 510 B.C., in the period of the tyranny of the Pisistratids. The Athenian warrior, wearing a crested helmet, is carrying a round shield and spear. (Athens, Acropolis Museum)

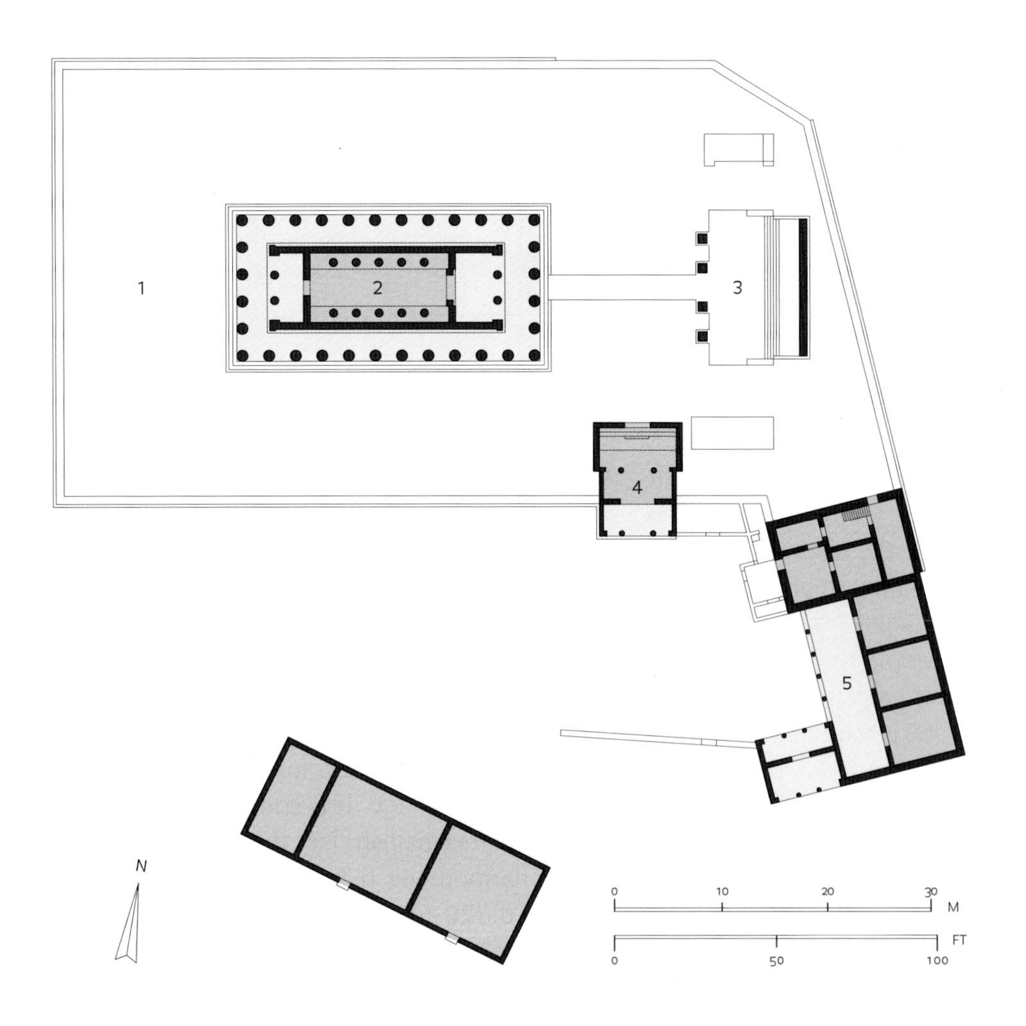

The temple of Aegina and its *peribolos*
Plan of the Doric Temple of Athena Aphaia (the Invisible), on the island of Aegina, dating from 495 B.C.
1 *Peribolos*
2 Temple of Athena Aphaia
3 Sacrificial altar
4 *Propylaea*
5 Lodgings for the priests

like the parts taken from the small Temple of Nike – that the use of color also applied to the Ionic order.

Then Hittorff asserted that polychromy was a standard phenomenon: it was no longer confined just to blue triglyphs, metope backgrounds, blue and red capitals and entablatures; soon he observed brightly colored architraves, ceilings and coffers, where the azure blue was set off by gold. Now he started to extrapolate. In supposing that the temples of Segesta and Selinus were entirely polychromatic, he imagined huge panels covered with scenes produced using encaustic paint. This exaggeratedly hard and fast theory stemmed from poorly understood ancient writings, as well as from the interest in painting made manifest by the neo-classicists – Schinkel, Semper, and von Klenze – who dreamed of producing works where they could call upon the services of the masters of academicism.

In this way, Greek architecture – which was for too long regarded as a somewhat pallid art form, as white as the Parian marble or stucco – suddenly became polychromatic. It offered brightly-coloured highlights. The whole image of the Greek temple changed and came alive.

In the same way, the superb sculpture of the pediments of the Temple of Aphaia (in the Glyptothek in Munich) stood out against the colored tympana. These compositions, with their themes of Heracles and Ajax in the Trojan War, marked one of the high points of Greek statuary. The purity of the drawing and design, the fullness of the volumes, the sacred hieratic nature of the arrested action, freezing the mythical gesture in eternity, all were part of the blaze of polychromy, as Furtwängler's reconstruction conceived it.

An engraving of the sanctuary of Aegina
As seen by the English painter Edward Dodwell, in 1805, the Temple of Aphaia before the modern restoration work.

The Doric structure
At the end of the Archaic period, the temple of Aegina showed a distinctive style, close to Classicism. The Doric column became more refined beneath the entablature, as did the spacing of the triglyphs and metopes.

The lightness of the hexastyle façade
The Doric temple of Aegina, dating from the early fifth century B.C., marks a clear advance in the way structures were becoming less cumbersome, columns more slender and refined, and the intercolumniation more widely spaced. The building, made of shelly tufa, was stuccoed and covered with lively polychromatic work.

Sketch of the façade of the Temple of Aphaia
The spare structure of the temple of Aegina, with its doors which take up not only the entrance to the *cella* but also the spacing of the intercolumniation of the façade, announces the Age of Pericles.

A "committed" publication
The large, three-volume folio edition titled *Expédition scientifique de Morée*, Paris, 1831–1838, by Blouet, Trézel, Ravoisié *et alii*, made a major contribution to the dispute about polychromy in Greek architecture. The color re-creations of the temple of Aegina, in 1833, provided arguments for those in Hittorff's camp.

Expression of geometry
The perspective view of the corner of the Temple of Aphaia highlights the rigor of the Doric style, while at the same time setting off its elegant dynamism beneath the sun of the Saronic Gulf. The architecture here pulses and vibrates in the light.

The double Doric order
The two levels of the inner colonnade, seen through the doorway of the *cella* of the Temple of Aphaia. This was one of the earliest uses of the two-storey system, applied to the inner area of the temple – although the small dimensions of the sanctuary of Aegina did not really call for this formula.

A necessary correction
In order to deal with "the contradictory demands at the corners of the colonnade, where the triglyph had to be at once the axis of the column and form the corner of the entablature" (Roland Martin), the Greeks opted for a shortening of the distance between axes at the ends of the peristyle.

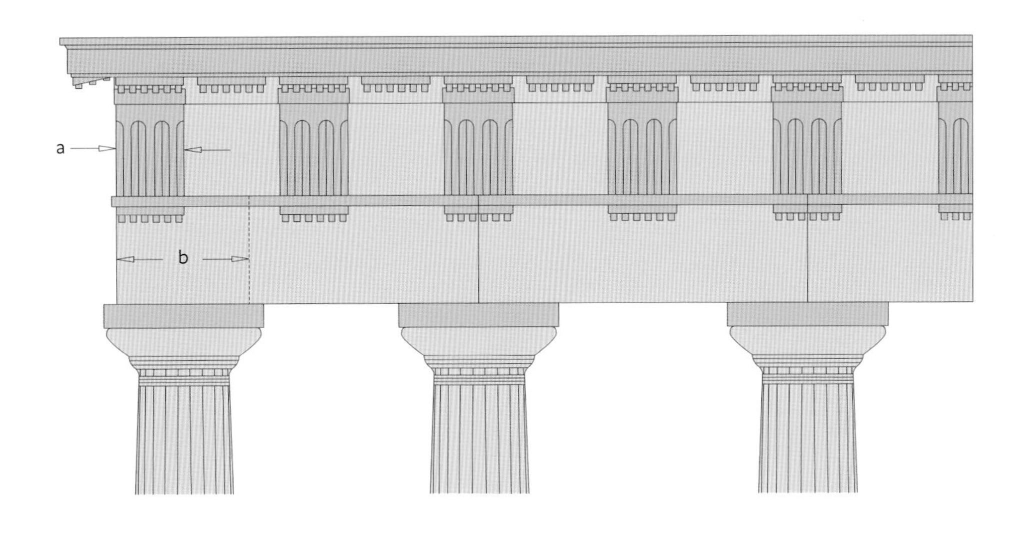

A view stretching to the sea
Taking full advantage of its island site, the temple of Aegina towers over the surrounding countryside and, from its colonnade offers a view which sweeps over the vastness of it, as far as the horizon.

The Uncertain Transition of the Corner

The research undertaken by Greek architects continually tended to make the Doric style the expression of clarity, logic and coherence of forms and structures. The builders of the Archaic and then the Classical period also consistently came up against difficulties resulting precisely from the rigor and restrictions of the interplay of alternative elements in the Doric entablature. Above the architrave of the temple, the frieze was formed by triglyphs separated by metopes. In some cases the triglyphs surmounted a column, in others an intercolumniation. The metopes, which were usually decorated with mythical scenes in relief, provided panels of a constant width. But at the corners of the peripteral temple this fine layout became confused as a result of contradictory demands and constraints: the structural logic no longer tallied with the rhythmic regularity.

An example will help us to grasp the dilemma with which the Greek builders had to wrestle. Mindful that the motif of the triglyphs represented the "petrified" survival of the ends of the beams of the wooden structure, statics dictated that this element should rest precisely on the axis of the column. Furthermore, coherence demanded that the metopes form a homogeneous series of panels of the same size. Lastly, this well-wrought theoretical organization issued from intercolumniations set at regular intervals. In practice, however, these different conditions were mutually exclusive, and created what the experts call the "angle conflict".

One thing strikes any onlooker straightaway. By admitting that, on each side of the entablature surrounding the edifice, the frieze ends in a triglyph, the corner has to be made up of two perpendicular triglyphs, with one of them visible on the façade and the other on the long side. In this configuration, the corner triglyphs cannot surmount the axis of the column without the latter appearing to be thrust outwards. So they have to be put out of alignment. Not only does this solution clash with the structural coherence, but it also means enlarging the last metope. So we have a lack of order which satisfies neither logic nor aesthetics.

The solution usually espoused by the Greek architects involved two options: on the one hand, an acceptance – for want of any better course – that the corner triglyphs should be put out of alignment, towards the outside, and on the other, in order to retain evenly sized metopes, the adoption of a shorter intercolumniation at the corners of the building. This arrangement, which Greek architectural theoreticians have called the "angle contraction", satisfies the eye by lending a greater density to the corners of the temples. It would be rounded off by optical rectifica-

The Poseidon of Livadhostro
This fine Archaic bronze, contemporary with the temple of Aegina (*circa* 490 B.C.) was discovered near Plataea. Like the lips which are "polychromed" with the help of a copper leaf, the eyes must have been inlaid. Detail of a statue measuring 1.18 m in height, which clearly illustrates the severe style dating from the end of the Archaic period. (Athens, National Museum)

tions, such as the strengthening of the diameter of the angle column, its slight inclination towards the diagonal axis and the curvature of the stylobate. These arrangements gave the building aesthetic cohesion. They conveyed the primacy of the perceptible aspect over the purely architectonic aspect. We are witnessing operations which sacrifice the logic of construction to a concept that favours visual perception. The lesson implicit in this option is comforting: it marks a humanization of the coldly mathematical character that Greek architecture could display. It tempers the numerical rigidity of the plan. Paradoxically, aesthetics holds sway over the purity of the concept.

At Aegina, the solution to the problem of the corner involved a reduction of 22 cm in the intercolumniation. The angle columns were 2 cm thicker and included, at the top, an inclination of 3 cm towards the interior of the building (G. Gruben). But the stylobate was not curved.

Bassae and the Corinthian Capital

The Temple of Apollo Epicurius – the Helper – at Bassae, in Arcadia, was built in a very isolated place in the mountains of the Peloponnese, at an altitude of 1100 m. The nearest town, Phigaleia, is 6 km away. The building was probably started in 429 and completed between 400 and 390 B.C. According to Pausanias, it was the work of the architect Ictinus, who designed the Parthenon. Roland Martin emphasizes the contrast between its surprisingly Archaic features and its innovative aspects, which seem to back this attribution.

The temple is a hexastyle peripteral building with fifteen columns on the sides, measuring not more than 14.48 by 38.25 m. The proportions are thus more elongated than those of the temple at Aegina. It is aligned on a north/south axis. The *cella* which precedes the quite deep *pronaos* is followed by an *opisthodomos*. Both have a pair of columns *in antis*. But the most original aspect is to be found in the interior of the *naos*. It has lateral niches formed by ten engaged columns at the end of low walls (five on each side). To left and right, the first four walls are perpendicular to the side walls, with the fifth, set at 45°, facing the entrance. At the back of the *naos*, these two oblique reinforcements frame an axial column, which we shall describe in due course. This structure seems to separate the *naos* from an *adytum*, or *sekos*, which was lit by a side door situated to the east. This odd arrangement may have had to do with an oracular system.

The ten engaged lateral columns of the *cella* have broad, flared bases of a type

In the heart of the Peloponnese
This print by Edward Dodwell shows the Classical Temple of Apollo Epicurius at Bassae in 1805. Work on this building, which would appear to be the work of the brilliant architect Ictinus, started in around 429 B.C., at a height of 1100 m, in Arcadia.

not found elsewhere, resting on a socle slightly raised around the central flagstones. They have strange Ionic capitals with volutes descending very low on the sides. Once again, this formula points to a tendency to combine the Doric style, used for the outside parts, with the Ionic style, used solely for the interior of the sanctuary.

But the onlooker has further surprises in store. For the very first time in Greece, the axial column, mentioned above, in front of which must have stood the statue of Apollo Epicurius, had a capital in the Corinthian style. This consisted of a basket of foliage with small corner volutes supporting the abacus. This association of the Corinthian style for the *naos* and the Doric style for the peripteral colonnade recurs in the *tholos* at Delphi, with its twenty columns, and in the large monopteral building of Epidaurus, known as the Thymele, with twenty-six outer columns in all.

The presence of the three orders – Doric, Ionic, and Corinthian – brought together in a single building is striking, to say the least. If we add to this the fact that

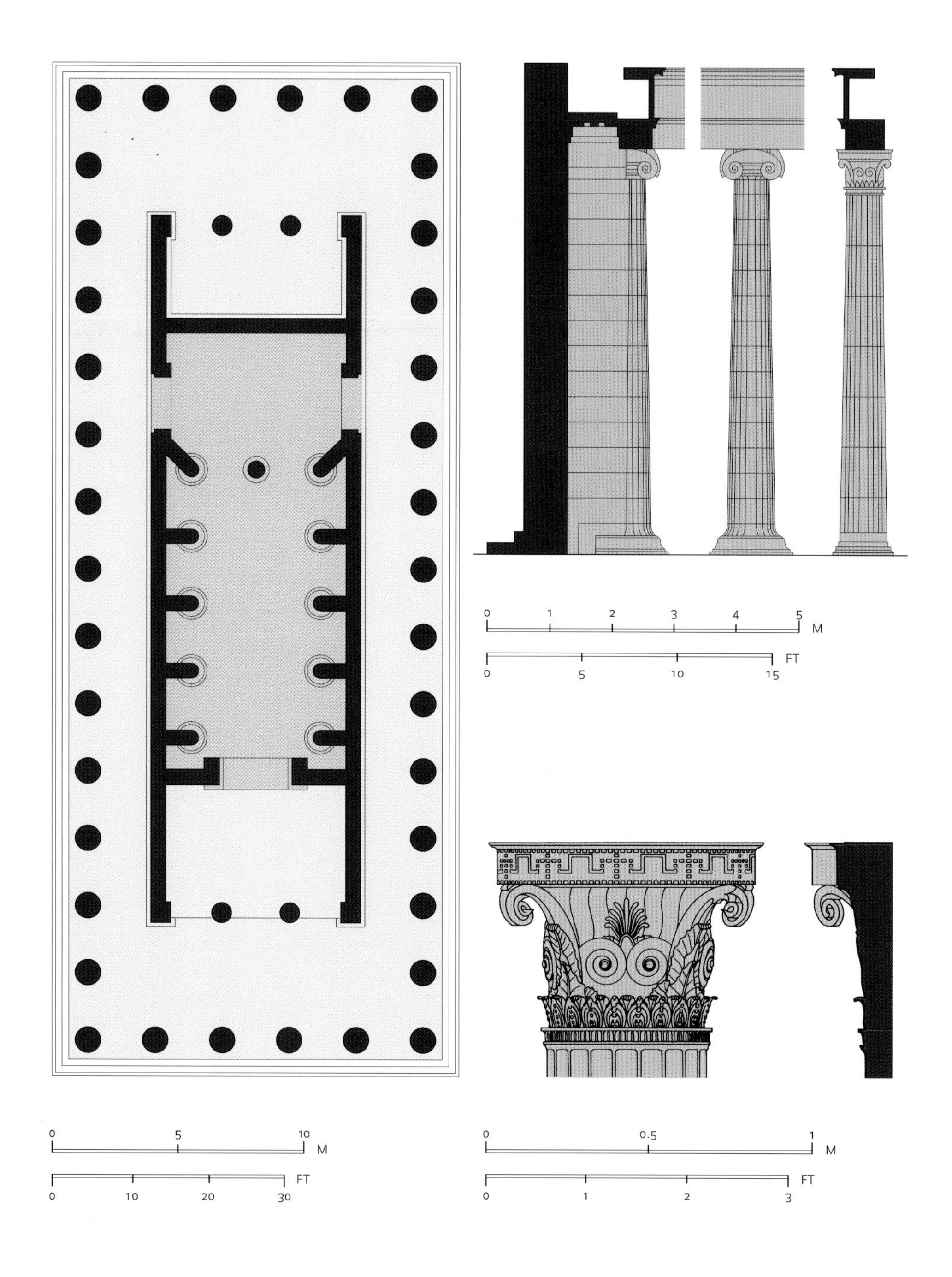

An erudite eclecticism
Plan of the temple of Bassae, with its curious *naos*; section and elevation of the inner Ionic columns, and view and section of the Corinthian capital.

Pending restoration
Shifting ground has taken its toll on the porticoes of the temple of Bassae, the columns are no longer quite vertical. At the present time, the building is covered with a plastic "bubble", while it is dismantled and completely re-erected by archaeologists.

the temple of Bassae also had handsome pediment sculptures and, more particularly, an interior frieze, it would seem, judging from the evidence, that this was a kind of laboratory for new research. In it, Ictinus – whose place was possibly taken by the sculptor Scopas (fourth century B.C.) – worked on his innovative solutions to the various formal and aesthetic problems.

At the end of the fourth century B.C., with the appearance of the Corinthian order, we cannot help but think about the basic significance of the peripteral colonnade, as described early on in this study, associating it with the concept of the sacred wood. For nothing shows more clearly the profound semiological value of the column in relation to the primitive worship of the tree which the pantheistic system regarded as the first abode of the deity.

This association – attested to by such examples as the *daphnephorion*, the laurel tree of Apollo, the oak of Zeus at Dodona, and the olive tree of Athena at the Erechtheum – was henceforth expressed with a vigour and precision conveyed by the stylized foliage of the capital crowning the shaft. It was at the top of the tree trunk that young shoots sprouted forth. These illustrate the vitality of the "petrified" vegetation that would encircle the temple.

This idea, symbolized by the encircling portico, is best illustrated in the Corinthian-style boughs. For the foliage is much more present in the scrolled baskets of acanthus than it ever was in the Doric style, where only the shaft, with its fluting evoking the spreading of a trunk and the falling leaves of the primitive gorgerins, calls to mind the original tree.

The base of a column of the *naos*
At Bassae, the internal arrangement, with its Ionic columns abutting a low wall, and perpendicular to the outer wall of the *naos*, lends an unexpected appearance to the room where worship was conducted, so that it resembles the early formula of the Temple of Hera at Olympia. The base of the shafts, with its flared outline, has no equivalent anywhere. To all appearances, it is the daring contribution of a builder looking for novel solutions.

Needless to say, being a product of Aeolian volutes, the Ionic order retained the image of rolled-up vine branches. But never before had its identification with natural foliage been so straightforward. For plant forms stamp their character on the Corinthian style, attributed, according to Vitruvius – to the sculptor Callimachus, a disciple of Phidias, and author of the bronze palm tree of the Erechtheum.

So the last style to appear in Greek architecture marks a real resourcefulness and clarifies what is left unsaid in the Doric and Ionic styles.

Attempted reconstruction
In the publication entitled *Expédition scientifique de Morée*, which appeared 1831–1838, the temple of Bassae is the object of a reconstruction project showing (above) the façade of the sanctuary, and (below) a hypothetical cross-section view of the *naos*, showing the axial Corinthian column at the end of the *cella*.

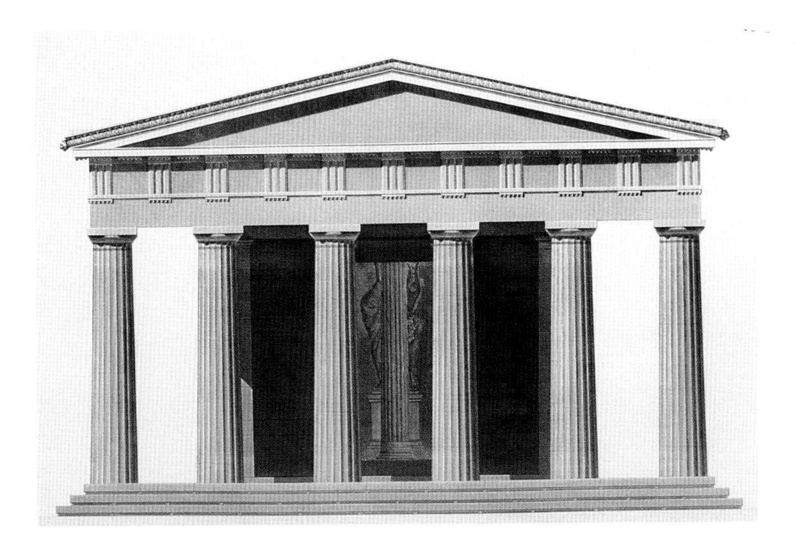

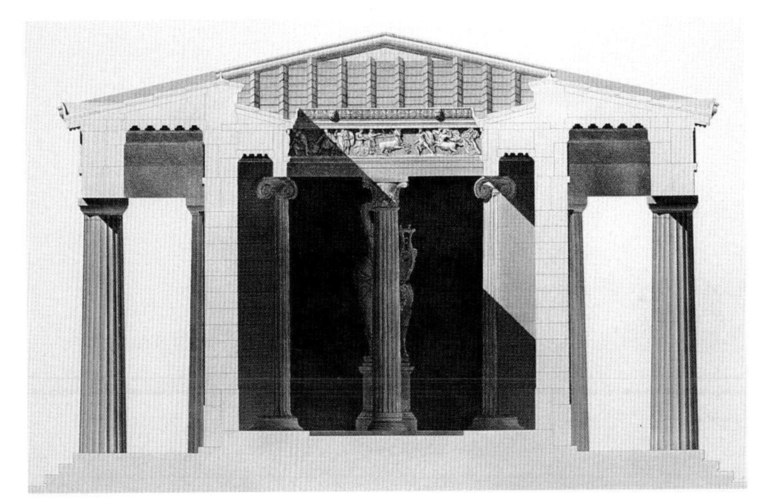

A frieze of the Ionic type
Bassae also made innovations in terms of decoration. A continuous frieze, in the Ionic spirit, runs around the east entablature. It shows the battle between the Greeks and the Amazons depicted in a lively style. (London, British Museum)

The seat of prophecy
The Temple of Apollo, built during the fourth century B.C. (in its sixth version), was the seat of the Pythia, centre of Greek divination, where citizens and sovereigns alike would come in search of signs that might enable them to decipher their fate.

Page 156
The sanctuary of Apollo
The polygonal wall, built in 548 B.C., rises up in the majestic landscape of Delphi. An Ionic portico was added close to it in 478 to house the trophies brought back by the Athenians after their naval victories over the Persians. This impressive terrace acted as a foundation for the various temples which the Greeks erected to Apollo of Delphi.

Delphi, the Sanctuary of Apollo

The wild and mysterious splendour of the rugged, majestic landscape at Delphi, where temples, treasuries, theatre and stadium grace the slopes of Mount Parnassus, is the ideal setting for the oracle of Apollo, who long guided the destiny of the Greek world.

Once the "holy war" had freed the sanctuary, this site, where the gods themselves appear to talk, became thick with monuments between the sixth and fourth centuries B.C. In the middle of this sacred land stands the great Temple of Apollo, itself built on a broad excavated area consolidated with 6000 m^3 of fill, which is retained by a mighty polygonal wall. Next to this latter, which dates from the Archaic period (early sixth century), the Portico of the Athenians was built in the Ionic style in 478. Beneath it the victors in the Persian wars housed the trophies they had captured from the Persians.

The temple, whose ruins are still very much in evidence, was the sixth in a series of buildings whose foundations have been unearthed by archaeologists. It was here that the oracle, known as the Pythia, made her prophecies, in the *manteion* or place of divination. Built between 370 and 320, after an earthquake followed by a fire which destroyed Temple V, this sanctuary – one of the most venerable in all ancient Greece – borrowed the exact plan of its predecessor. Although Delphi may have been the seat of the oracle, which led to the presence of a whole host of outstanding monuments, the Ancients were not offended by the Archaic aspects resulting from this traditionalism.

The building, measuring 58.18 by 21.68 m, is a hexastyle with fifteen columns on the sides, with *pronaos* and *opisthodomos* preceded by pairs of columns *in antis*. The Doric shafts had a diameter of 1.6 m and stand 10.5 m high, whereas the columns of Temple V did not exceed 8 m. They clearly show the development towards a remarkable refinement, peculiar to the end of the Classical period.

The inner dimensions of the *cella* (11 by 25 m) justified the presence of two porticoes which divided the area into three naves. At the back, the *adytum*, intended to be used by the Pythia, was designed to accommodate the instruments of divination, and, in particular, the famous bronze tripod which bore away, "in spirit", the pythoness, messenger of the gods. This venerable temple also contained the *omphalos* or cosmic egg symbolizing the centre of the world.

Treasuries and Offerings

To show their gratitude, the Ancients would take precious *ex voto* offerings to Delphi and leave them there – offerings made to the gods for successes achieved following the "revelations" of the oracle. In addition they erected monuments to house these offerings. These are known as treasuries – small temples usually with two columns *in antis* or four façade columns (prostyle), which might be either Doric or Ionic, and, in the latter instance, have caryatids instead of shafts (as in the Treasury of Siphnos, dating from 525 B.C.).

One such treasury – the Treasury of the Athenians – was successfully restored at the beginning of the twentieth century. It shows a very "straightforward" concept of *anastylosis,* by clearly stressing the difference between the original and the reconstructed parts. Standing on the Sacred Way leading to the Temple of Apollo,

A commemorative chapel
The Treasury of the Athenians at Delphi was built in 487 B.C. in gratitude to the gods for the victory at Marathon over the Persians. Like most treasuries, this small Doric temple contained *ex votos* dedicated to the gods.

The Charioteer of Delphi
This bronze statue, offered in 478 or 474 by a tyrant of Gela (Sicily) to the Delphic sanctuary, in commemoration of his victory in the chariot-races at the Pythian Games, was discovered quite by chance at the site of Delphi. Measuring 1.80 m in height, this work, at once motionless and mobile, with its severe drapery, marks the high point of an age in which the hieratic spirit would be transformed into action. (Delphi, Museum)

this small Doric edifice, built in Parian marble, measures just 6.6 by 9.7 m. Built by Athens after the victory at Marathon, it dates from 487 and is an assertive example of the Classical style. Beneath its pediment, the entablature bears triglyphs and metopes, these latter sculpted with the glorious scenes marking the heroic deeds of Theseus, the Attic hero *par excellence*. The balance and harmony of this building clearly show the maturity of Greek architecture at the time of the Persian wars.

The gifts offered by sovereigns and important persons who dedicated *ex votos* to the oracle and to the gods of Delphi came in various shapes and sizes: statues of *kouroi* and goddesses, the huge effigy of a silver bull embellished with gold, commemorative columns supporting an Archaic sphinx on its Ionic capital, or dancing figures springing from a bunch of Corinthian acanthus plants, ivory sculptures, gold

The *tholos*: a round temple
On the site of Marmaria, below the centre of the Delphic site, the *tholos* built in about 370, of which three of the twenty columns have been re-erected, is the first of a type which would subsequently be developed, especially at Epidaurus. In the sanctuary of Athena, at Delphi, this *tholos* marries the Doric style of the surrounding outer colonnade with the Corinthian style of the capitals which surmount the inner half-columns.

Page 161
A concentric composition
Designed by the architect Theodorus of Phocaea the plan of the *tholos* of Athena Pronaia at Delphi is easy to make out on the base of the building. The circular system, with its extreme refinement as far as these formal developments were concerned, certainly contained a significance about which we learn little from writings or excavations. The round form may relate to chthonic, or underworld, rituals.

A stadium dominating the city
Dominating the city of Delphi, set into the steep mountainside, a stadium designed for the competitive events of the Pythian Games was constructed in the Classical period. But it was not until the Roman period that the stadium was fitted out with the tiered steps which line one side of the track.

jewellery, and so on. One of the most striking finds made at Delphi is none other than the famous bronze *auriga,* offered in Sicily in 476 by Polyzelus, tyrant of Gela, after his victory in the chariot race at the Pythian games. All that has come down to us is the charioteer, but he is miraculously intact and well illustrates the concern for "truth" shown by Classical art: the folds of the tunic, the head with its head-band, the enamel eyes surrounded by bronze lashes, and so on. These features combine with a refusal to accept the strict frontal pose and symmetry as conveyed by the position of the head which is turned to the left in relation to the feet.

The Tholos of Theodorus

On the site of Delphi, one of the staggered terraces in the mountainside – the so-called Marmaria terrace – accommodated, alongside the Sanctuary of Athena Pronaia, the magnificent *tholos*, or round temple, dedicated to the goddess. The monopteral building, surrounded by twenty Doric columns, measures 13.5 m in diameter at the stylobate, while the *cella* attains a diameter of 8.6 m. The height at the cornice is 8.32 m. This round temple, erected *circa* 370 B.C., is built entirely of Pentelic marble. Inside, the Doric order is replaced by ten engaged Corinthian columns. In this masterpiece, it has only been possible to re-erect three columns on the beautiful base with three concentric steps. We know that the architect of this *tholos* at Delphi was Theodorus of Phocaea, author of a treatise about its building. Sadly, this work has not survived, but it is referred to by Vitruvius.

Further up the mountainside at Delphi, the great theatre, as if coiled within a natural recess in the crag, looks out on to an outstandingly beautiful landscape. It was also built in the fourth century, but was restored and embellished in the Hellenistic period by Eumenes II of Pergamum, and enlarged during the Roman period. As in all the great Greek sanctuaries, this theatre was used for both worship and culture. Designed to accommodate the Pythian games, during which playwrights and poets competed with another, it could also be used for large gatherings of up to 5000 people. The seven *cuneus* or wedge-like divisions of the *cavea*, demarcated by stairways fanning out from the *orchestra*, punctuate the tiers of seats.

Going still higher, we come to the stadium, also lined with tiered seats and dating from the third century B.C. In its original state it contained no more than a track 178 m long (6 *plethra* of 100 feet), where runners vied with one another. It was developed and improved during the Roman period.

A stunning site

The dazzling view from the great theatre of Delphi stretches away as far as the valley of the river Pleistus. Built in the fourth century B.C., the *cavea* was embellished and enlarged under the reign of Eumenes II, king of Pergamum, and then refitted in the Roman period. Dominating the great Temple of Apollo, the site has retained its wild look, at the foot of Mount Parnassus, on a fault, where the rock houses the spring of Castalia.

The Temples of Sunium and Lindus

At the south-eastern tip of Attica, surveying the Aegean Sea, stands the Temple of Poseidon, erected on Cape Sunium, in one of the most picturesque sites of ancient Greece. Demonstrating an outstanding sense of how to make use of the landscape, the sanctuary dedicated to the god of the sea and the wind is the outcome – like the Parthenon – of a magnificent effort to rebuild the ruins resulting from the Persian Wars. A first temple had in fact been built here at the beginning of the fifth century B.C., but it was still in the stages of being finished when it was destroyed. Built of limestone *(poros)*, it was rebuilt – entirely in marble – in 449, as the result of a decision taken by Pericles. Once again, it was a Doric hexastyle. It had thirteen columns on the sides and measured about 100 feet in length (13.47 by 31.12 m at the stylobate), giving a proportion of 5:9. Its columns – fifteen still survive, and have been reconstructed – are 6.02 m in height, and have a diameter of 1.04 m. They stand on a socle formed by two superimposed terraces, which lend the building its lofty aspect on the top of the cliff overlooking the waves below.

At Sunium, several innovative features point to the creativity of the "Age of Pericles" – the architrave of the *pronaos* spans the side galleries; inside, an "inverted" frieze – turned, in other words, towards the *naos* – indicates the use of a formula stemming from the Ionic order, as at Bassae; there were no columns at all in the *cella*. It must have contained a statue of Poseidon, possibly similar to the large bronze retrieved from the sea off Cape Artemisium, in Euboea, which came from

To the glory of the god of the sea
The great bronze of Poseidon, discovered by fishermen in 1928 in their nets, off Cape Artemisium, at the northern end of the island of Euboea, is one of the masterpieces of Classical sculpture. Dating from about 460 B.C., this work, which measures more than 2 m in height, is attributed to the sculptor Calamis. It lends the god, holding his trident, an image that is at once potent and serene. (Athens, National Museum)

Dominating Cape Sunium
At the eastern end of Attica, the Temple of Poseidon, eroded by sea winds, raises its colonnade above the Aegean. Completed in 449 B.C., it was part of the building programme embarked upon by Pericles immediately after the Persian Wars.

Histiaia. The sculpted decoration that has been positively identified was based on the traditional themes of duels between giants and centaurs, as well as the heroic deeds of Theseus.

Set in an even more majestic geographical location, the Temple of Athena at Lindus, in the south of the island of Rhodes, is also in the Doric style. Although close to Ionia, the site is in fact a Dorian settlement. The Sanctuary of Athena Lindia, erected in the fourth century B.C. on the edge of a sheer cliff that dominates the sea, was a prostyle, whose four extremely elegant columns had an altogether Ionic proportion of 6.5 diameters to height, as in the great Temple of Apollo (VI) at Delphi. In the Hellenistic period, the temple at Lindus was preceded by a monumental *propylaeum,* interspersed with terraces and porticoes.

On top of the cliffs of Lindus, on the island of Rhodes
The Temple of Athena Lindia, which soars over the sea on the island of Rhodes, was constructed at the end of the fourth century B.C. It was built in the Doric style, despite the proximity of the Ionian shores. The top of the acropolis, which stands on a southern headland of the island, offers an outstanding view from the temple.

Epidaurus, the Perfect Theatre

During the fourth century B.C., near the city of Epidaurus in the north-eastern part of the Peloponnese, an important sanctuary of Asclepius, the god of healing, sprang up in just a few years. Various buildings for worship and medical care were erected in this famous place of pilgrimage. The Doric Temple of Asclepius was a hexastyle with eleven lateral columns, built by the architect Theodotus, with porticoes for incubation, intended for fumigation treatment, the Temple of Apollo, and so on. We have already mentioned the *tholos* attributed to an architect by the name of Polyclitus (known as "the Younger", to avoid confusion with the sculptor). This was a noteworthy building, now in a very ruined state, which had twenty-six Doric columns outside (diameter 21.82 m) and a ring-shaped portico made up of fourteen Corinthian shafts in the *naos*. Known as the Thymele, this monopteral building was one of the most accomplished circular buildings of Greek architecture.

But the present-day fame of Epidaurus is due above all to its splendid theatre. Built at the end of the fourth century B.C., the sumptuous hemicycle, whose *cavea* fits perfectly into the surrounding landscape, could accommodate 15000 spectators. The subtle interplay of geometry and numbers, revealed by an analysis of the structure, led Pausanias to attribute it to the same architect who built the thymele. Its graceful and balanced hollowed form, which rises up from the perfectly round central *orchestra*, is slightly greater than a half-circle. The flared, shell-like auditorium of the construction with a diameter of 120 m and a 24 m drop from the topmost tier to ground level is divided into two areas, upper and lower, by a walk-way forming the *diazoma*. In the lower part, the hemicycle is divided into twelve *cunei*, or wedge-like sections, each one consisting of some thirty tiers, while in the upper section there are twenty *cunei* each with some twenty tiers.

This tight organization and strict system, which seem to be governed by purely geometric laws, show the subtle treatment used by the architect. On closer inspection, there are symmetrical variations in the width of the *cunei* and in the curvature of the arcs opening imperceptibly outwards toward the edges of the *cavea*.

Lending an ear to the Tragedians
On the tiered seats of the theatre of Epidaurus, the 15000-strong audience which used to gather in the city of Asclepius, god of health and healing, would follow dramatic competitions, where the great masters of Greek comedy and tragedy would vie with one another at the *agones* (public contests).

Miraculous harmony at Epidaurus
Around the *orchestra*, the shell-like theatre set into the hill of Epidaurus fans out like a radial structure, whose concentric rows of seating are all focused on the stage, where the dramatic action would unfold. With its diameter of 120 m, the theatre of Epidaurus is one of the finest semi-circular buildings of Antiquity. Its design, the work of Polyclitus the Younger, according to Pausanias, dates from the end of the fourth century B.C. It is based on a series of mathematical principles and proportions, such as the Golden Section and the so-called Fibonacci Sequence. Its harmony is thus the result of a *symmetria* in the real sense of the term.

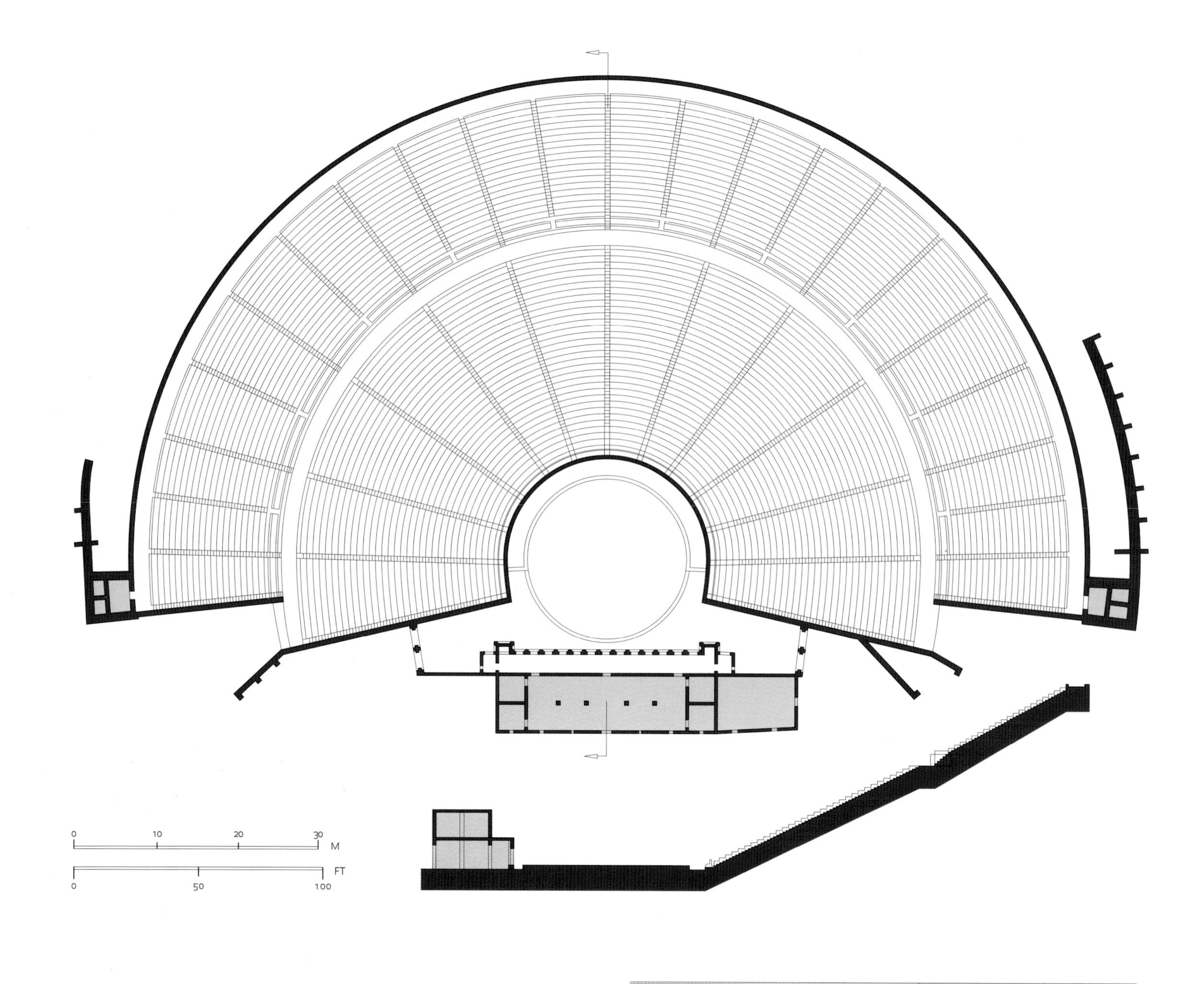
0 10 20 30 M
0 50 100 FT

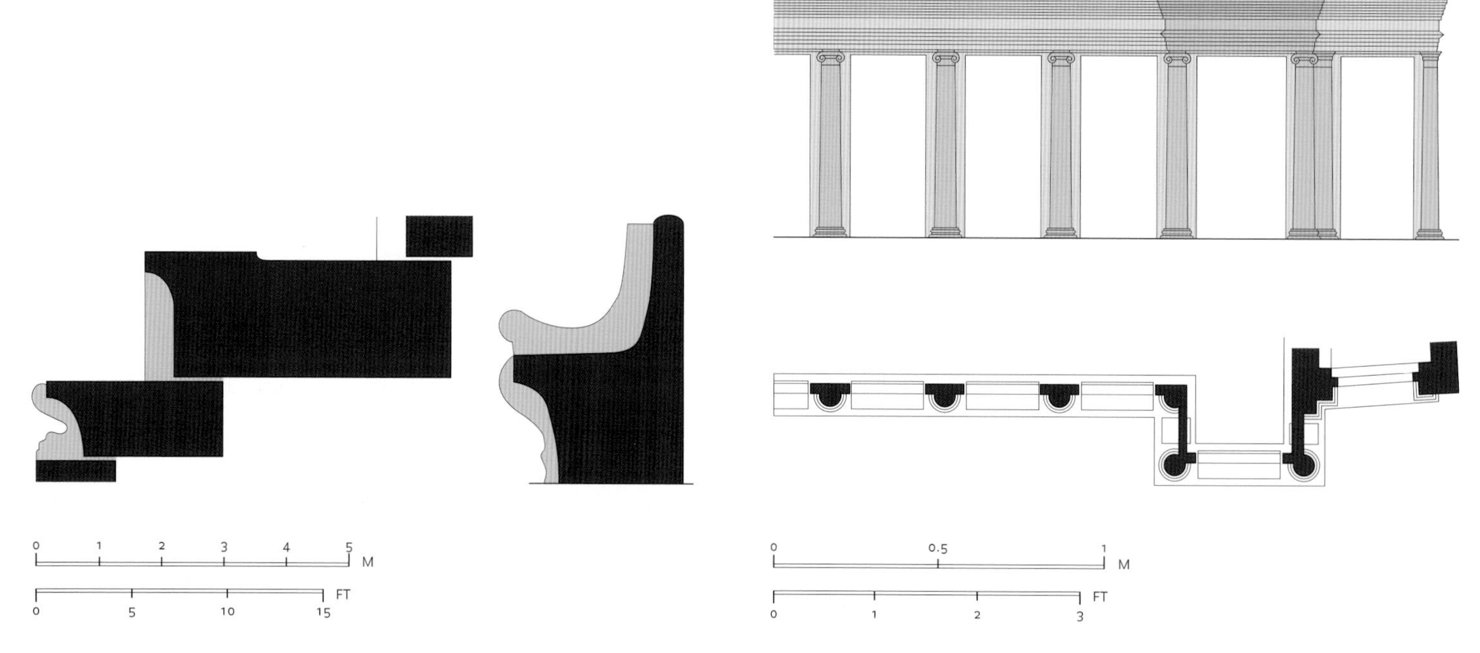
0 1 2 3 4 5 M
0 5 10 15 FT
0 0.5 1 M
0 1 2 3 FT

Page 170
The design of the theatre of Epidaurus
Plan and section of the building, with a detail of the tiered steps and seats, and the layout of the *proscenium*. The *cavea* covers a semi-circular area which extends well beyond 180° C. Despite the perfection of this shell set into the hillside, the link between the *cavea* and the stage is still not successfully achieved. It was not until the Roman period that theatres finally achieved architectural unity.

The seating at Epidaurus
Two types of seats were available for spectators at Epidaurus: those for ordinary people and those for city councillors and officials.
Left: The rows of tiers forming the bulk of the seating in the *cavea* of the theatre, with edges at the ends of the *cuneus*.
Right: Seats with backs and arms, reserved for political figures and city officials.

These irregularities are possibly due to a rhythmic pursuit, akin to the variations described as "optical corrections". What comes through, however, is the harmonious perfection of this immense and tranquil auditorium. By referring to Vitruvius' formulae for the composition of ancient theatres, it is possible to get some idea of the refinement of the principal lines and layout which govern these buildings.

Conversely, between the tiers designated for the general public (*cavea*) and the stage structure *(proscenium)*, there is, at Epidaurus, as in all Classical Greek theatres, a none too pleasing solution to the problem of continuity: the link between circular and concentric elements, or *orchestra*, on the one hand, and the rectangular *scene*, on the other, can only be reached by crossing the passages which led to either side of the *orchestra*, forming the *parodos*. This is not a very integrated concept, for it relies essentially on crossing to the *orchestra* and thus has no truly logical architectural order. This problem would not be solved until the Roman period.

Classical Military Architecture

In the wake of the Persian Wars, Athens emerged victorious but ravaged. It was clear that she must have the means to defend herself against any kind of threat. Accordingly, in 478 work started on the construction of a wall around the city itself. Next, Athens was linked to the Piraeus by the defensive system called the Long Walls. These works consisted of four basic parts: a 6 km fortification around the capital, the reinforcement of the walls of the Acropolis, the wall around the Piraeus, which was 13 km long, and the construction of the Long Walls measuring 7.5 and 6.5 km. These works would take thirty-five years, and the resulting fortifications enabled Athens to "rise to the rank of a great power" (E. Lévy).

But almost nothing remains today of this impressive undertaking embarked upon to promote Athenian imperialism. Later, however, a series of forts and fortresses was built in the fourth century to protect Attica from raids. These included, Aegosthena at the end of the Gulf of Corinth, followed by Glyphtocastro or Eleutherae on the Thebes-Eleusis road, Panactum and Phylae on the road linking Thebes to Athens, and then a succession of small mountain forts extending to the fortress of Rhamnus overlooking the sea opposite Euboea, as well as Corone, Thoricus, and Sunium, at the southernmost tip of Attica.

These constructions had similar features: they were fortresses with curtain walls topped by a parapet walk-way punctuated by square towers and fitted with embrasures for archers and an upper floor supporting machines of war. The salient towers made it possible to fire ballistae in quick succession or produce flanking fire. They had loopholes and were surmounted by merlons. The gates, usually backed up by a postern set just behind the opening, were made by experts in the art of siege-craft and siege warfare. The whole gate unit, often with three parts – the outer

The fortress of Aegosthena
The fourth century B.C. Boeotian fortress of Aegosthena is one of the major defences of Attica against seaborne troops.

Unscathed towers in the landscape
Military architecture has only rarely interested historians. At Aegosthena, however, the tallest "keep" is still intact. Its fine rusticated stonework is evidence of the care called for by its construction. All that is missing is the upper floors and the roof.

Barring the road from Thebes to Athens
Eleutherae: the fourth-century fortress which guards the thoroughfare that links Boeotia with Attica has a powerful wall punctuated by salient towers. The curtain-walls are 2.60 m thick and built, like the towers, in fine regular rusticated stonework.

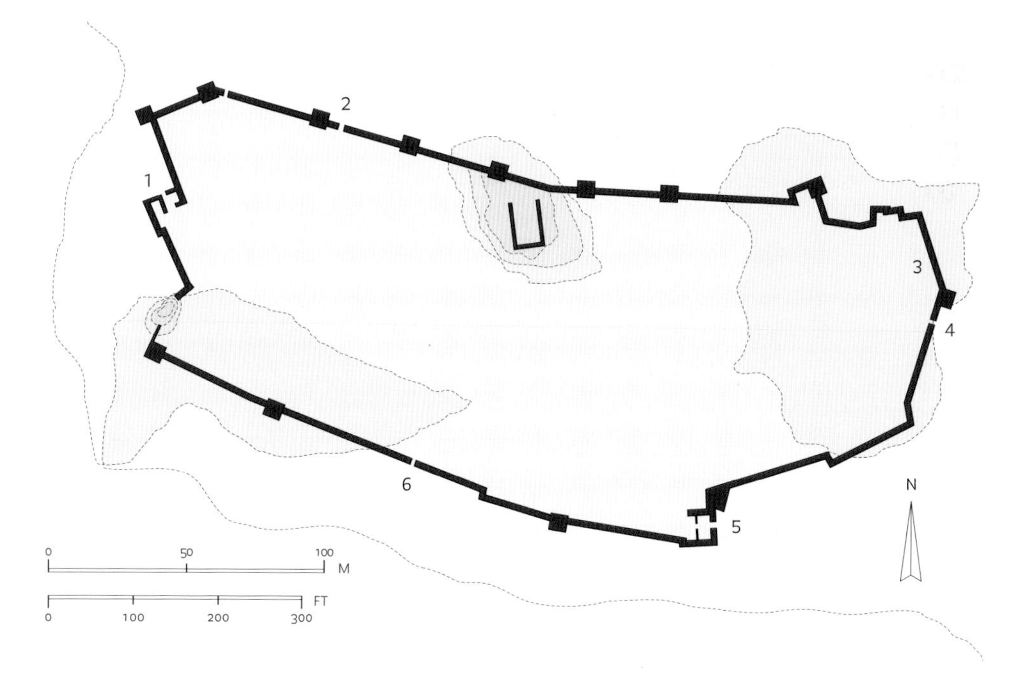

Fortifications stand guard
Plan of the fortress of Eleutherae, west of Athens, with its towers jutting out from the curtain-walls:
1 Thebes Gate
2 North postern
3 Water-tank
4 East postern
5 Athens Gate
6 South postern

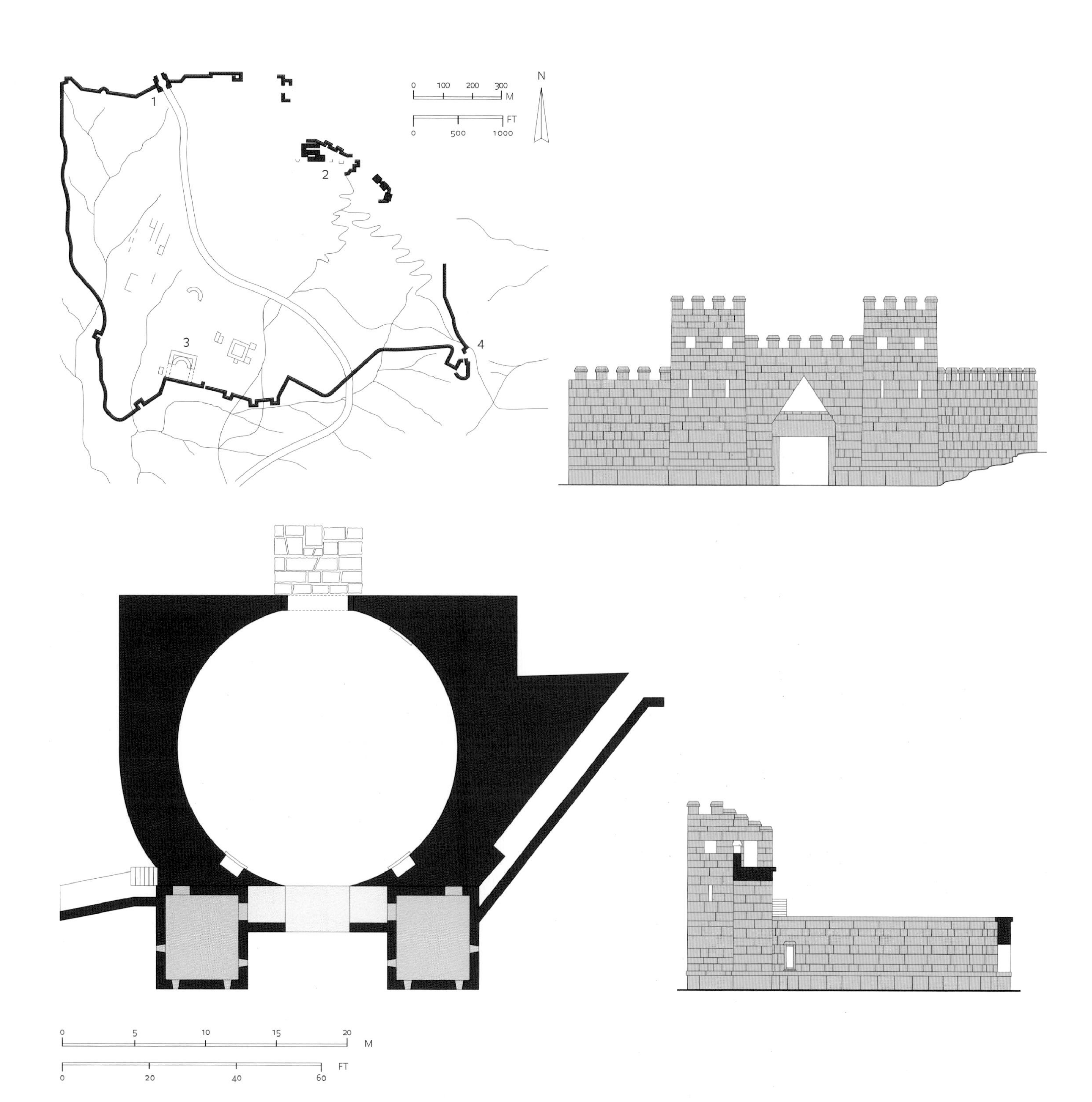

The wall of Messene, built by Epaminondas

The wall of Messene, in the Peloponnese, was built in the fourth century B.C., as part of the expansion policy of Sparta. *Above left*: Overall plan of the perimeter wall which measures some 9 km in length and climbs more than 400 m between the Arcadian Gate (396 m) and the Acropolis of Mount Ithome (802 m).

1 Arcadian Gate
2 Acropolis and Altar of Zeus
3 *Agora* and Messenian Gate
4 Laconian Gate

Below and right: Plan, elevation and section of the Arcadian Gate at Messene, with its round bastion system, access to which is guarded by two towers.

faces being connected by bond-stones – or alternatively just two – with two facings enclosing filler – was formed by large rusticated blocks, set in regular courses using the dry-stone technique and with carefully dressed angle rabbets.

But a stronghold such as Aegosthena, with its square wall with one side facing the sea, had an upper curtain wall fitted with a sort of keep, which was tall and imposing. This advance post was to provide warning of any landing on one of the few stretches of shore where there was a beach offering access to enemy troops.

Inland, the fortress of Eleutherae barred the road to Thebes, here dominated by towering crags. It occupied an area measuring 300 by 120 m, and its northern wall was defended by eight towers.

Phylae, north of Athens, was an impressive eyrie surveying a steep ravine – a key position in a defensive system which enabled small detachments to control the mountain. Rhamnus, with its positions staked out by defensive marble structures, guarded the Strait of Euboea, and its walls plunged straight into the sea.

All these structures are in a remarkable state of preservation. In some cases, the military installations seem to be completely intact – all that would be needed would be to rebuild floors in the towers, replace a few toppled merlons and repair the parapet walks a little to make these military buildings look exactly as they originally did twenty-three centuries ago.

The most spectacular complex, however, in the heart of the southwestern mountains of the Peloponnese, is the city of Messene, built in 369 by the Theban general Epaminondas to withstand the Spartan threat. The wall around the city, situated at the foot of Mount Ithome (802 m) which forms the acropolis, measures all of 9 km. Much of it is still standing and shows curtain-walls 2 m thick and up to 6 m high punctuated by towers, which are sometimes square and sometimes round and projecting, rising to a height of 9 m.

The Arcadian Gate, flanked by two square towers, provided a defensive system

The Arcadian Gate at Messene
In front of the round courtyard of the Arcadian Gate, a huge toppled lintel marks the main access. Note the stonework using very large blocks forming the first course in the form of orthostats or vertical slabs, on which the regular layers of rusticated blocks were then laid.

The organization of the defences at Messene
In the stronghold of Messene, splayed arrow-slits, loopholes and doors giving access to the parapet walk are made of drystone blocks of limestone.

organized around a circular courtyard. Any attackers who managed to break down the first gate found themselves in an enclosed area ringed by a round wall and forming a sort of barbican. From the top of this round wall, the defenders could focus their fire on the assailants and prevent them from gaining the second gate.

Military architecture forms an often-forgotten chapter of Greek art. It contains useful lessons about the permanent state of war that reigned between the Greek cities, and it attests to the considerable efforts undertaken by the powers of the day to stabilize a situation that was in a constant state of flux.

Page 177
A wall punctuated by towers
The long wall of Messene, in the Peloponnese, is punctuated by round and square towers. The ancient fortifications encircled not only a city but also large open spaces, where peasants from the surrounding area put their livestock to protect them from enemy attacks.

The Fortress of Euryalos at Syracuse

It was the tyrant Dionysius I who in 400 B.C. equipped Syracuse with its mighty 27-km long wall. In addition to the sea walls of the island of Ortygia and the lower city (Tyche), the land-based walls of Epipolae (the upper city) thrust westwards in the form of a quoin or wedge. Euryalos was situated at their extremity, forming a daunting pivot in this defensive system. It was a huge "castle" foreshadowing by a millennium and a half the colossal building endeavours of the Crusades to the Holy Land.

The defence of Syracuse was dominated by this huge system made up of three ditches hewn in the bare rock and forming a spur of limestone. The third man-made ditch, some 15 m deep, measured at least 70 m in length and 16 in width. A stone pinnacle supported the apron of a draw-bridge. A series of deep underground tunnels enabled those defending the place to make unexpected sorties at the bottom of the ditch, or else to fall back unnoticed on to the "castle". This massive structure consisted of three stone towers (*tripylon*) set side by side to bar the way to any foe who might have managed to cross the ditches. According to the reconstruction made by Luigi Mauceri, it is possible that these three towers were joined together by means of wooden structures designed to accommodate archers.

The fortress of Syracuse withstood all the attacks and onslaughts made against it, until the day when the Romans took possession of the city in 212 B.C.

Page 178
An impressive trench
The "castle" of Euryalos – an outpost defending the city of Syracuse, in Sicily – was built in about 400 B.C. by the tyrant Dionysius, to complete a huge construction programme including a 27 km wall. Three ditches were dug right through a jutting spur, in the form of trenches hewn in the living rock. The third one, 70 m long, 16 m wide and 15 m deep, is the outcome of the hard labor of thousands of slaves who were taken prisoner during the disastrous expedition mounted by Athens in Sicily in 415 B.C., and later during battles against the Carthaginians.

A stone pinnacle at Euryalos
In the middle of the trench hewn by human hands, the Syracusans left a stone pinnacle to support a drawbridge. With this device, the entrance to the fortress of Euryalos was stoutly defended.

A network of underground passages
Beneath the vertical walls of the trenches of Euryalos, the defenders carved out passages hewn out of the rock, which enabled their troops to carry out sorties to repel attackers.

The Acropolis of Pericles

Architecture at its Zenith

Page 181
Bearing the effigy of the owl of Athena
Thanks to its silver mines at Laurion, Athens developed an "economic imperialism" based on a sound currency – the famous tetradrachms which the city coined in the fifth and fourth centuries B.C., bearing the effigy of an owl, emblematic of the goddess Athena. (Geneva, Museum of Art and History)

When the Persians withdrew from Greece in 48, not a stone was left standing on the Acropolis of Athens. Before Xerxes' troops were defeated at Salamis and Plataea, they had razed the temples to the ground, including some which were still unfinished on top of this impressive stone "table" with its sheer sides. This hilltop had been fortified since earliest times and dominated the plain below from a height of 80 m.

On the site of the original city of Athens, where civic, military and religious buildings jockeyed for position in Mycenaean and Homeric times, from the Archaic period onward the Acropolis contained only the sanctuaries of the Athenians. For the upper city, now deserted by its inhabitants who preferred the surrounding plain, had become a sacred site. It was here, on a plateau levelled by human hand and measuring 300 by 175 m, that there now sprang up the temples to the goddess Athena who presided over the destiny of the city.

Pericles and the City-planning Programme

After the havoc wrought by the Persians, it took the Athenians a full thirty-three years before they started to act. Despite their victory, they did not know where to begin with the ruins confronting them. The efforts of the Pisistratids to endow the city with a series of grand monuments came to nothing. It was not until the arrival of Pericles at the head of the Athenian government that construction of the new Parthenon was embarked upon in 447. This project was undertaken with the co-operation of the architects Ictinus and Callicrates, and the sculptor Phidias.

As a result of the contributions of the different members of the Delian League, set up immediately after the Persian wars with Athens at its head, a series of sumptuous monuments was erected on the Acropolis. The transfer of the federal coffers from Delos to Athens (in 454) helped the Athenians to put their programme of grand designs into action – a programme partly funded by tributes paid by League members. These contributions were complemented by the mining activities at Laurion in Attica.

Pericles was a stirring orator and a shrewd strategist, who championed democratic ideas but nevertheless contributed to the establishment of the hegemony of Athens and the creation of an imperial policy that made the effective stranglehold of Athens look like a form of centralizing power. This policy helped to turn the League into nothing less than an empire. At the same time, the autonomy of the Greek cities of Ionia from the Great King was guaranteed by the signing of the Peace of Callias (449).

With his team of artists and builders, Pericles came up with a grandiose project: the dedication of the "great Temple" of Athens to the glory of the goddess of Athena Polias, patron and protectress of the city, by glorifying the Parthenos, the venerable virgin who had saved the Greeks; and a new design for the whole "city plan" of the Acropolis, with its sanctuaries and sacred areas.

The first, or old Parthenon – started by Pisistratus, tyrant of Athens from

A pensive Athena in front of a stele
Athena, goddess of war (helmeted and armed with a spear) symbolizing the supremacy of Reason, is the city deity of the Athenians. It was she who presided over the fate and destiny of the city, and it is her temples which stand on top of the Acropolis. This marble stele, 48 cm high, dates from 460 B.C. (Athens, Acropolis Museum)

561/560 to 528 – the remains of which are still there under the temple which can be seen today, went through two phases. The first involved a temple built of *poros*, whose base measured 31.39 by 76.82 m. Only the infrastructure was completed. The second, in marble and slightly smaller (23.53 by 66.94 m), was a hexastyle edifice with sixteen lateral columns. Its construction had been started in about 520 under the reign of the Pisistratids Hippias and Hipparchus. This unfinished building, which was ravaged by Xerxes, included a series of solutions which would be retained in the Parthenon of Phidias and Ictinus. Behind the six-columned façades, a second row of four more slender columns replaced the shafts *in antis*. To the east, the narrow and very elongated *naos* consisted of three naves separated by two porticoes of ten inner columns on two levels. To the west there was an *opisthodomos*, followed by a square room, the roof of which was supported by a group of four columns.

The Classical Parthenon, in the Doric style, retains these different parts. But to them Ictinus added a modification of paramount importance: he enlarged the whole structure which, instead of six façade columns, now had eight. He opted for an octostyle temple with six columns forming the second row of shafts set behind the façades. Each side had seventeen columns. The much wider *naos* now measured 19 m instead of 12. The back of the room represented a return to the square format of the lateral porticoes on two levels with five columns rising up behind the statue of Athena. The four-columned room – the actual Parthenon – had tall and elegant Ionic shafts. The measurements of this building at the stylobate were 30.88 by 69.50 m, which is relatively small compared to many Archaic temples, and those in Ionia in particular. But the distinctive feature of this building was its quality, which was carried down to the very smallest details. The height of the forty-six

The Acropolis inhabited
In about 1805, when the English painter Edward Dodwell visited the Acropolis, there were still dwellings amid the ruins, as is shown by this print published in 1821.

Page 185 above
Fortress and sanctuary?
This angle-shot taken from the Plaka district of Athens gives the Acropolis a powerfully military image, with its soaring walls encircling the large flat structure on which stood only the temples of the Greek deities.

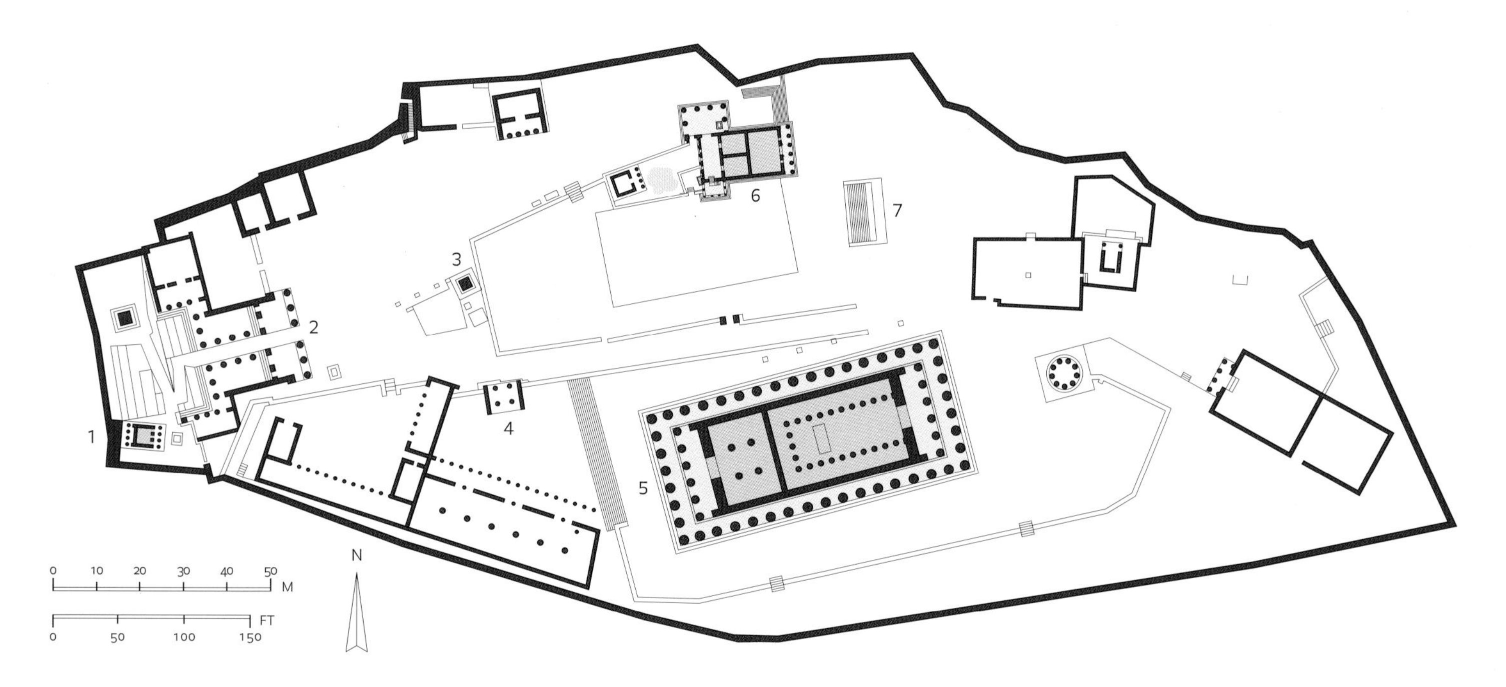

Plan of the Acropolis of Athens
Since the Age of Pericles, the whole of the upper city – site, in the Mycenaean period, of the city proper – was given over exclusively to the gods:

1 Temple of Athena Nike in front of the Propylaea
2 Inner façade of the Propylaea
3 Colossal statue of Athena Promachos
4 *Propylon* of the Chalkotheke
5 Parthenon, or Temple of Athena Parthenos
6 Erechtheum
7 Altar of Athena

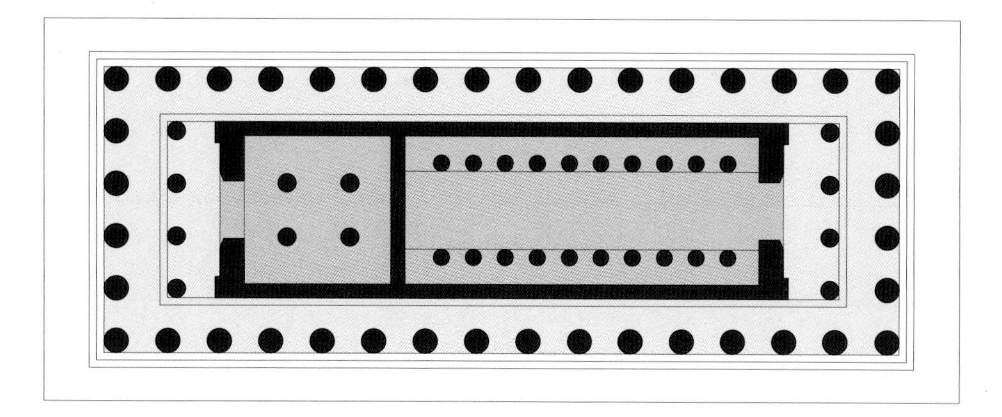

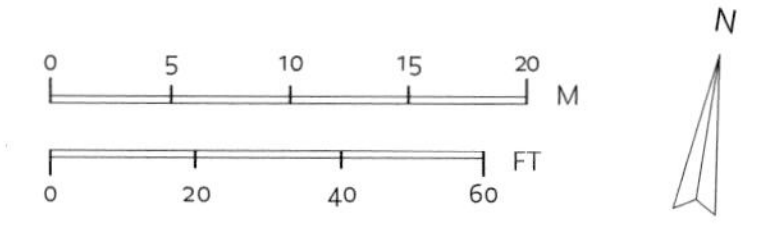

The first Parthenon
Plan of the first Temple of Athena Parthenos (known as the Pre-Parthenon). Built of marble, work on it started in the early fifth century on the Acropolis, to replace an early *hecatompedon* made of tufa. This building was still being worked on – or so it would seem – when the Persians destroyed it in 480. This Pre-Parthenon was the same length as the building erected by Phidias and Ictinus (67 m). But it is a hexastyle, whereas its successor would have eight columns on its façade. The essential structure remained the same, however, with a *cella* with three naves to the east, and a Hall of Virgins to the west, which was originally square, and then became oblong at the hand of Ictinus. This latter hall had a roof supported by four tall Ionic columns.

columns of the peripteral portico was 10.43 m, and the cornice reached a height of 13.72 m. The building, constructed in dazzlingly white Pentelic marble, was set off by bright polychromy in the upper parts such as capitals, triglyphs, metopes and pedimental tympana.

Proportions and Numbers

The numbers and proportions of Pythagorean *symmetria*, harmony and symbolism were probably realized more coherently in the Parthenon than anywhere else. Many works have been devoted to analyzing the systems governing the making of this masterpiece. The mathematical formulation, whose strength resides in its simplicity, is based on the numbers two (the first even number) and three (the first odd number), and on their squares, four and nine. Based on this 4:9 ratio, which applies both to the dimensions of the stylobate and to those of the *naos* without the *antae*, everything follows an absolute logic. This proportion is divided into three "Pythagorean" rectangles with sides of three, four, and five (their squares being nine, sixteen and twenty-five).

Ernst Berger of Basle provides us with a remarkably illuminating key. The author shows that the composition is based on a module: the largest common denominator of the length, width and height of the Parthenon (length 69.50 m; width 30.88; height 13.72). This common denominator is established, respectively, with 81 modules (that is 9^2), 36 modules (6^2) and 16 modules (4^2). This same module (of 0.858 m) is applied to the width of the triglyphs and the height of the capitals. There are 5 inter-axial modules (5.148 m) between the columns; 12 modules for the height of the columns, and 21 modules for the overall height of the temple; the proportions of the *naos* are 25 by 60 modules.

The diameter of the shaft of the columns is 1.905 m and the inter-axial distance 4.293 m, so the ratio is again 4:9. Similarly, the *naos*, without the *antae*, measures 48.3 m in length by 21.44 m in width, that is a proportion of 4:9.

Research has helped to develop this analysis to such a point that we can now fully grasp the extreme refinement of the interplay of these proportions. It would be tedious to offer further examples here. Suffice it to say that these measurements express a determination to set the entire building within a sort of numerical grid. The *commodulatio*, or application of a module which recurs in all essential measurements, and the *ordinatio* contribute to the success, or *eurhythmia*, the aesthetically perfect balance.

A proud composition
The north-west corner of the Parthenon, with its cluster of Doric columns made of pentelic marble. This is the glorification of a rhythmic spacing which underpins a perfect harmony. Built between 447 and 432 B.C., the Sanctuary of Athena rises to a height of 13.72 m at the cornice.

In reality, the applications show that all these dimensions – length, width, height, proportions of the *naos*, diameter and height of the columns, height of the capitals, and so on – stem from a unitary system. This system was more than a "formula" for masterpieces. It was – for Greek architects – a way of endowing their work with a meaning, a far-reaching significance connecting the microcosm of the temple not only with the macrocosm of the universe but also with the eternal ideas that govern the mighty celestial mechanics and the rhythms of the world.

Never, perhaps, has concern for detail been taken so far in the quest for visual harmony and in the manipulation of perspective and optical effects. What is more,

Manifest strength
The façade of the Parthenon, with its eight columns which support the entablature and the pediment, thrusts itself forward as a Classical paradigm. Set at the very heart of Pericles' grand design, the purpose of this project was to sweep away the humiliation suffered by the Persian invasion and the sack of Athens. The shafts in fact have a smaller distance between their axes than might be expected of the Parthenon when it was constructed (latter half of the fifth century), and the reason for this (according to Roland Martin) is that the architects – Callicrates and Ictinus – had to use marble drums already made for the Pre-Parthenon, whose diameter was not wide enough.

Dominating the Acropolis
Seen from the Hill of the Muses in Athens, the Parthenon rises up above the supporting walls and the Theatre of Herodes Atticus, and forms a magnificent marble crown surmounting the whole city. It asserts the pre-eminent role of the goddess Athena and underscores the perfection of Classical proportions with the elegance of its porticoes, enhanced by an interplay of light and shadow.

Page 191
Geometry and proportions
Above: Side elevation and plan of the Parthenon. The Temple of Athena Parthenos, designed by Phidias and built by Ictinus and Callicrates, is at once traditional and innovative. Its peripteral Doric portico (8 by 17 columns), behind which stand six more refined and slender Doric shafts, is matched by the four Ionic columns of the Hall of Virgins to the west, while, to the east, the principle of the three naves is adopted, based on two superimposed Doric colonnades. These – which form a right-angled sequence at the back of the hall – are the frame for the cult-statue: the colossal chryselephantine statue of Phidias.
1 East vestibule
2 *Cella*
3 Site of the chryselephantine statue of Athena
4 Hall of the Virgins
5 West vestibule
Below: The set of numbers which is involved in the composition of the Parthenon. The plan is based on the 4:9 ratio, which is divided into three Pythagorean rectangles, whose sides 3 and 4 have a diagonal 5 (the hypotenuse). In addition, the longitudinal juxtaposition of two Pythagorean rectangles provides the proportion 3:8. Lastly, the module the whole composition is the outcome of the largest common denominator of the length, width and height. This module is contained 81 times (9^2) in each square resulting from the basic proportions: 4 by 9. In the Parthenon it measures 0.858 m.

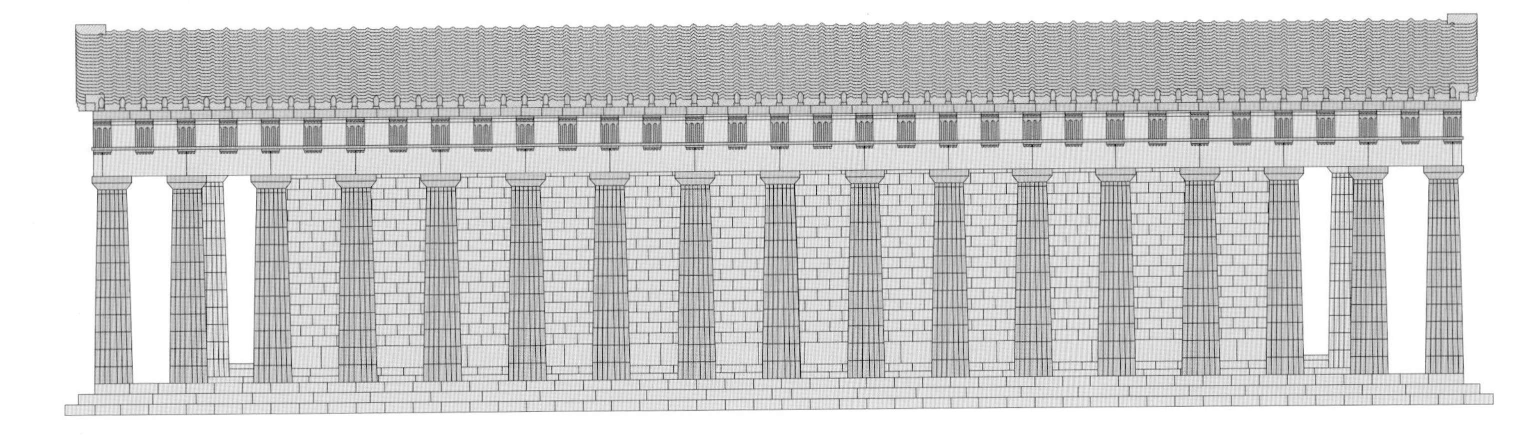

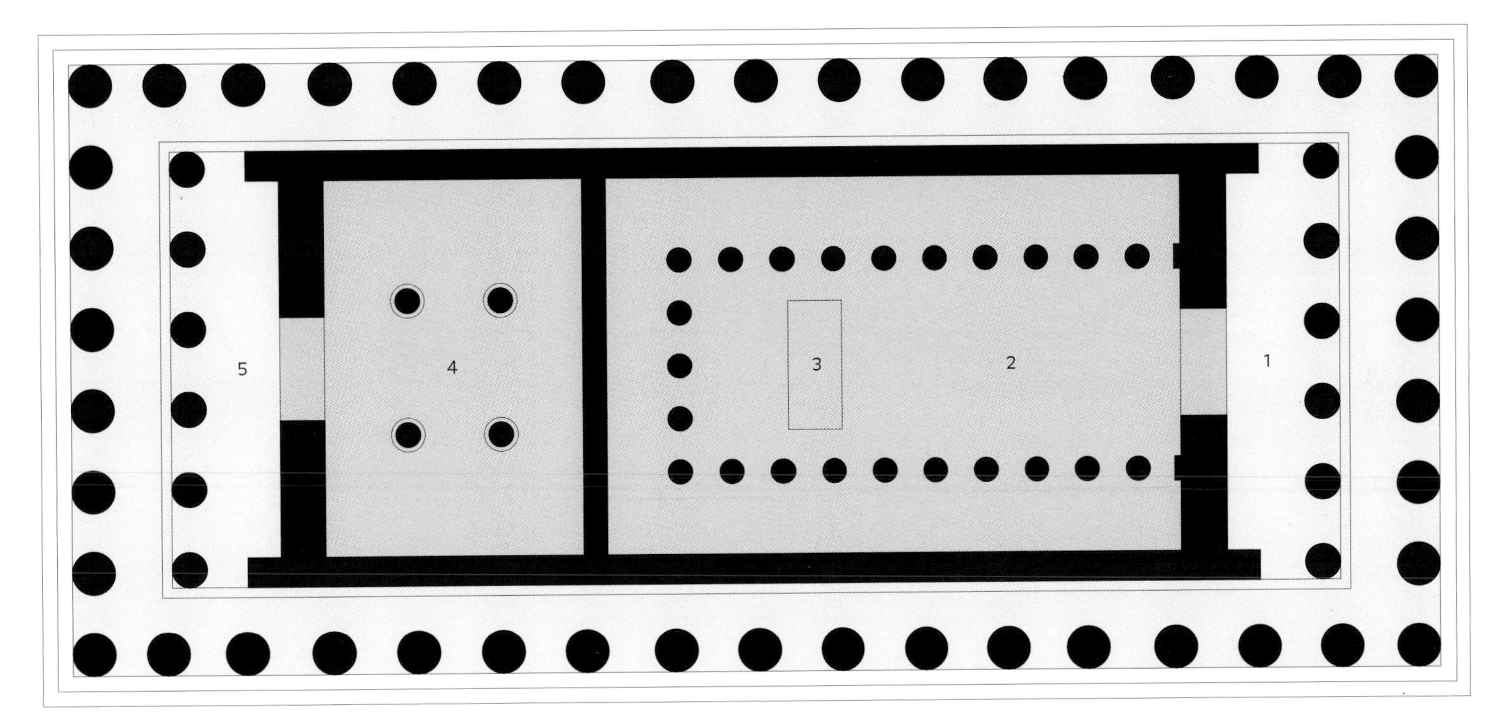
5
4
3
2
1

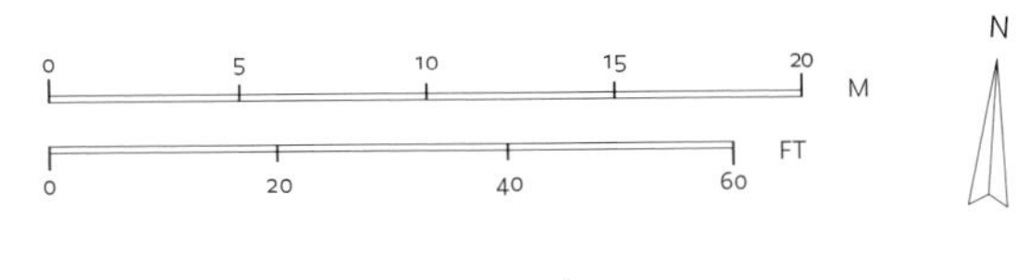
0
5
10
15
20
M
0
20
40
60
FT
N

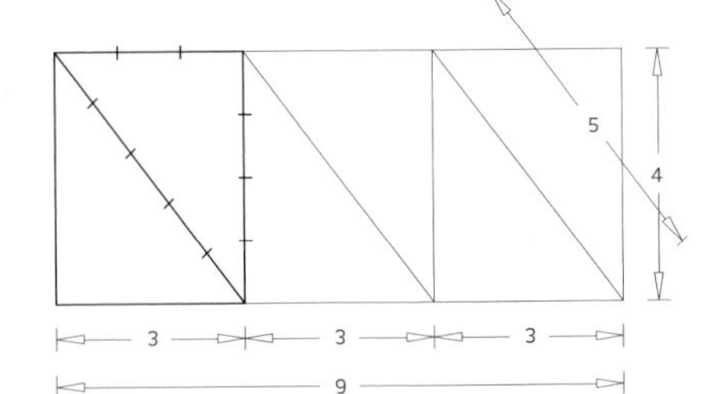
5
4
3
3
3
9

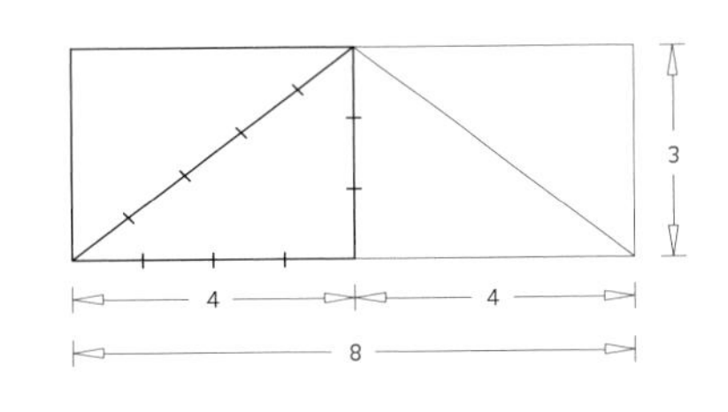
3
4
4
8

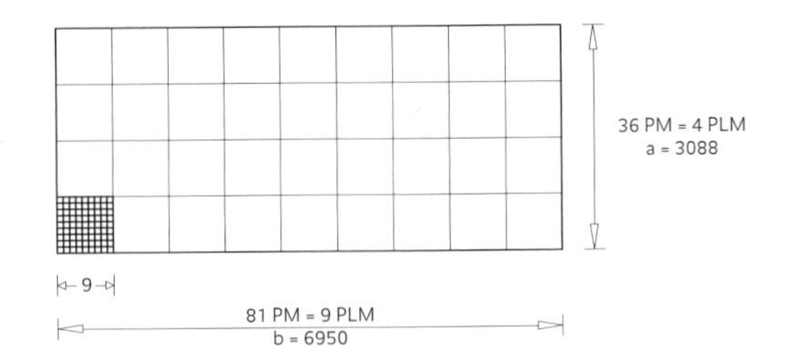
36 PM = 4 PLM
a = 3088
9
81 PM = 9 PLM
b = 6950

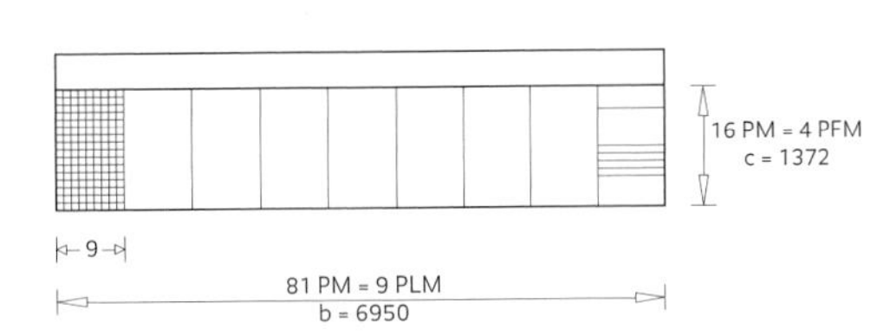
16 PM = 4 PFM
c = 1372
9
81 PM = 9 PLM
b = 6950

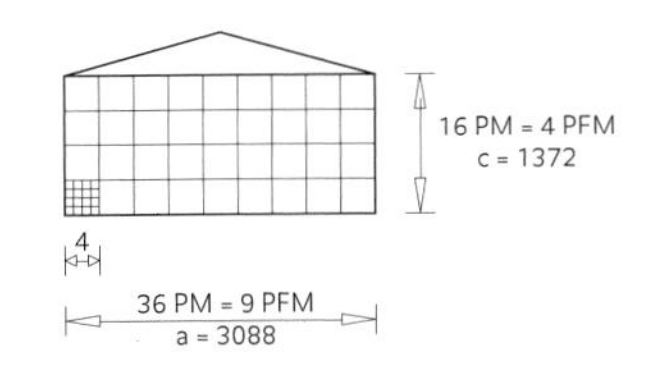
16 PM = 4 PFM
c = 1372
4
36 PM = 9 PFM
a = 3088

there is every reason to suppose that they may have a functional factor. One thinks, in particular, of the curvature of the stylobate, called for by rainwater run-off, and the reinforcement of the corner columns, designed to withstand the diagonal thrusts more effectively. Everything here is purity and serene perfection.

The east pediment of the Parthenon
The sculpture of the west pediment of the Parthenon depicted the confrontation between Athena and Poseidon. That of the east pediment represents the birth of Athena. In the south corner (above), we see the horses drawing the chariot of Helios emerging from the stone, marking the dawn of a new era. The horse is also a theme which recurs again and again like a *leitmotif* in the Parthenon – the horse of Selene (the Moon) (at the other end of the same pediment) and especially the horses in the cavalcade forming the procession of the Panathenaea, which takes up most of the north and south friezes.

The Decoration of the Parthenon

As the Sanctuary of Athena Parthenos, the Parthenon presents an outstanding array of sculptures. Firstly, the pediments and the statuary of the tympana depicting, to east and west alike, a series of gods and heroes: the birth of Athena, and her rivalry with Poseidon to rule over Attica. By offering the olive, the symbol of peace, Athena won the day. Here the tree regains its redemptive significance.

Then we have the series of ninety-two metopes, with their sculpture in the round, produced between 447 and 442. These represent the fight of the Centaurs and the Lapiths, heroes and Amazons, symbols of the struggle between gods and giants, which assumes its full import in the clash between Greeks and Persians, East and West. For the Parthenon is also a trophy, and a temple with an apotropaic (or evil-averting) significance, whose role was to exorcize the Achaemenid threat.

Lastly, under the portico of the outer peristyle, there runs the huge relief of the Panathenaic Procession. This is a colossal continuous composition – based on the principle of Ionic friezes – which runs around the whole *cella* of the temple. It represents a ritual event to which the entire city was summoned to take part in – the Festival of the Great Panathenaea. On this occasion, a sumptuous embroidered *peplos* was offered each year to the goddess Athena during a procession which brought together all the representatives of the city. The cortège started out from the Agora, made its way up the slopes of the Acropolis to pay homage to the patroness of the city and included great sacrifices involving the immolation of four oxen and four ewes. The festival took place after the harvest and represented an act of thanks for the blessings granted.

On a surround of 160 m, the sculptor depicted gods, heroes, horsemen, people making sacrifices, maidens weaving the *peplos*, animals, gift-bearers, musicians and chariots. The festival, not unlike New Year ceremonies in the East, marked the moment of a close communion between everyone in attendance and Athena Polias. Because of its "civic" nature, this ceremony deserves more detailed discussion at a later stage. For its significance turns out to be profoundly political.

Last of all, in the *cella*, Phidias produced his masterpiece: the idol, the divine statue representing Athena Parthenos standing – a colossal work about 11 m in height. Here, once again, Greek art played on proportions, this time involving the harmony of the human body. The laws governing *symmetria* comply with the Canon of Polyclitus, a treatise which codified statuary and set down its numerical ratios.

The impressive chryselephantine effigy depicting the virgin goddess, made entirely of gold and ivory on a wood and metal frame, was highlighted by bright polychromy. It stood on a pedestal decorated with bas-reliefs depicting the epic story of Athena.

The Challenge of the Frieze of the Panathenaea

Any student of comparative art history is duty-bound to examine the famous Frieze of the Panathenaea – which runs round the *cella* of the temple – in its socio-political context. It would seem relevant to resituate it in the Graeco-Persian conflict, because the Parthenon itself was, in some ways, the outcome of the victory of the Greeks over the Achaemenids.

Is it not, after all, plain to see that this procession is a "response" to the frieze forming a border to the great stairways of the Apadana at Persepolis? In order to get a clear grasp of the extent to which the two works form the two parts of a great diptych produced half a century apart, it is necessary to make an altogether new comparison. The prototype is the Apadana of Persepolis, with its great stairways flanking the Reception Room of the Nations, created by Darius, in about 513 B.C. Over a width of 80 m, forming the socle of the building on three superimposed levels, we find the bas-reliefs of the famous Procession of the Tributaries. The twenty-three nations parade before the Great King to deliver offerings which symbolize the tribute paid to the empire.

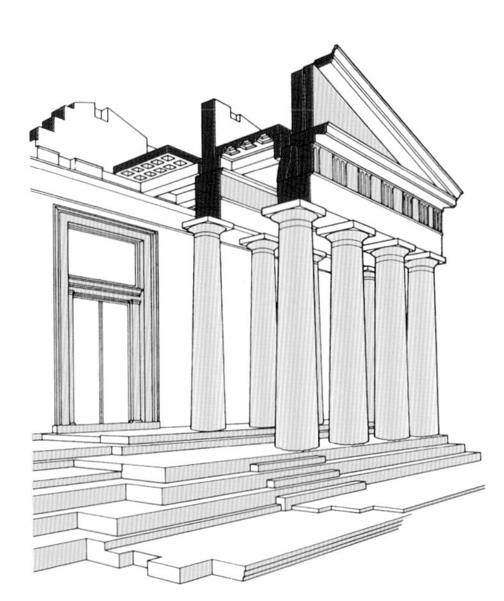

The arrangement of the sculpted decoration
Sculpture is present in the Parthenon on the two tympana, the ninety-two metopes which ring the building and alternate with the triglyphs, and the 160 m of frieze which surround the *cella*.

The centre of this vast unfurling of sculpted motifs is filled by a royal inscription, the text of which is carved in three languages: Old Persian, Elamite, and Babylonian. In the corners, lions slaying bulls express the victory of Good over Evil. The whole scene is set against a pine-clad landscape.

To the right, Persian dignitaries advance behind a battalion of the armed "Immortals" who form the guard of the King of Kings. In their wake come horses, grooms, ceremonial chariots, the bearers of the sovereign's throne, as well as leading figures at the court. For the Persian people were the master of the empire.

To the left, we follow the procession of the delegations with their attendants, each nation being separated from the next by a pine tree. The delegates, who carry "samples" of the tribute, show the whole range of products coming from the vast empire of the Achaemenids. Those from Susa offer weapons and lions, the Armenians offer metal vases and horses, the Babylonians embroidered fabrics and buffaloes, the Ionians fine cloth and jewels, the Phrygians apparel and horses, the Sakas gold artefacts clothes and horses, the Abyssinians perfume vases, an ivory tusk and a giraffe, the Somalis of Punt a goat and a two-horse chariot, the Arabs a dromedary and bolts of fabric, the Thracians lances, shields, and a horse, the Medes bracelets, clothes and a horse, the Bactrians a camel, the Egyptians a buffalo, the Sogdians a camel and hides, the Parthians, also a camel and hides the Elamites a lioness and two cubs, as well as daggers, the Scythians a dagger, hatchets and a horse, the Assyrians a humped ox and a lance, the Cilicians two rams and tanned hides, the Indians a donkey, the Arachosians vases and a camel, the Lydians of Sardis

At Persepolis as on the Acropolis
The presence of horses and horsemen is striking in the Procession of the Tributaries in the Apadana. These two horse's heads, complete with harness, and drawing the chariot of the Lydians, are Greek in style.

Page 195 above
The Procession of the Tributaries
At Persepolis, the representatives of each country brought gifts typical of their region: horses, gold and silver plate, fabrics, perfumes, spices, and so on. Each delegation was introduced by a Mede or a Persian.

fine cloth, the Cappadocians a horse and raiment, and the Phoenicians gold, bracelets and a chariot.

This fantastic "fresco" of peoples forms a huge procession, which was supposed to have taken place at the feet of the Achaemenid sovereign. As we mentioned earlier, this Procession of the Tributaries occurred during the festival of the Now Ruz, or Persian New Year, glorifying imperial unity.

The refinement of the sculptural work, the perfection of the detail, the delicacy of the gestures and the accurate rendering of the costumes of each country mean that this document is an inexhaustible fount of information. We should also add that this frieze was originally entirely polychromatic.

While the plan for the work commissioned by the Achaemenid sovereign was based on dictates that differed from those of the Greek friezes, this is essentially because it was not looking for movement, but, on the contrary, order and rigor.

Below

The Panathenaic Procession

A principle akin to that of Persepolis, based on the march-past of participants, enlivens the frieze of the Parthenon: on the left, horsemen on prancing mounts head towards the site of the ceremony; on the right, young people carry water-pitchers containing offerings to the goddess. (Athens, Acropolis Museum)

So we are dealing with a certain degree of state control, which conveys the organization of the empire. But the way the faces, hands and head-dresses are treated and the quality of the horses and wild animals are such that this work is an outstanding achievement. We said earlier that large numbers of Ionian artists and craftsmen were undoubtedly involved in this project. So it is not possible that, even if the Athenians never refer to it in any writings that have come down to us, they did not get wind of this magnificent undertaking to the glory of the unity of the Persian realm.

To match the artistic "manifesto" of the Achaemenids, and aware of the need to exalt a strong Greek entity around the savior-deity represented by Athena Polias, the victorious Parthenos, Pericles thus elected to embellish the Parthenon with a frieze which, from every point of view, would outdo and eclipse the work at Persepolis.

The Panathenaic Procession, produced between 442 and 438, commemorates a religious and civic festival. What exactly does it show? On the west side of the Parthenon, we see the procession starting out: horsemen prepare to mount their steeds which are often rearing up. They calm the animals, then set off. On the north side, the mounted troop moves forward in a lively procession, with no rigidity. They are followed by the animals bound for the sacrificial altar – ewes and oxen – as well as vase-bearers, musicians and war chariots. On the east side, young maidens carry incense-burners, and, coming from the north, gift-bearers head for the mythical heroes who walk ahead of the twelve gods. In the middle, Athena receives the sacred *peplos*. Coming from the south, the Ergastines, who had woven the ritual vestment, advance, followed by maidens carrying libations in phials. Lastly, the south side – with several gaps, but reconstructed thanks to the drawings made by Jacques Carrey in the seventeenth century – shows mounted horsemen, chariots and citizens carrying olive branches – the olive being Athena's tree – as well as sacrificial animals being led to the altar. The whole work expresses the unity of the four tribes making up the city of Athens, just as the Apadana glorifies the unity of the peoples of the Achaemenid Empire.

Judging from the numbers of the figures in these two works – the Procession of the Tributaries at Persepolis, on the one hand, and the Panathenaic Procession at Athens on the other – one gets the impression of a real "trophy" that the Greeks were keen to take away from the Persians once more. Whereas at Persepolis the procession of the nations includes a total of 250 figures, about fourty animals, and a few chariots, on the Acropolis, the ritual frieze of the Parthenon assembles 360 figures, including 143 horsemen and a total of 220 animals and about ten chariots.

At Persepolis, the bas-reliefs, which are on three levels each 0.9 m high, would cover a length of 125 m if they were laid end to end. In Athens, the frieze around the *cella* measures 1.06 m in height and has a total length of 160 m. By any measure, the work produced by Phidias and his team surpasses the creation of the Achaemenids.

On the other hand, it is surprising to see the Greek frieze arranged beneath the ceiling coffers covering the peristyle of the Parthenon, in a rather dark area which never receives direct light, whereas the reliefs of Persepolis are fully lit by direct sunlight. From a political standpoint, the antithetical stance of these two works is quite clear. The one takes the form of a military march-past, a kind of triumphal procession, while the other is a civic and religious festival. Just as the strict arrangement of the Immortals contrasts with the joyous disorder of the Greek horsemen, so the meticulous perfection of the Achaemenid drapery breaks with the graceful quality of the loose and flowing clothes of the Athenian citizens. As expressed by the sculptors, this conveys the antagonism between the strong centralized power of the Persian kingdom and the almost anarchic freedom of the Greeks in their independent city. With just one slight qualification: the reliefs of Persepolis are con-

Page 197
Light and shadow on the fluting
The north portico of the Parthenon, caressed by the fierce clarity of the Attic sky. The image of the "forest of columns" is haunting and unforgettable. Here it forms a veritable curtain that vibrates in the sun's rays.

Survival, Destruction and Restoration of the Parthenon

The Temple of Athena Polias was turned into a church in the sixth century A.D. This involved doing away with the great statue of Phidias, which was taken to Constantinople. The Crusaders subsequently dedicated the building to Catholic worship in 1208, and the Ottomans turned it into a mosque in 1460.

Before that, the Parthenon had bravely survived the 2000 years of its lively history. Sadly, the Turks had turned the Acropolis into a fortress and used the Parthenon as a warehouse for munitions. During the attack mounted in 1687 by the Venetians, led by the Swede Koenigsmark, a shell landed on the powder magazine and the building was extensively damaged by the explosion. Lastly, in 1802, with the agreement of the sultan, Lord Elgin took possession of fifty-six panels of the frieze and fifteen metopes, which he had shipped to the British Museum.

The restoration work got under way in the nineteenth century, by way of "pictures" made by resident Villa Medici students such as Alexis Paccard (1845) and Benoît Loviot (1879), who drew attention to the importance of the monument. Archaeologically speaking, it was not possible to start excavating until the Acropolis had been relieved of the various constructions that had been encumbering it since the Christian and Turkish periods. The palaeo-Christian apse and the small mosque erected in the temple itself were torn down, and the Ottoman bastion was destroyed. Work proper started in 1835, shortly after Greek independence had been declared. In 1885, a major campaign culminated in the discovery of the Archaic statuary of the old Parthenon. Between 1923 and 1933, Greece embarked on the task setting up the columns again. Today, another major programme is under way, called for in the wake of the 1981 earthquake. This programme has made it possible to use drums and blocks found in the meantime, to re-erect certain columns, and to prepare for the re-erecting of the columns of the *pronaos*, largely with the help of original materials.

temporary with the Severe style in Greece, whereas the frieze designed by Phidias glorifies Classical dynamism in all its fullness.

This frieze, like the tympana and metopes, with their chromatic highlighting, is an integral part of the architecture. The whole decoration serves the building and lends it its religious significance as well as a social and political character in the clash between East and West, and in the gradual winning back of freedoms embarked upon by the Greek city.

In this way, the Parthenon, as if suspended between heaven and earth on the top of the Acropolis, offers its triumphant majesty. Its lofty and powerful octostyle façades, with their forest of shafts, its long lateral perspectives, which are at once repetitive but endlessly variable (the width of the interaxial distances proceeds from small at the ends and centre to considerable at the fourth and seventh intervals from each corner on the south side), and its elegance springing from an evident balance obtained from the laws of *symmetria*, are the reflection of a rarely achieved perfection.

This masterpiece needed a prelude, a preparation allowing the onlooker to grow slowly accustomed to the sublime. Such an outstanding "introduction" was formed by the Propylaea.

A monumental portal
The inner portico of the Propylaea of Mnesicles provides a hexastyle response to the façade of the Parthenon: same order, same spacing, same mouldings. The "prelude" announces the "symphony" by design.

The Creation of the Propylaea and the Temple of Nike

The operation conducted by Pericles was not limited to the construction of the Parthenon alone. It included a programme that encompassed the whole of the Acropolis, starting with the Propylaea – or monumental gate – which formed the access way to the uppermost area, via the Sacred Way used by the Panathenaic Procession.

The design of the Propylaea was entrusted to the architect Mnesicles, and work got under way in 437, as soon as the Temple of Athena Parthenos was completed. It was then interrupted in 431 by the Peloponnesian Wars, and the building remained unfinished.

The Propylaea responded to a series of contradictory constraints which posed testing problems for the architect. It formed a grand entrance, while at the same time serving – symbolically – as a defensive structure, because it formed part of the wall around the Acropolis. Moreover, by being on the edge of the uppermost area of the hill, this symbolic building was situated on a threshold, on a borderline marking the limit between the gradient of the ascending path and the horizontal plane. So it played the part of a complex intersection. Its western (outer) façade was set lower down than its eastern (inner) façade. Last of all, the processional thoroughfare that crosses it from one end to the other was reserved for the carts used for ritual processions, while also providing steps for pedestrians to left and right.

The Propylaea thus had the awkward task of visually "fudging" the difference in level between the outer face and the inner. Seen from below, the formula adopted

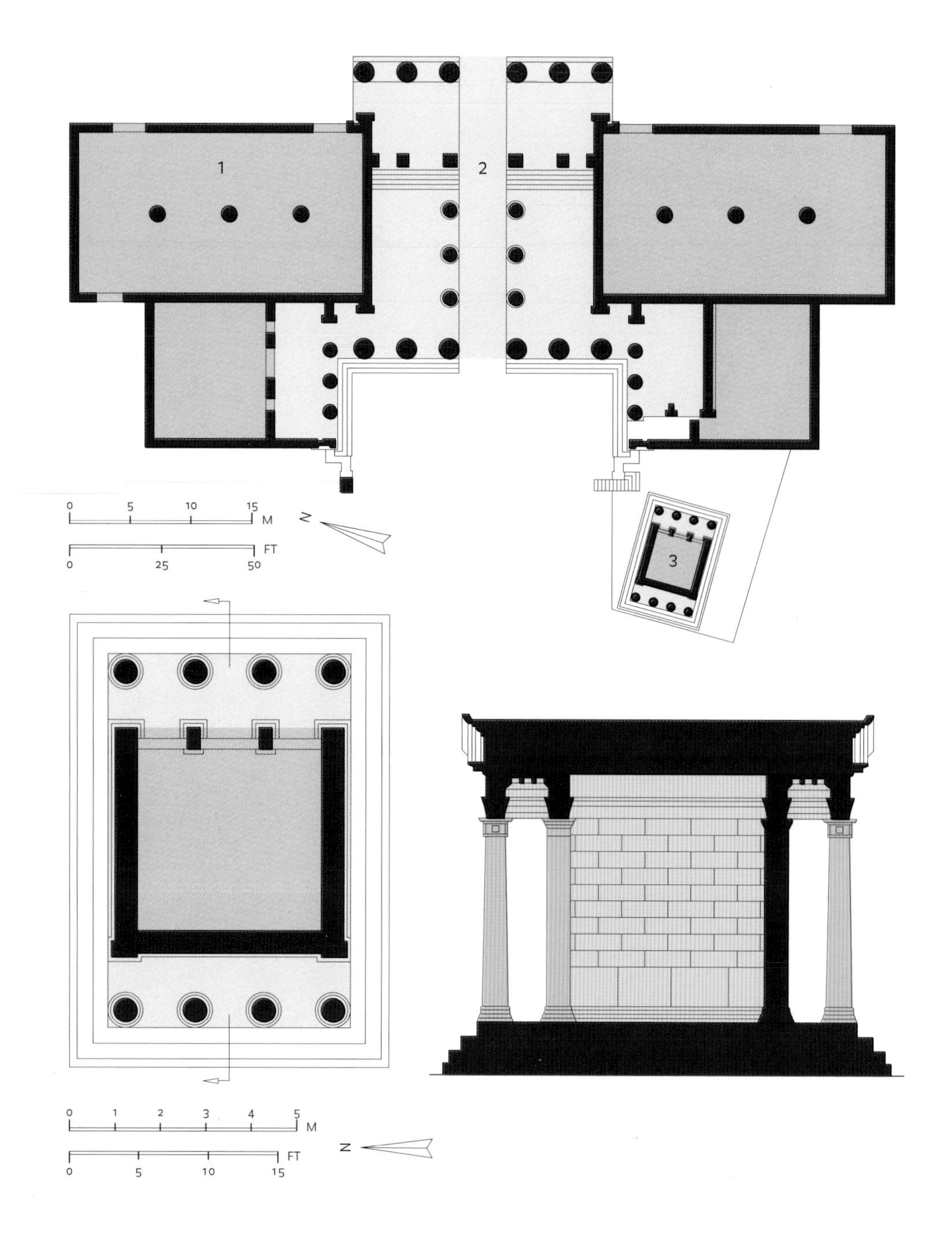

The entrance to the realm of the gods

Above: A reconstructed plan of the Propylaea of Mnesicles, built from 437–432 B.C. on the sill marking the edge of the plateau of the Acropolis. Access was gained along a thoroughfare climbing up the last projection, between six tall Ionic columns. On both sides, the rooms of the painting and sculpture galleries (based on a reconstruction that is generally agreed upon).

1 Hall of the picture-gallery or *pinakotheke* (matched, conjecturally, by the symmetrical hall of the sculpture-gallery or *glyptotheke*)
2 Colonnade running along the axial passage of the Propylaea
3 Temple of Athena Nike

Below: Plan and longitudinal section of the small Temple of Athena Nike (the Victorious) in the Ionic style, dating from *circa* 421 B.C. This is an amphiprostyle building (with porticoes at each end, but without columns along the sides).

presents a Doric hexastyle façade, with angle shafts formed by three more slender columns. Axially, the access way called for an intercolumniation that was wider at the centre. Inside the Propylaea the ramp was flanked by two Ionic porticoes with three large columns on either side. Because of their height, these Ionic shafts helped to overcome the difference in level, while still retaining a shaft diameter similar to that of the Doric columns which form the façade. As at Bassae, and in the square room of the Parthenon, the Ionic style was called for in the interior areas.

At the top of the ramp rose the actual gate formed by five apertures: a wide central passage between two pillars flanked, on either side, by two smaller passages which were narrower and terraced. Access was thus gained to the upper floor, behind the east façade. Its hexastyle colonnade corresponded to the octostyle of the Parthenon. Before emerging from the Propylaea, the visitor glimpsed, as if framed by the fluted shafts, the Temple of Athena Parthenos offset to the right. Rising up in all its beauty, it offers its three-quarter perspective and surveys the rocky plateau; to the left appears the busy silhouette of the Erechtheum, punctuated by its caryatids.

A marble framework
Borrowed from the techniques of carpentry, the ceilings of the Propylaea imitate wooden forms, with their caissons and beams.

A technological *tour de force*
The Propylaea clings to the slope that climbs up the last projection of the Acropolis. Bold terracing made it possible to anchor the two wings of the monumental entrance to the rock.

Mnesicles skilfully solved the tricky equation posed by the placement of the Propylaea. In particular, he successfully achieved an apparent symmetry between the asymmetrical wings framing the entrance portico. At the outset, he was keen to include, on either side of the axial passage, two majestic rooms measuring about 22 by 13 m, with three inner columns supporting the ceiling. These rooms, which were never built, were to have formed the *pinakotheke* or picture gallery (which was finally installed in the north-west room) and, in all probability, the *glyptotheke* or sculpture gallery, containing the *ex votos*.

The decoration of the Propylaea was limited, where the façades were concerned, to just the proportional features peculiar to the Doric style: no bas-reliefs on friezes and no sculptures on metopes. The purely architectural austerity was intended both to be in harmony with the Parthenon and to contrast with the Parthenon's ornamental opulence, as if to underscore the difference between a civic edifice and a religious building. Apart from the traditional polychromy, the marble ceiling coffers were covered with a lapis lazuli blue, set off by gold stars which emphasized the wealth of this work.

Page 202 and 203
Dominating the city of Athens
Commanding the steep sides of the Acropolis, transformed by supporting walls into a sacred fortress, the Propylaea and the Temple of Nike proudly glorify Athenian Classicism.

Like a sacred bastion towering over the visitor on his right, the small Ionic Temple of Athena Nike (the Victorious) stood proudly on a natural promontory in front of the Propylaea. Its remarkably elegant, four-columned amphiprostyle façades framed a tiny square *naos*, 5 m by 5, the entrance to which, without any *pronaos*, was preceded by two slender marble pillars.

Erected in about 421, shortly after the death of Pericles, this small temple was decorated with a continuous sculpted frieze all around it. It depicted, around Athena and the assembly of the gods, battle scenes alluding to the Persian wars. It was, in reality, a triumphal hymn offered to the patron goddess Athena Polias.

The Complexity of the Erechtheum

Opposite the north portico of the Parthenon, which stands above it, the Erechtheum is at once one of the most complicated and one of the most refined temples of Classical religious architecture. It was built between 421 and 406 B.C. The building forms a marked contrast with the Parthenon, both because of the difference in scale and because of its busy structure, as compared with the powerful unifying volume of the temple built by Ictinus.

Made entirely of Pentelic marble – like the other buildings of the Acropolis – this sanctuary, with its puzzling plan, developed not only on two right-angled axes, but on two levels as well. It was dedicated to sundry gods and heroes, starting with Athena Polias, Erechtheus-Poseidon and Hephaestus, not forgetting either the tomb of King Cecrops or the enclosure of Pandrosos, his daughter, who is alleged to have invented weaving, and who was paid homage by the *ergastinai,* the young maidens of the Athenian nobility called upon to weave the *peplos*. This same holy enclosure was also associated with the cult of the olive – venerated as the emblem of the goddess – and an olive tree actually grew in the *temenos* of the temple.

These multiple functions involved a host of specific areas and rooms which were spread throughout the building, whence the complexity of its organization. Just as the Parthenon stood close to the southern crag, the Erechtheum was built on the edge of the chasm to the north of the Acropolis. The building is oriented east/west. To the east it has a handsome Ionic hexastyle façade in the purest Classical style. Behind the six prostyle columns, the side walls of the *cella* are bare. Inside is the oblong *naos* dedicated to Athena, in which stood the cult statue.

At the back of the *naos*, which takes up the front part of the huge *cella* which is

An unusual organization
Considered disconcerting by travellers in the early nineteenth century, the complex forms of the Erechtheum, on the Acropolis, still leave modern historian perplexed. But the charm of the caryatids never failed to seduce onlookers, as is clear from this engraving by the English painter Edward Dodwell.

The very opposite of Doric "sobriety"
The visitor looking at the Erechtheum from the Propylaea discovers an asymmetrical composition, the structures of which defy logic, but stem from an almost "picturesque" organization. It was erected between 421 and 406 B.C., after Pericles' building programme, in an altogether innovative spirit.

now completely empty, there were, it would seem, two twin areas, one dedicated to Hephaestus, the other to Boutes, brother of Erechtheus. These two rooms adjoined the *naos* of Athena, rather than the chevet of the temple. Because of the steep slope to the west of the plateau of the Acropolis, they were in fact situated 4 m above the rocky floor of the western room of the temple. This part of the building has an unusual façade. Beneath the pediment, four engaged columns separate the openings set half-way up, like windows.

The organization of the Erechtheum on its east/west axis is part of a strictly rectangular plan, and its dimensions do not exceed 22.76 m in length and 11.63 m in width, which is very small when compared with the Parthenon.

Let us now take a look at the structure governed by the north south axis, which is no less unusual. It starts from a lower level and crosses the axis which determines the upper level. To the north, noticeably lower than the sanctuary of Athena Polias and offset towards the west, there is a salient portico which projects some way towards the cliff. It is an Ionic tetrastyle with an angle shaft on either side. In the direction of the empty space which it overlooks, it forms a sort of open canopy. Its six tall and slender columns, set well apart, help to make up for the difference in level. They measure 7.63 m in height, with a diameter of 0.82 m, in other words a proportion of more than 1:9. The intercolumniation measures 3 m.

Following on from this portico, a long covered area, dedicated to Erechtheus-Poseidon, occupies the lower level of the temple at its chevet. We should point out that Erechtheus, the Athenian hero who presided over the city's origins, was associated with Poseidon who, like Athena, laid claim to the city of Athens. This narrow room, delimited by the west façade with its windows, ended in a stairway offering

A "Baroque" composition
The west façade of the Erechtheum: between a large north wing in the shape of a canopy forming the north portico, and a small shrine-like building whose roof is supported by six statues of women – the caryatids – to the south, the end of the main body of the building has engaged columns between which there are tall windows. A decidedly uncommon and surprising architectural formula!

Page 207
The Ionic elegance of the Erechtheum
Conversely, the east façade of the Erechtheum shows a dazzling purity: the hexastyle portico in the Ionic style, with its slender columns standing on moulded bases and its capitals with their lofty volutes, contrasts strongly with the west side.

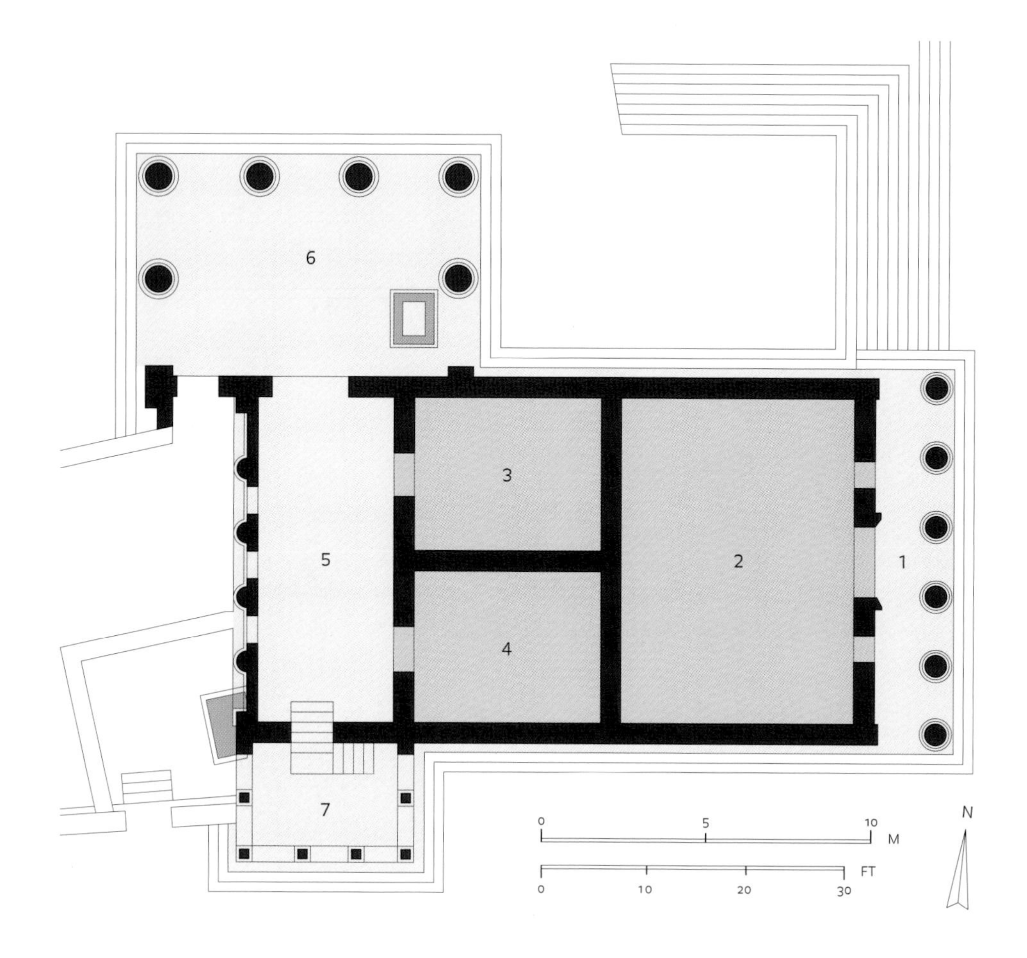

Open to the four winds
Plan of the Erechtheum, on the Acropolis of Athens. The building combines various places of worship, connected with rituals to Athena, which have shaped the construction of many elements which all have a specific orientation.
1 Prostyle columns
2 Sanctuary of Athena
3 Sanctuary of Boutes
4 Sanctuary of Hephaestus
5 Sanctuary of Erechtheus-Poseidon
6 Sanctuary of Poseidon
7 Caryatid Porch

Page 209 above
Dawn on the south façade
Recently restored with meticulous care, the Erechtheum, where damage to its marble stonework has been dressed, like so many wounds, offers the sight of its powerfully worked-out asymmetrical layout to the admiration of the visitor.

Page 209 below
Ionic moulding
The subtle moulding at the base of the Ionic columns of the Erechtheum: the tori, with their scotias, introduce a dialogue with the fluted grooves.

access to the famous Caryatid Porch situated opposite the Parthenon. This porch constitutes a counterpart to the northern canopy in the sense that it, too, has four façade supports and a shaft on each side at the corner. This arrangement emphasizes the north-south axis, of which it forms the southern extremity.

This Caryatid Porch, which is inaccessible from the outside, is accentuated by six statues of young maidens or *korai*. It is in the purest Ionic tradition – like the Treasury of Siphnos at Delphi, where the caryatids predate those of the Erechtheum by a century.

The Erechtheum is a far cry from the Classical programme of the peristyle sanctuary and its sober incorporation in a rectangular layout, governed by a colonnade with a succession of repeated shafts resting on the stylobate. Here, the façades sometimes present an Ionic hexastyle and sometimes engaged columns forming, in relief, part of the masonry of a wall pierced by windows, and sometimes, too, an Ionic tetrastyle awning that is salient, or on the other side the Caryatid Porch.

In a word, the architectural organization is completely reversed. The space explodes, as it were, in different directions, and the levels grow in number, like internal linking structures. A certain "Baroque" spirit suffused this late fifth-century art, heralding new solutions which would be entertained by the Hellenistic age and then the Roman world. There was a movement towards a light style and a refined elegance, which was underpinned by this overall return to the Ionic model. From this point on, this latter was no longer confined to the inner structures of Doric buildings. It took the place of a certain "monopoly" of the Doric style in Greece.

So the Ionian spirit that underscored the ethnic kinship between Athens and the cities of Asia was asserted, not unlike a kind of manifesto, to exalt Greekness in its

Lightness rediscovered
The Caryatid Porch, which is completely off-centre and stands out against a bare wall, is the Ionic version of the humanized tetrastyle. Young women with elegant drapery take the place of columns. From this time on, casts took the place of the originals, but the disappearance of ungainly supporting "posts" restores the building to its original quality of lightness.

Page 211
Maidens honoring Athena
Attributed to the workshop of the sculptor Alcamenes, the caryatids, wearing the *peplos*, effortlessly support the canopy-shaped roof of the south shrine of the Erechtheum.

Contemporary with the Parthenon
The Hephaesteum – long known as the Theseum because of its sculpted decoration devoted to the hero Theseus – stands on the edge of the Agora of Athens. Built between 449 and 444, it is a Classical Doric hexastyle which has come down to us virtually intact. It is dedicated to Hephaestus, god of fire and forge – in other words of craftsmanship.

A Classical peripteral temple
The south portico of the Hephaesteum: the marble structure has survived above the colonnade which runs around the building, and consists of thirty-four shafts. The *cella*, still in place, is only missing the inner columns which used to divide it into three naves.

A lofty façade
The wide intercolumniation that is a feature of the portico surrounding the Hephaesteum in Athens is typical of the development of the Doric style in the middle of the fifth century B.C.

opposition to the Achaemenids. Once again, this *leitmotif,* which embraced connotations contrasting democracy with autocratic systems, would illuminate the architecture of the period with a far-reaching significance.

The Agora and the Temple of Hephaestus

As the starting point of the Panathenaic Procession, the Agora was both the political hub of the City and the seat of democracy, where the Citizens' Assembly would meet. It was not a development in terms of city-planning, but rather a series of works occurring at intervals over several centuries. After the departure of the Persians, it was important to reconstruct civic and religious buildings alike.

Pericles commissioned, in particular, a Doric temple dedicated to Hephaestus, god of craftsmen and potters, which discreetly dominates the square. The Hephaesteum (often called the Theseum), which was built between 449 and 444 B.C., was a Classical peripteral hexastyle of marble throughout, measuring 100 feet in length (*hecatompedon*) and governed by the 4:9 proportion like the Parthenon. Its dimensions (14.45 by 32.51 m) and its plan (six columns widthwise and thirteen lengthwise) accentuated the presence of a "vestibule" preceding the *pronaos,* whose oblong area was in turn emphasized by an architrave running the whole length of the building, as in the Temple of Poseidon on Cape Sunium. Although only slightly larger than this latter, the Hephaesteum shows an inner organization of the *naos* that borrows the principle adopted by Ictinus for the inner colonnade of the Parthenon – the area was divided into three naves and a portico running crosswise behind the cult statue (seven columns lengthwise, and four widthwise). This arrangement vanished when the temple was converted into a church.

The decoration includes an "Ionic" frieze decorating the *cella* with high reliefs, depicting the heroic Deeds of Theseus and the war against the Centaurs. The metopes represented the Labors of Heracles and the Feats of Theseus.

Sacred City-planning

So the work planned by Pericles, with the help of architects and sculptors who carried out the programme for the renovation of Athens after the Persian wars, and of the Acropolis in particular, culminated with the dedication to the goddess Athena of all the buildings now covering the sacred outskirts of the upper city. The actual organization of this holy city, which took full advantage of the complicated lie of the land, had taken into account the location of the cliffs and the steep slope of the upper plateau, to give birth to an energetic and unexpected complex.

Unlike the grid system governing the Hippodamian city designed for human beings, here, for the sacred city, the planning was refined and subtle. Thus, for anyone emerging on to the Acropolis, after negotiating the Propylaea, the two temples – Parthenon and Erechtheum, whose converging perspective had the effect of intensifying the space – formed the framework for a main upper square, which is where the annual Panathenaic Procession ended. This very loose organization also contrasted with the rigour of the overall plan of Persepolis, which was different in every way. Once again – as in the contrast between the strict arrangement of the bas-reliefs of the Procession of the Tributaries and the free quality of the procession dedicated to Athena on the Parthenon frieze – the antithesis between autocracy and democracy burst forth in an exemplary symbolic – not to say semiological – demonstration.

Rigor and repetition
On its south façade, looking out over the Agora of Athens, the Hephaesteum plays on the horizontal layout of the lines which punctuate the Doric columns. The fact that the ceiling caissons are no longer there creates a play of shadows, as the marble structure above is projected on to the wall of the *cella*.

Page 215
A broad projecting vestibule
The lightening of the structures is clear to see in the Hephaesteum of Athens. Note the absence of any support in the second row of columns, forming a wide covered area which precedes the *pronaos*.

Conclusion

Reason – the Great Organizer

Page 217
Hermes leading the dance
A votive relief included beneath the silhouette of an architectural pediment surmounted by acroteria. Behind Hermes, the Cecropides and the child Erechthonius hold hands as they perform a dance. Late sixth–early fifth century B.C. (Athens, Acropolis Museum)

Throughout their history, the Greeks have built a great deal – sanctuaries, theatres, and fortifications, often constructed from magnificent materials, strewn over the various regions of the eastern Mediterranean, from the shores of the Aegean and Anatolia to Sicily and southern Italy. A pervasive stylistic unity and a fundamental consistency and coherence provide this heritage with its own specific character.

This survey of Greek architecture, which consists for the most part of temples – as opposed to much rarer civic and military buildings – may give the reader the impression of an abundance of solutions to a simple form. These variations which affect the religious building, and the peripteral temple in particular, raise two questions: why are no two temples the same? And why were the architects forever intent upon revitalizing the plans of their sanctuaries?

The answer to these questions is probably that, in the thinking of the Ancients, each place of worship had to be unique. This would also be the case in the Middle Ages, when each church differed from the next. In each instance, people would attempt to offer the deity an even more perfect work. A passage from Plato's *Republic* clearly expressed this desire for constant renewal. The task of the architects, wrote the philosopher, is to "produce bodies which did not previously exist". There is no better way of defining the role of the builder.

Furthermore, architectural concerns are omnipresent in Plato's work. When it is a matter of defining beauty, he specifically states, in the *Philebus*: "What I understand here by beauty ... is not what the common man generally understands by this term, as, for example, the beauty of living things and their representation. On the contrary, it is something rectilinear ... and circular, with the surfaces of solid bodies composed by means of the compasses, the cord, and the set square. For these forms are not, like the others, beautiful under certain conditions; they are always beautiful in themselves." What better definition of architecture could Plato have come up with? For the terms which he uses – "compasses, cord and set square" – are the very tools which symbolize the work of the architect, the instruments of geometric and mathematical design, which give rise to the *symmetria* and harmony of creation.

And as if in confirmation of all this, does not Anaxagoras of Clazomenae (500–428) – who had numbered Pericles, Euripides and perhaps Socrates among his disciples in Athens – assert this supremacy of the intelligence by making everything subordinate to "organizing reason"? For the clear organization of the building is nothing other than the key to *eurhythmia* and *commodulatio*. In architecture, as in philosophy, the mind tends to construct a system where everything flows from a single principle, where "everything is in everything", to use the words of Anaxagoras.

A victorious young athlete
This stele, discovered at Cape Sunium, south of Athens, which dates from about 450 B.C., shows a naked young man putting on the victor's crown. (Athens, National Museum)

Proof of this rationalization of building is to be found in the famous Skeuotheke, or stone Arsenal designated for Athenian galleys, which the architect Philon had built at Piraeus, and whose precise description, dating from the latter half of the fourth century B.C., has come down to us in the form of a stele with a ninety-seven-line inscription. The quantified description of the work, conceived as rigorous

Page 220
The Theatre of Dionysus
The *cavea* set on the southern slope of the Acropolis has undergone lengthy developments since it was moved, in 498 B.C., from the site where theatrical works in honour of Dionysus were performed, which was originally located in the Agora. The main features of this building – as it can be seen today – are from the Graeco-Roman period.

"Reserved" seats
In the Theatre of Dionysus, the rows of seats earmarked for distinguished spectators are distinctively furnished with nothing less than "armchairs" on the edge of the *orchestra*. The theatre, a place for ideological debate, where the concepts of freedom and democracy were aired, would undergo a gradual political transformation, when it was used for meetings of the *ecclesia*, that is the community of citizens wielding executive power.

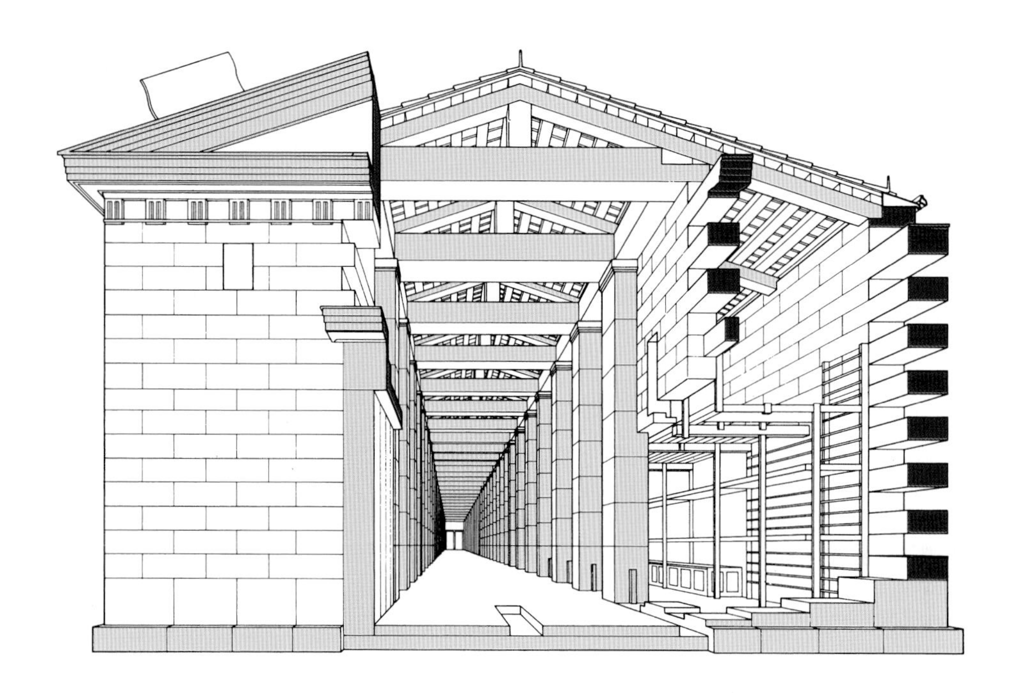

The Arsenal of Athens
Known as the Skeuotheke, or "galley store", built by the architect Philon at Piraeus, the building dating from the latter half of the fourth century B.C. was so well described by an inscription discovered on a stele that it has been possible to reconstruct how it looked. But was the description just a draft?

"quantity surveying", shows that architectural creation operates by way of a concept, well before it takes on the tangible form of a building. Based on a three-dimensional system verbally set forth by the architect, a contractor must be in a position to carry out the project, basing his work on the current rules governing the technique of building. We are dealing here with a formulation which is akin to the architecture dictated in great historical or revealed writings – the Arch of David, the Temple of Ezekiel, the Temple and the Palace of Solomon, and so on.

This architecture, which is verbal rather than conceived on the drawing-board, explains, in a straightforward manner, the use of key proportions, and measurements and modules expressed in round figures, as we have come across them throughout this study: the *hecatompedon*, or 100-foot temple, the Heraion of Samos, measuring 100 by 200 Samian feet, and so on.

This primacy of the concept or design includes and involves the role of the philosopher in architectural creation: "Let no man venture here if he is not a geometer", wrote Plato, as if to underline the importance of the grasp of eternal ideas in the process of creation.

With the advent of an ideal architecture, it was the ideal city of *The Republic* which was brought together with the "conceptual" monument. The organization of space governed the organization of society. And there was good cause to contrast the democratic approach of Athens, illustrated by Aeschylus' tragedy *The Persians*, which was staged in the Theatre of Dionysus, at the foot of the Acropolis, to extol the Greek victory at Salamis over the Achaemenids with the despotic power of Darius and Xerxes even if it was Ionic columns which presided over the construction of the Apadana at Persepolis and Greek sculptors who worked on the Procession of the Tributaries.

For in the great clash between Greeks and Persians, the least we can do is acknowledge a shared desire to transcend the human condition through art and architecture.

An Athenian funerary stele
Quite removed from the movement of action, the art of funerary steles in the fourth century B.C. embraced a calm hieratic quality, conjuring up the sadness of mourning – a melancholy which the prospect of haunting the Elysian fields fails to overcome. (Athens, National Museum)

The Monument of Lysicrates in Athens
This marble *tholos*, which stands at the foot of the Acropolis in Athens, was erected in 335–334. A purely emblematic work, it was built as a shrine designed to house a bronze Dionysiac tripod. Its cylindrical mass is flanked by Corinthian columns, surmounted by a frieze illustrating a hymn to Dionysus.

Chronological Table

The Lion Gate at the Acropolis of Mycenae

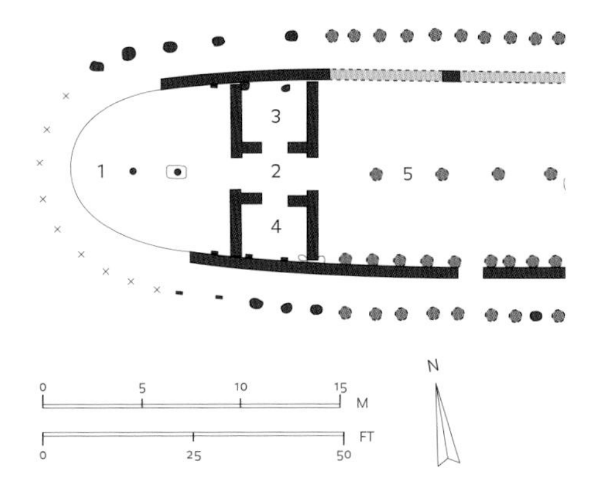

Detail of the plan of the Heroon of Lefkandi with its "apsidal" colonnade

Monuments

2200–1000 B.C.
The Age of the Mycenaeans

16th century	Mycenae: First architectural works, pit graves, Royal Circle, and treasuries
1250–1220	*Tholos*-tombs: "Treasury of Atreus", "Tomb of Clytemnestra"
13th century	Hight of architectural achievement at Mycenae: cyclopean masonry: palace and *megaron*
12th century	Destruction of the Mycenaean monuments

1000–600 B.C.
Colonization

11th–8th century	First "apsidal" rooms with rounded chevet
8th century	Surrounding (peripteral) porticoes of the so-called "veranda" type on wooden pillars: Megaron A and Megaron B at Thermum, Heroon at Lefkandi, Palace of Apollo at Eretria
Late 7th century	Temple of Apollo at Thermum, *Hecatompedon* of Ephesus Birth of the peristyle

Historical Events

2200–1000 B.C.

c. 2200	Arrival of the Achaeans in Greece
c. 1650	Linear A script
c. 1600	The Achaeans in the Peloponnese
c. 1500	Destruction of Thera (Santorini)
c. 1450–1400	The Mycenaeans plunder Crete
Late 15th century	Decline of Cnossus Linear B script
c. 1400–1200	Mycenaean expansion in the Mediterranean
c. 1230–1180	Invasion of the "Sea Peoples" in the Near East
12th century	Dorian and Ionian invasions in Greece: decline of the Mycenaeans

1000–600 B.C.

8th century	Work of Homer Alphabetic script Foundation of Carthage (Phoenicians)
776	First Olympic Games
8th century	Start of the colonization of the Mediterranean basin
756	Foundation of Cumae (southern Italy)
c. 750	End of the royalty in Athens
740	Foundation of Zancle (Sicily)
733	Foundation of Syracuse (Sicily)
710	Foundation of Tarentum
700	Chalcidice (Macedonia) colonized

The entrance to the "Treasury of Atreus" at Mycenae

A fresco discovered on the Acropolis of Mycenae

600–550 B.C.
The Archaic Period

c. 600 Heraion of Olympia: "petrification": columns transposed into stone
c. 595 Aeolic capital in Asia Minor
c. 590 Temple of Apollo at Syracuse
Appearance of the Ionic and Doric orders
580 Pediments of the temple of Corfu
570–560 Rhoecus and Theodorus build the dipteron of Samos (abandoned in 540)
560 Artemision D at Ephesus by Chersiphron, Metagenes and Theodorus
c. 560 Pre-Parthenon of Pisistratus (1st phase)

c. 600 Legislation of Draco in Athens
Foundation of Marseilles
c. 585–525 Anaximenes
582 Pythian Games at Delphi
c. 580 Foundation of Agrigentum
566 Great Panathenaea in Athens
561–547 Reign of Croesus in Lydia
c. 561–528 Pisistratus, tyrant of Athens
559–529 Reign of Cyrus II of Persia

The "petrified" columns of the Temple of Hera at Olympia

550–500 B.C.
From Paestum to Persepolis

540 Second Heraion of Samos, built by Polycrates
From 540 Palace of Pasargadae for Cyrus
c. 540 The "Basilica" at Paestum
535 Tunnel of Eupalinus at Samos
530 First Temple of Apollo at Didyma
c. 530 Peplos-clad *korai:* Acropolis of Athens
525 Eleusis: first Telesterion
525 Delphi: frieze of the Treasury of Siphnos
c. 500 Paestum: Temple of Athena ("Ceres")
520–510 Susa: Achaemenid palace
520–480 Athens: Pre-Parthenon, in marble (2nd phase)
513 Persepolis: Apadana of Darius
510 Smiling *kore*: Acropolis of Athens
510–470 Selinus: Temple G, Apollonion
before 500 Agrigentum: Temple of Heracles

547 Croesus clashes with Cyrus II: Ionia taken by the Persians
Death of Thales of Miletus and Anaximander
539 Cyrus takes Babylon
529–522 Reign of Cambyses II, king of the Persians
c. 530 Pythagoras at Croton and Metapontum
521–486 Darius I, king of the Persians
511 The Greeks of Thrace conquered
510 Athens: fall of the tyranny
508/507 Athens: reforms of Cleisthenes

The façade of the Archaic Temple of Athena at Paestum

500–480 B.C.
The Dawn of Classicism

c. 500 Persepolis: reliefs of the Procession of the Tributaries, Hall of the Nations
c. 500 Delphi: polygonal wall
495 Aegina: Temple of Athena Aphaia
Sunium: first Temple of Poseidon
487 Delphi: Treasury of the Athenians
480 Paestum: "Tomb of the Diver"
Agrigentum: Olympieion

499 Revolt of the Greek cities of Ionia
c. 498 The temple of Sardis burnt
497–493 Persian repression: Miletus razed to the ground
491–490 Darius attacks Athens and Eretria: first Persian War
490 Greek victory at Marathon
c. 480 Death of Pythagoras
486–465 Reign of Xerxes, king of the Persians
c. 483 Athens: Themistocles builds a fleet
481–478 Xerxes: second Persian War
480 The Acropolis of Athens destroyed
480 Greek victory at Salamis

Detail of the Frieze of the Tributaries in the Apadana of Persepolis

The façade of the "reassembled" Temple of Hera at Selinus

480–450 B.C.
Classicism

c. 480 *Ecclesiasterion* at Metapontum and Paestum
479 Hippodamus rebuilds Miletus
478 Delphi: portico of the Athenians
City wall built around Athens
470 Coroebus enlarges the Telesterion
465–450 Selinus: Temple E dedicated to Hera
460–440 Paestum: second Temple of Hera

480 Theron defeats the Carthaginians
c. 480–406 Euripides
479 Greek victory at Plataea
478 Hieron tyrant of Syracuse
478/477 Foundation of the Delian League
472 *The Persians* by Aeschylus
c. 469–399 Socrates
467/466 Victory of Cimon over the Persians
465 Xerxes assassinated: reign of Artaxerxes
461/460 Reform of Ephialtes in Athens
454 Athenian disaster in Egypt
454 Transfer of the federal Treasury of Delos to Athens

450–430 B.C.
The Age of Pericles

c. 450 Agrigentum: Temple of Hera Lacinia
449 Sunium: Temple of Poseidon
449–444 Athens: the Hephaesteum
447–438 Athens: construction of the Parthenon by Phidias, Callicrates and Ictinus
447–442 Phidias: the metopes of the Parthenon
438 Phidias sculpts the Athena Parthenos
438–432 The pediments of the Parthenon
437–432 Athens: the Propylaea of Mnesicles

449 Peace of Callias with the Persians
446/445 Thirty Years' peace with Sparta
443–429 Pericles becomes Head of State in Athens
c. 432 Death of Phidias
431–421 Peloponnesian War (I)
430 Plague strikes Athens

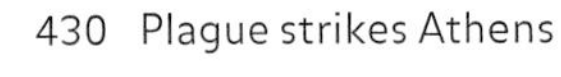

North-west corner of the Parthenon on the Acropolis of Athens

430–400 B.C.
The Decline of Athens

429–390 Bassae: Temple of Apollo Epicurius
c. 430 Agrigentum: "Temple of Concord"
Segesta: unfinished temple
421–406 Athens: the Erechtheum
420 Xanthus: Nereid Monument
421 Athens: Temple of Athena Nike
Caryatids of the Erechtheum
415 Segesta: work on the temple is halted
From 400 Syracuse: fortress of Euryalos

429 Death of Pericles
423–404 Reign of Darius II in Persia
419 Alcibiades appointed general
415 Catastrophic Athenian expedition in Sicily
413–404 Peloponnesian War (II): defeat of Athens
411 Oligarchy of the Four Hundred in Athens
409 Selinus razed to the ground by the Carthaginians
408 Cyrus II governs Asia Minor
406 Agrigentum taken
405–367 Dionysius I, tyrant of Syracuse
405 Lysander defeats the Athenians
401 Revolt of Cyrus II and retreat of the Ten Thousand

The Temple of Athena Nike on the west of the Acropolis of Athens

The east façade of the Erechtheum on the Acropolis of Athens

Monuments

400–360 B.C.
A World of Fortresses

c. 400 Friezes at Bassae
380 Epidaurus: Temple of Asclepius
4th century Fortresses in Attica: Phylae, Aegosthena, Eleutherae, Rhamnus
c. 370 Delphi: *Tholos* of Marmaria
378 Delos: Temple of Apollo (VI)
370 Wall of Messene built by Epaminondas

360–330 B.C.
The End of Classicism

356 Ephesus: destruction of the Artemision
From 350 Halicarnassus: Tomb of Mausolus
c. 350 Epidaurus: *Tholos* of Polyclitus the Younger
342–330 Lindus: Temple of Athena (Rhodes)
c. 340 Priene:Temple of Athena Polias
335/334 Athens: Monument of Lysicrates
330 Ephesus: work starts on the new Artemision
330 Eleusis: portico of the Telesterion by Philon
330 Paestum: painted tombs (Lucanian influence)
330 Epidaurus: theatre

Historical Events

400–360 B.C.

399 Socrates condemned to death
387 Plato founds the Academy
386 The King's Peace
377 Mausolus, satrap of Caria
371 Battle of Leuctra (Thebans defeat the Spartans)
367–365 Plato visits Sicily
362 Battle of Mantinea (defeat of Thebes)

360–330 B.C.

359 Philip II, king of Macedonia
353 Death of King Mausolus
348 Philip II takes Olynthus
347 Death of Plato
Alexander becomes a student of Aristotle
336 Alexander general of the Greeks
333 Battle of Issus
331 Foundation of Alexandria
330 Fire at Persepolis

The *tholos* of Athena Pronaia at the site of Marmaria at Delphi

The *tholos*-like Monument of Lysicrates in Athens

Glossary

Abacus: Upper part of the capital in the form of a square flat slab which bears the load of the entablature.
Acanthus: Mediterranean plant with very indented leaves, the shape of which inspired the decoration of Corinthian capitals.
Achaeans: A Greek people who, in about 1600 B.C., invaded the region of the Peloponnese and gave birth to the Mycenaean civilization.
Achaemenids: Dynasty of three Persian kings descended from the legendary Achaemenes. Cyrus II (559–529) founded the Persian Empire which would hold sway from the frontiers of India to Egypt and Asia Minor until 330 B.C.
Acropolis: In Greek cities, this term describes the "upper town" which was the hub of political, religious and military life. Subsequently, it was where there were often only the community's sanctuaries.
Acroterium: Architectural ornamentation in relief, which surmounts the corners and top of a pediment.
Adytum: Secret room in a temple, reserved exclusively for priests.
Aeolic (capital): An Archaic Greek capital formed by two volutes projecting vertically and separated by a palmette.
Agora: In the Greek city, the public place where citizens' assemblies were held. Describes the political hub of the city.
Amazonomachy: A fight involving Amazons, in which barbarian warriors of Antiquity mount horses and are armed with bow and sword.
Amphiprostyle: Describes a temple whose front and rear façades include two rows of columns.
Anaktoron: Sacred shrine housing statues of worship.
Anastylosis: An operation consisting in reconstructing an ancient building mainly with materials found on the spot.
Annulets: Small mouldings or grooves which surround the base of a Doric capital.
Antae, in antis: The *antae* are front walls, which end in a pilaster. The Latin term *in antis*, "between the *antae*", is used for columns set between two *antae*.
Apadana: Throne room of Achaemenid palaces, usually with a large number of columns (a hypostyle area).
Apsidal: Describes the chevet of a rounded apse-shaped building, by analogy with the form of the sanctuary.
Architrave: Beam or lintel resting on supports (columns or pillars) and forming the lower part of an entablature.
Auriga or charioteer: The driver of a chariot in ancient races.
Baldachin: Light structure or shrine-like aedicula designed to house an altar or statue.
Barbarians: Describes, for the Greeks of Antiquity, any foreign people. It did not originally have derogatory connotations.
Basket: Main feature of a Corinthian capital formed by a flared body shaped like an upturned, truncated cone. Acanthus leaves sprout from the basket.
Bastion: Part of a fortification which forms a salient projection in a wall.
Bouleuterion: A meeting hall where the council (or *boule*) of a Greek city would sit. An area designed for political assemblies.
Bracket (corbel): Decorative feature in the form of a support placed beneath the cornice of a frieze or beneath the slope of a pediment.
Bronze Age: The period characterized by the use of bronze-working; in the Mediterranean, between the third and second millennia B.C.
Caisson: An element embellishing the lower part of a ceiling, consisting of a panel edged with projecting beams and mouldings.
Campaniform: Describes the base of a column with the shape of a bell. May also be applied to a capital whose basket is flared.
Canon: Law of proportions governing the human body in the Greek sculpture of Antiquity. Ratios of dimensions making up a conventional code of harmony applied to the depiction of men and women.
Capital: Decorative feature surmounting the shaft of a column or pillar on which the architrave rests. The capital consists of an echinus or basket which supports an abacus. Its decoration is governed by the Classical orders.
Caryatid: In architecture, a support in the form of a female statue. According to Vitruvius, the name derives from the women of Caryae, who were reduced to slavery as a punishment for having collaborated with the Persians.
Casing (door): Architectural term describing the uprights or frame of a door.
Cavea: The concave semicircular auditorium of the theatre, where the audience was seated on tiers.
Cella: The main body of an ancient temple which, in addition to the *naos*, housing the statue of the deity, also contains a *pronaos* forming the vestibule, an *opisthodomos* at the chevet, and in some cases an *adytum*, or secret area, and a treasury.
Centaur: Mythological creature formed by the torso of a man and the body of an animal (a horse).
Centauromachy: Legendary fight against the centaurs who symbolized brutality and savagery.
Chimaera: Mythical monster with fantastic shapes, combining various fearsome animals: lion, snake, and so on.
Chryselephantine (statue): Describes a sculpture enriched with gold and ivory.
Commodulatio: Use of proportions based on the multiples of a single module, designed to obtain formal and rhythmic harmony.
Corbelled vault: Describes a vault made with horizontal courses, one jutting out beyond the last. The corbelled vault is a false vault.
Corinthian: Architectural order characterized in particular by the capital with a basket decorated with acanthus leaves and horns of plenty at the corners, the crockets of which are akin to the volutes of the Ionic order.
Course: In the stonework of a wall, a horizontal row of blocks of the same height. A wall is made up of several superimposed courses.
Cuneus: In an ancient theatre, the corner-shaped division of the *cavea*, delimited by radial stairs.
Curtain wall: Straight section of wall in a city wall, situated between two projecting towers.
Cyclopean: Describes the stonework of a colossal wall, built with huge, irregular blocks, reckoned to be the work of the Cyclopes.
Cyclops: Legendary giant with just one eye in the middle of the forehead.
Daphnephorion: From *daphnephore*, meaning one bearing laurels, whence: a sanctuary dedicated to Apollo wearing a crown of laurels.
Decastyle: Architectural term describing a building whose façade has ten columns.
Dentils: Decorative features formed by a series of cubic, salient teeth, set apart, embellishing a cornice.
Diazoma: Promenade in the form of a semicircle, horizontally dividing the *cavea* of an ancient theatre.
Dipteral: Describes a building surrounded by a double row of peripteral columns.
Dorians: Greek-speaking people who, in several waves, invaded Greece between the thirteenth and eleventh centuries B.C., laying waste to the Mycenaean kingdoms.
Doric: In architecture, one of the Greek orders, characterized by columns with no base, with a

capital consisting of a gorgerin (necking grooves), an echinus and an abacus.

Dromos: Describes the access corridor – in a stair cavity lined with tall walls – of a domed Mycenaean tomb.

Drum: Cylindrical element forming the shaft of a column. Its diameter is always greater than its height.

Echinus: Main part of the Doric capital in the form of a small cushion or bell, bounded by a round moulding between the gorgerin and the abacus. Its outline would develop from a flattened torus into a more elongated half-heart.

Egg and dart: Decorative relief moulding in the form of juxtaposed eggs and darts.

Ecclesia: Assembly of the people in the Greek city.

Emporion: A place for trading, market-place.

Engaged (or embedded) column: Describes a column or other feature partly embedded in a wall, from which it projects.

Entablature: In classical architecture, the various horizontal parts which surmount the supports (columns or pillars). From bottom to top it consists of the architrave, the frieze, and the cornice.

Epipole: The upper city, in particular at Syracuse.

Erinyes: The Greek goddesses of vengeance.

Eros: Deity of love. God of amorous passion. Also describes physical attraction between people.

Eurhythmia: Harmonious combination of proportions.

Exedra: In ancient architecture, generally describes a semicircular or rectangular space in a building, forming a recess in an external elevation. Often with a semicircular seat lining it.

Ex voto: Art object – picture, sculpture, crown – dedicated to a god following a wish by the donor.

False (vault): Corbelled vault. Does not use radial archstones.

Flutes: Vertical and parallel grooves which decorate the surface of the cylindrical shaft of a column, lending it a rising motion and an energetic formal quality.

Foot: Unit of measurement generally used in ancient construction and architecture. The Doric foot equals 32.7 cm, the Samian foot 34.95 cm, and the Ionian foot 29.4 cm. The Greeks also used the cubit *(pechus)* of 52.45 cm.

Gable: Upper triangular part of a wall parallel with the trusses bearing the sloping surfaces of a roof. In the Greek temple, it merges with the pediment.

Geometric (pottery): Describes the decoration of Greek pottery (twelfth to eighth centuries B.C.) combining patterns obtained with compasses, triangles and meanders.

Gigantomachy: Legendary fight between mythical giants doing battle with the gods.

Gorgerin (necking grooves): In architecture, the lower part of a capital, extending the main part of the column.

Gorgon: Fearsome female monster whose hair consists of snakes. On Athena's shield, she symbolized the apotropaic power of the goddess, to ward off danger.

Gnomon: Vertical shaft whose shadow makes it possible to observe the height of the sun, the dates of the solstices, and even the time of day, thanks to the sundial.

Harpy: Winged monster with a woman's or bird's head. With her talons she could kidnap souls.

Hecatompedon: Literally: 100 feet long. A Greek temple with an actual length of 100 feet.

Heroon: Temple or monument in honor of a hero, which designates a deified figure, protector of a city.

Hexastyle: A building whose façade has six columns.

Hippodamian (plan): Describes a town or city plan inspired by Hippodamus of Miletus (fifth century B.C.), architect, geometrician, and surveyor, held to be the inventor of the orthogonal layout.

Holocaust: Sacrifice offered to the gods, to be consumed by fire on the altar.

Hybris: Excess, violence, exaggeration, which the Greeks contrasted with justice (*dike*), and regarded as the source of upheaval and evil.

Hypaethral: Describes an enclosed, but open-roofed, area.

Hyperoon: Dwelling occupying the upper floor of a palace, often reserved for women.

Hypostyle (area): Describes an area whose roof is supported by rows of columns or pillars.

Interaxis: The space between the axes of two columns.

Intercolumniation: The open space between two columns.

Intrados: Concave inner surface of an arch or vault.

Ionic (order): In architecture, the Ionic order is characterized principally by slender columns with a base, a capital embellished by volutes, and an entablature with a continuous frieze.

Isonomia: Political system based on the equality of one and all before the law.

Joist: Diagonal timbers supporting the roof.

Kore: Archaic Greek statue representing a young girl clad in rich apparel, constituting an offering to the gods.

Kouros: Archaic Greek statue representing a young man, standing, sometimes of colossal dimensions. These sculptures were arranged as offerings to the gods in temples.

Lantern: Structure surmounting a roof and pierced by apertures, designed to illuminate the interior of a building.

Lapiths: Legendary people of Thessaly, believed to have put up a valiant fight against the Centaurs.

Libations: Offering made to the gods of a liquid poured over the altar or ground.

Linear B (script) : System of Mycenaean syllabic writing transcribing the early Greek language.

Lintel: Horizontal load-bearing feature in stone or wood surmounting an aperture.

Logos: Source of ideas, and universal reason, among Greek philosophers.

Manteion: Place where the future is consulted, seat of the oracle.

Mausoleum: Huge funerary monument deriving its name from king Mausolus, Graeco-Persian satrap of Caria (377–353 B.C.).

Medusa: Mythical female figure, whose head was covered with snakes, and whose gaze turned her foes to stone. One of the three Gorgons of Greek mythology.

Megaron: Main room of the Mycenaean palace, comprising the hearth and the throne, preceded by a vestibule and an inner courtyard.

Metope: Panel, often sculpted, alternating with the triglyphs in the Doric frieze.

Mimesis: Greek term describing the imitation of reality in artistic representation.

Minoans: Term deriving from Minos, legendary King of Cnossus, used to designate the ancient Cretan civilization (2600–1200 B.C.).

Module: In ancient architecture, a common measurement, traditionally accepted, applied to the various proportions of a building. A unit of measurement governing the ratios between the parts of an building.

Monopteral: Describes a round temple (*tholos*) with a single row of outer columns which support the roof.

Museum of painting ***(pinakotheke):*** Building or room where a collection of paintings was displayed, for example, inside the Propylaea on the Acropolis at Athens.

Museum of sculpture ***(glyptotheke):*** Collection of sculptures. Room where they are shown.

Mutule: Support in the form of a flat corbel, arranged beneath a cornice. In the Doric style, the lower surface – or soffit – was decorated with guttae in relief.

Mycenean: Stemming from the civilization or art of the Achaeans and Mycenae (1500–1100 B.C.).

Naïskos: In Greek architecture, a sacred aedicula or shrine forming an independent chapel inside the temple. It usually contained the effigy of the god.

Naos: In Greek architecture, abode of the god, which takes the form of an inner area containing the divine statue. The holiest part of the *cella* of the temple.

Nomos: Greek term meaning law and justice.

Numen: Pure thought, in its higher form; object of understanding.

Octostyle: A building whose façade has eight columns.

Omphalos: The cosmic egg, navel of the world; at Delphi, the *umbilicus* in the form of a sacred stone.

Opisthodomos: Greek term describing the area in the rear part of the *cella* of a temple. It is often set between the antae (*in antis*), at the chevet of the sanctuary, and could receive offerings.

Orchestra: In Greek theatres, the round area situated at the bottom of the tiers, in front of the stage.

Ordinatio: Latin term describing, in both architecture and art, a common basis for the measurement of the different parts of the work. Often equivalent to the module.

Orders (the): In ancient architecture, describes various structural systems for organizing the proportions of buildings in Doric, Ionic or Corinthian style. Also, a modular system applied to the elevation of a building and its supports, in particular the columns and pilasters with their bases, capitals and entablatures.

Orthogonal: Term describing a right-angled configuration, or a system based on a chessboard layout.

Orthostat: Upright slab, usually decorated with reliefs, covering the bottom of a wall.

Palmette: Decoration in the form of stylized palm leaves.

Panta rhei: "Everything flows", "Everything changes": expression of the pre-Socratic philosopher Heraclitus of Ephesus.

Pantheism: Philosophical system whereby the deity merges with the world and is one with the universe.

Pantheon: Temple dedicated to all the Greek or Roman gods.

Parodos: Side entrance of a Greek theatre, adjoining the *orchestra*.

Peplos: Piece of female Greek attire. Tunic made in a rectangle of woollen fabric, puffed out at the waist by a belt. This is the traditional garment of Athena, woven by the Ergastines for the festival of the Panatheneae.

Peribolos: Enclosure planted with trees surrounding a temple.

Peripteral: Describes a temple surrounded on all sides by a row of columns, forming a peristyle.

Peristyle: Colonnade surrounding a building. The outer peristyle corresponds to the peripteral colonnade.

Phial: Cup used for making libations

Pilaster: Pillar engaged or embedded in the stonework of a wall, from which it projects. It usually has a base and a capital.

Pillar: Vertical stonework support, square, rectangular or cross-shaped, which usually has a base and a capital.

Pithoi: Greek term describing large ceramic vases or crocks, used for storing grain, olives, wine and oil.

Poliorcetics: Military technique to do with the art of besieging cities, with special reference to weaponry and fortifications.

Polis: In Greek, means, literally, the city. Whence: the city in its political sense.

Polygonal (wall): Describes a type of ancient structure formed by large irregular blocks, carefully put together. Often confused with the cyclopean structure, which is less rigorous.

Portico: Alignment of vertical supports connected by lintels or arches. The portico forms an open gallery on the long side of a building.

Postern: In military architecture, a structure with a hidden doorway.

Presocratics (philosophers): In ancient Greece, a group of thinkers prior to Socrates, whose main concern was to try to explain the nature of the universe.

Pronaos: Greek term describing the room or vestibule which precedes the *naos* of a temple.

Propylaeum: Monumental porch, often with a colonnaded façade, giving access to a Greek sanctuary.

Proscenium: Describes the stage, in an ancient theatre: it is the area set between the stage wall (*frons scenae*) and the *orchestra*.

Prostyle: Describes a temple which only has columns on its front façade.

Protome: Representation of the forequarters of a symbolic animal.

Pyre: In Antiquity, an altar of fire which was part of a temple.

Relieving (arch): In architecture, a relieving arch is used to relieve a load-bearing element over an empty area by laterally shifting the thrust on to solid piles.

Rhyton: Ancient horn-shaped drinking vessel, often decorated with an animal protome (lion, horse, bull, ibex). It usually had a ritual function.

Rough hewing: Cutting of a block of stone by roughly hewing the faces which will then be dressed and sculpted.

Saddle-roof: Describes a pitched roof with two slopes running from a single shared ridge.

Satrap: Governor of a Persian province or satrapy.

Sekos: Sacred enclosure, sometimes at the foot of an olive tree surrounded by a palisade. In the classical period, inner room of the temple (*naos*) where the cult statue was placed.

Siren: in Greek mythology, female sea demon and temptress personifying seduction and the dangers of the sea.

Scene: Corresponds first of all to the temporary tent housing theatrical shows, then became identified with the scene set before the *frons scenae*.

Skeuotheke: Arsenal, building constructed to house triremes of the Athenian war fleet.

Slanting cornice: Describes the sloping upper parts which crown a pediment.

Stoa (plural, stoai): Greek term describing a portico supported by columns.

Stylobate: Greek architectural term describing the foundation on which the columns of a building are set.

Symmetria: Arrangement and proportions of a building which lend it its harmony.

Symposion: Banquet during which the guests drink, make up and recite passages. It has given rise to a large *symposion* literature that has come down to us.

Techne: Art and technique, in a word, the science of construction.

Telesterion: Hypostyle building reserved for initiation in the sanctuary of Eleusis.

Temenos: Enclosure dedicated to the gods, area surrounding a temple.

Tetrastyle: Building whose façade has four columns.

Tholos: In Greek architecture, monopteral sanctuary: a temple whose plan is round and elevation cylindrical.

Torus (plural, tori): Semi-circular moulding.

Treasury: Small temple-shaped building which housed offerings in large sanctuaries.

Triclinium: Room in a Roman house serving as dining-room; by extension, a meeting held in it.

Bibliography

Trilithon: Literally: "three stones". Describes the architectural structure formed by two uprights (pillars or columns) joined by a horizontal lintel.
Triglyph: Decorative feature of the Doric frieze, which represents the end of a wooden beam, decorated with two vertical grooves, or glyphs, and bordered by two hemiglyphs. Triglyphs alternate with the metope panels.
Tripylon: Literally, "three doors", or triple door. Describes the entrance hall of a central palace in Persepolis.
Trusses: Timbers joined by a roof ridge, forming the system which supports the roof covering.
Tumulus: Mound covering a tomb or several burial places.
Tyche: Goddess of Fortune, she is often associated with a city, where a temple is dedicated to her.
Tympanum: In Greek architecture, triangular surface between a lintel and two sloping cornices.
Tyrant: A sovereign who has come to power illegally, with the backing of a force of mercenaries or part of the population. By extension, any despotic or autocratic sovereign.
Volute: Decorative spiral motif on the corners of Ionic capitals. Scroll-like ornament stemming from the motif of plant heads (acanthus, fern).
Xoanon (plural, xoana): Crude statue in wood or stone, depicting a deity.

Greece and the Greek World

Architecture et Société – De l'archaïsme grec à la fin de la République romaine, Paris, 1983.
Bammer, Anton: *Architektur und Gesellschaft in der Antike, Zur Deutung baulicher Symbole*, Vienna, 1985.
Bammer, Anton: *Die Architektur des Jüngeren Artemision von Ephesos*, Wiesbaden, 1972.
Bauplanung und Bautheorie der Antike, Diskussionen zur archäologischen Bauforschung, Berlin, 1983.
Berger, Ernst: Bauwerk und Plastik des Parthenon, Parthenon Congress at Basel, April 1980, in: *Antike Kunst*, 1980.
Betancourt, Philip P.: *The Aeolic Style in Architecture, a Survey of its Development in Palestine, the Halicarnassos Peninsula and Greece, 1000–500 B.C.*, Princeton, 1977.
Billot, Marie-Françoise: Recherches aux XVIIIe et XIXe siècles sur la polychromie de l'architecture grecque, in: *Paris – Rome – Athènes*, Exhibition catalogue Paris, 1982.
Carlier, Pierre: *Le IVe siècle grec jusqu'à la mort d'Alexandre*, Nouvelle histoire de l'Antiquité, Paris, 1995.
Chamoux, François: *La Civilisation grecque à l'époque archaïque et classique*, Les grandes Civilisations, Paris, 1963.
Demargne, Pierre: *Naissance de l'art grec*, L'Univers des Formes, Paris, ²1974.
Le Dessin d'architecture dans les sociétés antiques, Strasbourg, 1985.
Ducrey, Pierre: *Guerre et guerriers dans la Grèce antique*, Fribourg, 1985.
Ghyka, Matila C.: *Le Nombre d'Or*, vol.1: *Les Rythmes*, vol. 2: *Les Rites*, Paris, 1931.
Greek Sanctuaries, New Approaches, London, New York, 1993.
Gruben, Gottfried: Die Inselionische Ordnung, in: *Les grands Ateliers d'architecture dans le monde égéen du VIe siècle avant J.-C.*, Paris, 1993.
Gruben, Gottfried and Helmut **Berve**: *Griechische Tempel und Heiligtümer*, Munich, 1961.
Lévy, Edmond: *La Grèce au Ve siècle, de Clisthène à Socrate*, Nouvelle histoire de l'Antiquité, Paris, 1995.
Martin, Roland: *Monde grec*, Architecture universelle, Fribourg, 1966.
Martin, Roland: *L'Urbanisme dans la Grèce antique*, Paris, 1974.
Martin, Roland, Jean **Charbonneaux** and François **Villard**: *Grèce archaïque*, L'Univers des Formes, Paris, 1968.
Martin, Roland, Jean **Charbonneaux** and François **Villard**: *Grèce classique*, L'Univers des Formes, Paris, 1969.
Mauceri, Luigi: *Il Castello Eurialo nella storia e nell'arte*, Catania, reprint 1993.
Mertens, Dieter: L'Architettura del mondo greco d'Occidente, in: *I Greci in Occidente*, Exhibition catalogue, Venice, 1996.
Papaioannou, Kostas, Jean **Ducat**, Jean **Bousquet** *et alii*: *L'Art grec*, L'Art et les grandes Civilisations, Paris, 1993.
Payot, Daniel: *Le Philosophe et l'architecte, sur quelques déterminations philosophiques de l'idée d'architecture*, Paris, 1982.
Popham, M. R., P. G. **Calligas** and L. H. **Sackett**: *Lefkandi II, the Protogeometric Building at Toumba*, Athens, 1993.
Poursat, Jean-Claude: *La Grèce préclassique, des origines à la fin du VIe siècle*, Nouvelle histoire de l'Antiquité, Paris, 1995.
Robertson, Martin: *The Parthenon Frieze*, London, 1975.
Stierlin, Henri: *Grèce d'Asie, Arts et Civilisations classiques de Pergame à Nemroud Dagh*, Paris, Fribourg, 1986.
Stierlin, Henri: *Le Monde de la Grèce*, Paris, 1980.
Vernant, Jean Pierre: *Mythe et pensée chez les Grecs, Etudes de psychologie historique*, Paris, 1966.

Persia

Briant, Pierre: *Darius, les Perses et l'Empire*, Paris, 1992.
Briant, Pierre: *Histoire de l'Empire perse, De Cyrus à Alexandre*, Paris, 1996.
Broneer, O.: *The Tent of Xerxes and the Greek Theater*, University of California Publications in Classical Archaeology I, 12, 1944.
Deshayes, Jean: *Les Civilisations de l'Orient ancien*, Les grandes Civilisations, Paris, 1969.
Gall, H. von: Das persische Königszelt und die Hallenarchitektur in Iran und Griechenland, in: *Festschrift F. Brommer*, Mainz, 1977.
Gall, H. von: Das Zelt des Xerxes und seine Rolle als persischer Raumtyp in Griechenland, *Gymnasium*, 89, 1979.
Ghirshman, Roman: *Perse, Proto-iraniens, Mèdes, Achéménides*, L'Univers des Formes, Paris, 1963.
Ghirshman, Roman, Vladimir **Minorsky** and Ramesh **Sanghavi**, *Le Royaume immortel de Perse*, London, 1971.
Godard, André: *L'Art de l'Iran*, Paris, 1962.
Kleiss, W.: Zur Entwicklung der Achaemenidischen Palastarchitektur, *Iranica Antiqua*, 15, 1980.
Nielsen, Inge: *Hellenistic Palaces, Tradition and Renewal*, Aarhus, 1994.
Perrot, J.: L'Architecture militaire et palatiale des Achéménides à Suse, in: *150 Jahre Deutsches Archäologisches Institut*, Berlin, 1979, Mainz, 1981.
Stierlin, Henri: *Iran des bâtisseurs, 2 500 ans d'architecture*, Geneva, 1971.
Stierlin, Henri: *Le Monde de la Perse*, Paris, 1980.
Stronach, D.: *Pasargadae*, Oxford, 1978.
Stronach, D.: The Royal Garden at Pasargadae, Evolution and Legacy, in: *Archaeologia Iranica et Orientalis, Miscellanea in honorem Louis Vanden Berghe*, Ghent, 1989.

Index – Monuments

INDEX – Persons

Acknowledgements and credits

The author and photographer, and the publisher, are most grateful to the various institutions and museums which have granted permission to take photographs, and in particular:
The National Archaeological Museum, Athens
The Acropolis Museum, Athens
The Archaeological Museum, Delphi
The National Museum, Naples
The Villa Giulia Museum, Rome
The Archaeological Museum, Tarquinia
The Archaeological Museum, Paestum
The Archaeological Museum, Plovdiv
The Archaeological Museum, Izmir
The Archaeological Museum, Tehran
The Museum of Art and History, Geneva.
Certain documents come from the following archives, for which the author and the publishers are also grateful:
Pages 5, 24–25, 45, 47, 53, 131, 132 below, 133, 169, 217: © Giovanni Ricci, Milan.
Page 154: © Claude Bérard, Saint-Sulpice.
Pages 135, 137, 155: © British Museum, London.
Pages 62, 66: © Arthephot/Nimatallah, Paris.
Page 153: © Ken Takase/Arthephot, Paris.
Lastly, the plans published on pages 10–11, 21, 30, 34, 42, 43, 46, 49, 50, 68, 74, 99, 104, 105, 106, 112, 117, 125, 127, 128, 129, 136, 142, 144, 149, 152, 170, 173, 174, 185, 186, 191, 192, 200, 208 and 222 have been specially prepared by Alberto Berengo Gardin, Milan.

All 40 titles at a glance

Each book: US$ 29.99 | £ 16.99 | CDN$ 39.95

"... a truly remarkable publishing event in architecture"
The Architectural Review London

The Ancient World
- The Near East
- Egypt
- Greece
- The Roman Empire
- The Greco-Roman Orient

The Medieval World
- Byzantium
- The Early Middle Ages
- The Romanesque
- High Gothic
- Late Gothic

The Pre-Colombian World
- The Maya
- Mexico
- The Aztecs
- Peru
- The Incas

Islamic Masterpieces
- Islam from Baghdad to Cordoba
- Islam from Cairo to Granada
- Persia
- Asia Minor
- Mughal

The Splendours of Asia
- Hindu India
- Buddhist India
- China
- South-East Asia
- Japan

Stylistic Developments from 1400
- Renaissance
- Baroque in Italy
- Baroque in Central Europe
- Hispanic Baroque
- French Classicism

The Modern Age
- Neo-Classicism and Revolution
- American Architecture
- Art nouveau
- Early Modern Architecture
- Visionary Masters
- International Style
- Post-Modernism
- Green Architecture
- New Forms
- Contemporary Masters

- Collect 40 volumes of TASCHEN'S WORLD ARCHITECTURE in eight years (1996–2003) and build up a complete panorama of world architecture from the earliest buildings of Mesopotamia to the latest contemporary projects.
- The series is grouped into five-volume units, each devoted to the architectural development of a major civilisation, and introducing the reader to many new and unfamiliar worlds.
- Each volume covers a complex architectural era and is written so vividly that most readers will feel the urge to go out and discover these magnificent buildings for themselves.

TASCHEN'S WORLD ARCHITECTURE

"An excellently produced, informative guide to the history of architecture. Accessible to everyone."
Architektur Aktuell, Vienna

"...This is by far the most comprehensive review of recent years."
Frankfurter Rundschau, Frankfurt

"A successful debut of a very promising series."
Architektur & Wohnen, Hamburg, on *Islam from Baghdad to Cordoba*

"...each theme is presented in a very interesting, lively style... it makes you want to set off straight away to see everything with your own eyes."
Baumeister, Munich, on *The Roman Empire*

- TASCHEN'S WORLD ARCHITECTURE presents 6000 years of architectural history in 40 volumes.
- Each volume is a detailed and authoritative study of one specific era.
- The whole series provides a comprehensive survey of architecture from antiquity to the present day. Five volumes will be published each year.
- TASCHEN'S WORLD ARCHITECTURE is a must for all lovers of architecture and travel.
- Renowned photographers have travelled the world for this series, presenting more than 12000 photographs of famous and lesser-known buildings.
- Expert authors guide the reader through TASCHEN'S WORLD ARCHITECTURE with exciting, scientifically well-founded texts that place architecture within the cultural, political and social context of each era.
- The elegant, modern design and the clear, visually striking layout guide the reader through the historical and contemporary world of architecture.
- Influential architectural theories, typical stylistic features and specific construction techniques are separately explained on eye-catching pages.
- Each volume includes between 40 and 50 maps, plans and structural drawings based on the latest scholarly findings and are produced for this series using state-of-the-art computer technology.
- The appendix contains clear chronological tables, giving an instant overview of the correlation between the historical events and architecture of any given civilisation.
- A detailed glossary clearly explains architectural terms.
- An index of names and places ensures quick and easy reference to specific buildings and people.
- Each book contains 240 pages with some 300 color illustrations on high-quality art paper. 240 x 300 mm, hardcover with dust jacket.

Each book: US$ 29.99 | £ 16.99 | CDN$ 39.95

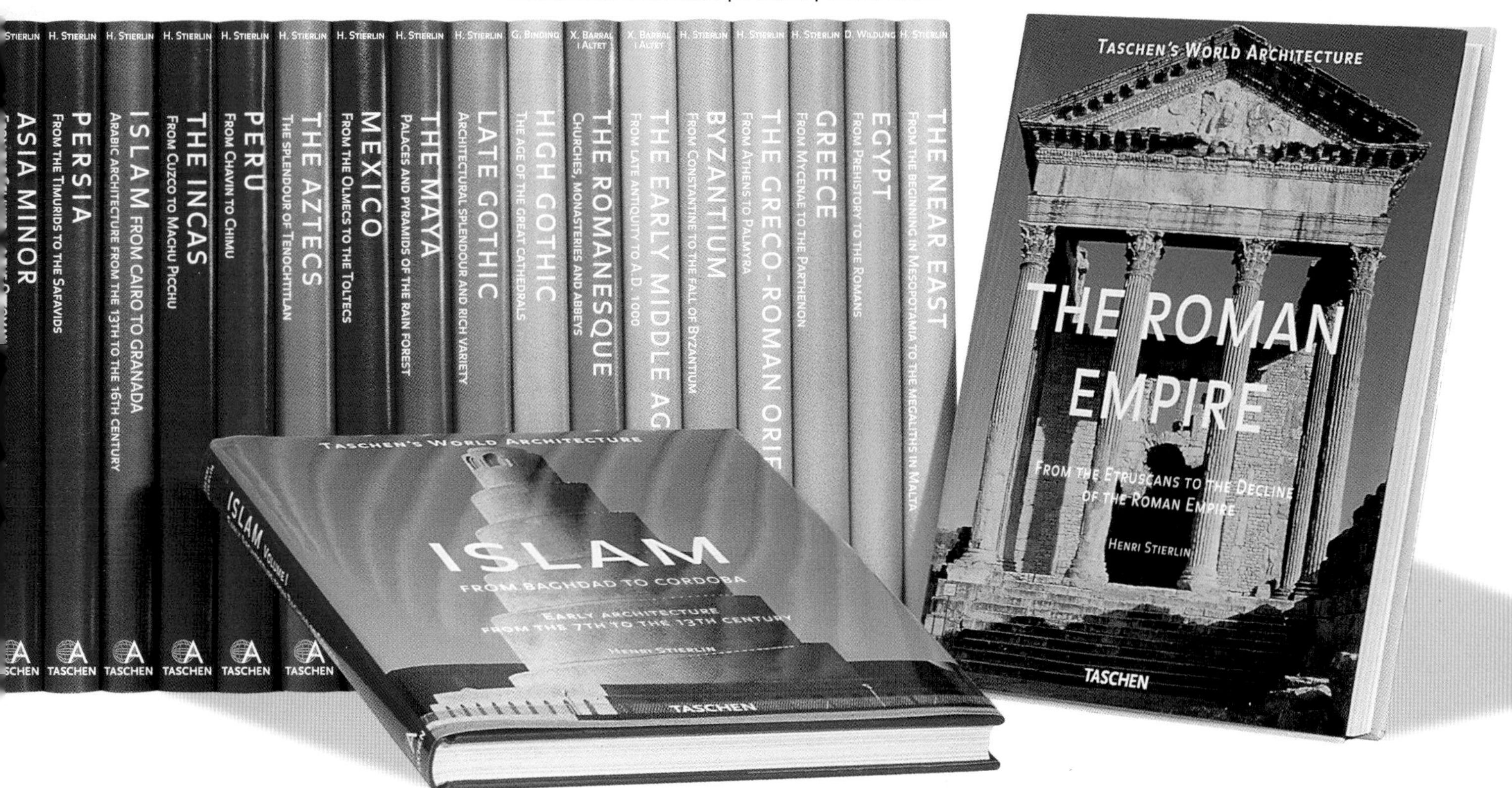